BEARING WITNESS

Anthropology, Culture and Society

Series Editors:
Professor Thomas Hylland Eriksen, University of Oslo
Dr Katy Gardner, University of Sussex
Dr Jon P. Mitchell, University of Sussex

BEARING WITNESS

Women and the Truth and Reconciliation Commission in South Africa

FIONA C. ROSS

Pluto **Press**

LONDON • STERLING, VIRGINIA

First published 2003
by PLUTO PRESS
345 Archway Road, London N6 5AA
and 22883 Quicksilver Drive,
Sterling, VA 20166–2012, USA

www.plutobooks.com

British Library Cataloguing in Publication Data
A catalogue record for this book is available from
the British Library

ISBN 0 7453 1892 4 hardback
ISBN 0 7453 1891 6 paperback

Library of Congress Cataloging in Publication Data
Applied for

10   9   8   7   6   5   4   3   2   1

Designed and produced for Pluto Press by
Chase Publishing Services, Fortescue, Sidmouth EX10 9QG, England
Typeset from disk by Stanford DTP Services, Towcester
Printed in the European Union by
Antony Rowe Ltd, Chippenham, England

CONTENTS

LIST OF TABLES

ACKNOWLEDGEMENTS

Indebtedness and reciprocity are core to social life. While acknowledgements cannot and perhaps never should do full justice to the intellectual debts incurred and the relationships which provide emotional sustenance during research and writing, and while I don't want to cancel my debts entirely, this page offers an opportunity to express thanks to particular people whose support has been invaluable in the making of this book.

The study on which the book is based was part of an ethnographic study of the Truth and Reconciliation Commission conducted by Professor Pamela Reynolds, then of the Department of Social Anthropology at the University of Cape Town. Her vision, determination, courage and intellectual stimulation have been inspirational and I am both grateful for her encouragement and glad to have worked with her.

My greatest thanks go to those with whom I worked closely in Zwelethemba: Nowi Khomba, Yvonne Khutwane, Nomeite Mfengu, Mirriam Moleleki, Neliswa Mroxiswa, Nokuzola Mtamo, Nothemba Ngcwecwe, Ntsoake Phelane, Noluthando Qaba, Thandiwe Silere, Ntombomzi Siwangaza, Nokwanda Tani, Xoliswa Tyawana, Vuyelwa Xuza, and Noluntu Zawukana. I also worked with some members of their families. I intruded on their time, their memories and their personal experiences – and on their kindness in allowing me to do so. I am especially grateful to Sylvia Khomba and Monica Qaba, who welcomed me into their homes, to Nana Khohlokoane and Xolile Dyabooi who assisted me in verifying data and obtaining permissions to conduct research, and to Mandoyi Tshandu for his assistance in arranging meetings. Mirriam Moleleki and Mawethu Bikane were important in establishing the initial contacts from which I generated my research network.

Thanks to all my colleagues, past and present, in the Department of Social Anthropology at UCT. Susan Levine gave freely of her knowledge of Zwelethemba and worked with me on a film about the young women with whom I worked, and Linda Waldman and Stuart Douglas read drafts of early chapters. I am grateful for Sally Frankental's critical eye, kind support and generous comments. Patti Henderson, friend, artist, performer, political activist and anthropologist, was my intellectual companion and emotional support. Thank you, too, to Colleen Crawford Cousins and Lindy Wilson, to my family, particularly Andrew Ross and to a circle of supportive and caring friends, especially Delia Marshall, whose encouragement sustained me in draining times.

Anne Beech and the staff at Pluto Press have been enthusiastic about this project and wonderful to work with. Thanks to Sandie Vahl for the indexing.

Richard Wilson, Jane Taylor and Peter Geschiere commented on the work in its previous incarnation as a doctoral dissertation. I thank them for their enthusiasm, advice and criticism. I am grateful too, to anonymous reviewers of the manuscript proposal for their comments and encouragement. I have tried to incorporate some of the suggestions – omissions etc. of course reflect my own failing.

I am grateful to Ingrid de Kok for permission to use her poem, 'Bandaged'; to the *Cape Times* for permission to use Roger Friedman's article 'ANC veteran tells of sexual abuse' and to SAPA for permission to reprint the report 'Woman tells truth body of sexual abuse'. The University of California Press granted me permission to use material earlier published in my paper 'Speech and silence: women's testimony in the first five weeks of public hearings of the South African Truth and Reconciliation Commission' in Veena Das, *Remaking a World: Violence, Social Suffering and Recovery*, copyright © 2001, the Regents of the University of California. The Truth and Reconciliation Commission granted permission to cite from its Report. Geoff Grundlingh's wonderful photographic exhibition of Zwelethemba and its youth activists remains inspirational and I am grateful for the cover picture that he provided.

And finally, thanks to Andy Hackland, whose love, support and caring sustained me during emotionally exhausting and intellectually challenging research, and whose critical engagement helped me better to envisage the import of both the TRC process and the roles of those who opposed the apartheid regime.

INTRODUCTION

An ear for this, an ear for that. Who to believe? ... The struggle for truth continues ever afterwards. Because afterwards is where we live ... Afterwards is where stories begin. (Nicol, 1995: 1)

As part of the effort to reorganise states and social institutions in the aftermath of violent or authoritarian political formations, recent decades have seen the emergence of new forms of enquiry. Alongside trials, tribunals, commissions of enquiry, courts-martial and other institutionalised forms, 'transitional justice', drawing on human rights discourse, has emerged as a mechanism in establishing democratic states. Within its ambit, phenomena glossed as 'Truth Commissions' are becoming important means by which political formations legitimate themselves and create a new sense of belonging (Wilson 1996, 2001). To date, 21 such commissions have been held world-wide (Hayner 2001), a number more have been mooted, and the model has been adapted and adopted in certain instances by the United Nations.

Truth commissions link together complex ideas about suffering, justice, human rights, accountability, history and witnessing. Alongside legal practices, they involve and invoke memorial and narrative practices that have important effects in shaping understandings and sculpting new social possibilities. The South African Truth and Reconciliation Commission (henceforth, the Commission), frequently described as offering an alternative to both 'amnesia' and 'Nuremburg trials' (Minow 1998), has captured the imagination of the international community. Close attention to its working offers a means to reflect on how suffering is given voice and acknowledged. Contemplating women's testimonies given before public hearings of the Commission's Human Rights Violations Committee (HRVC) and their local effects, my study questions conventional ways of attending to suffering and recovery. Its focus on women emerges from the Commission's work: as I show in Chapter 1, 'woman' was a category with a history. In tracing local effects, I chose to reflect on the Commission's work in Zwelethemba, which, since the 1950s, had been the epicentre of resistance in the Boland, the Western Cape's wine and fruit region. There, working with two generations of women who were involved in anti-apartheid organisations and activities, I examined how the Commission's grammar of pain, couched in terms of violations of human rights, permitted the expression of certain kinds of experience while eliding others.

There is already a large and growing literature on commissions, sometimes critical and sometimes adulatory, especially in relation to the South African experiment.[1] Unlike most studies of truth commissions, this book is not comparative. Comparative studies tend to homogenise and often are not sufficiently mindful of the particular – the grounds on which sociality is built. My aims are more intimate and immediate: I have paid close attention to testimonies generated before the Commission and to the experiences and words of women activists in order to reflect on the singularity of the local. The project would not have been possible without the 'politics of intimacy' (Appadurai 1997: 118) that frames anthropological thought and the ethnographic method; philosophical bearings that take seriously the shaping of local worlds and the socialities they enjoin. The book differs from most ethnographic studies in that it traces the work and social effects of an institution with a finite life, rather than focusing on 'a people' or 'a place'. I have used both conventional anthropological techniques and a multi-sited research method, a kind of travelling anthropology (Hastrup 1994; Augé 1995; Marcus 1995; Clifford 1997; Gupta and Ferguson 1997; Nordstrom 1998), following the Commission's public hearings from place to place around the country and then working closely with political activists in a small town to trace the ramifications of the Commission's work.

Data on women's testimonies and roles presented in Chapters 1 and 2 are derived from the public hearings that I attended,[2] from informal discussions during and after hearings, from the media and interviews. In addition to these sources, Chapter 3 draws on transcripts from selected public hearings carried on the Commission's site on the World Wide Web <www.truth.org.za> and the CD-ROM of the website (TRC (Truth and Reconciliation Commission) 1998). Material presented in Chapters 4, 5 and 6 is drawn from research conducted between 1996 and 1999 in Zwelethemba. The experiences and events people described were frightful. Suffering was great. Many people were brave in the face of violence and apartheid's devastating effects on social life. Many were hurt. Notwithstanding the rhetoric about healing that accompanied the Commission's work, and historians' claims of recording's emancipatory effects, people do not necessarily want their activities and experiences to be widely known. I have therefore refrained from naming or otherwise identifying those with whom I did not work closely in Zwelethemba. An effect of this strategy is a winnowing of generality that may seem discordant to readers familiar with broader ethnographic and historical claims. However, as I show in Chapter 5, it is difficult to come to a detailed understanding of the local and the singular in the present. The filtering I describe is a useful methodological tool to begin to access the complex ways in which people make and inhabit social worlds during and after violence and repression, and in the context of poverty and its enduring effects.

RESEARCH AS WITNESS

Stories of harm are intricate, oddly delicate. Their complexity emerges slowly over time, the product of careful and sustained mindfulness. Without focused attention, certain kinds of experience slip easily from the record. An example: siblings, a young man and a young woman, were detained and held in separate prisons in terms of Section 29 of the Internal Security Act No. 74 of 1982 that allowed for indefinite detention in solitary confinement for interrogation. Once, during an interrogation, the Security Branch interrogators played the young man a recording of a woman's torture. He recognised his sister's screams. His mother, coming to visit him in prison one day, heard his cries echoing down the corridors. She recognised her son's voice. The young woman does not know that her screams were recorded and played as part of the torture her brother endured. The young man does not know that his mother heard his torment.

A space of silence exists within the family. It may be respectful, a kind of will to silence, generated to protect one another from the knowledge of the extent of hurt. It may also be the silence of being unable or unwilling to meet the extent of pain suffered. To confront any member of the family with the knowledge would be to breach the barriers they have constructed and to force new spaces of acknowledgement that may not be beneficial to any concerned. Here, one can only acknowledge the strategies used to cope with violence, acknowledge the need for silence and amnesia of particular kinds.

Such cases suggest that research and writing may offer a form of witness, a term I use throughout in the general sense of recognising and acknowledging suffering. Witnessing requires attentiveness. Shoshana Felman and Dori Laub argue that it is a social process that rests on careful attention, 'listening' (1992: 70). Although what they write is addressed specifically to the testimonies of Holocaust survivors, it can apply in other contexts. They argue that 'Testimonies are not monologues; they cannot take place in solitude' (p. 71), and warn that 'The absence of an empathic listener, or more radically, the absence of an *addressable other*, an other who can hear the anguish of one's memories and thus affirm and recognise their realness, annihilates the story' (p. 68; emphasis in the original).

Writing about Argentina's 'Dirty War', and drawing from Felman and Laub's work, Diana Taylor (1997) points out that

The term 'witnessing' is highly problematic, both in the sense of the Western scientific ideal of the 'objective' observer and in the tradition of Greek tragic drama.[3] The first erroneously suggests that the viewer is ideologically and physically positioned outside the frame of the given-to-be-known/onlookers. And Greek tragedy ... casts viewers as passive onlookers, thus discouraging them/us from active involvement. [Taylor 1997: 25]

Taylor is not oblivious to the difficulties of witnessing in Argentina. She argues that during the 'Dirty War', Argentinians were forced to 'see' in some ways rather than others; to see 'subversion' rather than 'State violence'. Her description of 'seeing' as 'percepticide' emphasises the directionality of vision and its concomitant production of denial. To counter it, she seeks a space within which witnessing as 'an involved, informed, caring, yet critical form of spectatorship' (1997: 124) can occur. Her characterisation resonates with the aims of anthropological research and more widely: Dominick LaCapra makes an explicit link between witnessing and research, using the evocative phrase 'empathic unsettlement' to capture the effects on attentive witnesses of identification with others' experiences. Empathic unsettlement, an experience many anthropologists will recognise, is 'a kind of virtual experience through which one puts oneself in another's position while recognising the difference of that position, hence not taking the other's place' (1999: 722–3). It is potentially dangerous: too close an identification may usurp the position of the other, too great a distance may represent others negatively. I have deliberately written in a style that underplays my presence so as to give space to testifiers, respondents and testimonies to 'speak'.

Bearing witness is not spontaneous. Its difficulties are captured in a poem by the South African poet Ingrid de Kok.[4] The narrator in 'Bandaged' describes both an event of testimony that echoes those made before the Commission and the effects on the speaker and listener of speaking and attending to words of horror:

> Cut down as flowers,
> chopped up like wood
> burned in a blaze of fire.
>
> Bones unfleshed.
>
> Throat choked.
> Cheek charred
> in the cave of the mouth.
> Ear burst. Eye torn.
>
> Gravel. Grave in sand.
>
> O listen, let us not turn away
> from seeing and hearing
> the witness speak with bowed neck.
>
> Prayer, apostrophe, curse.
>
> A bandaged story about
> the broken world, stumps
> on which to hang our shame
> as useless hands, forever.

Horror closes the opportunities for witness: throat, mouth, ear, eye, all are destroyed. Despite its violent effects on the speaker and witness, the narrator-witness pleads for attention even when the story carries no hope, only the recognition of damage and the limitations of efforts to heal. Here witnessing calls for action – a 'not-turning away' from seeing and hearing. The book follows the call, drawing attention to the interplay between words, silence and absence. Its argument is layered, moving across time, space and genre. Tracing the emergence of particular grounds of possibility, its conclusions are, of necessity, tentative. It works at several levels: simultaneously an exploration of the Commission's assumptions and work, a consideration of women's roles and experiences under apartheid, a probing of the cadences of language and silence in relation to suffering and agency, and a critical assessment of ideas about harm and recovery. Chapters perform a double movement, considering both 'what happened' and how it is reported. Their temporality is dual: past events and their present conjuration. Interwoven with and implicit in these are expectations of and prospects for the future. In these respects, the discussion echoes some of the complex weaving of time through testimonies given before the Commission.

As I show in Chapter 1, 'Making the Subject', the Act that brought the Commission into being instructed a narrow understanding of the apartheid past. In construing apartheid as a particular violence whose effect was to produce victims, the Commission elided questions of agency and resistance and thereby precluded an assessment of power's work in constituting subjects. At the same time, it instantiated other subjects – perpetrators and victims. Some of the latter testified before public hearings. Here, women testified differently from men: speaking mainly of men's suffering, they addressed their own experiences of harm and activities of resistance to the Apartheid State only indirectly. As a result, 'women' emerged as a specific category in the Commission's work.

Henrietta Moore has warned that '"woman" cannot stand as an analytical category in anthropological enquiry', and that, 'What the category ... means in a given context has to be investigated and not assumed' (1988: 7; see also Butler 1990). In the remainder of the book, I take seriously both her warning and the effects of the instantiatory processes described in the first chapter. Chapter 2 explores the forms and content of women's testimonies, showing their subtlety in tracing the interpolation of violence into the quotidian world and pursuing the silences that shape and cut through testimonies. Critically engaging with the widespread idea that women did not testify about themselves, the chapter demonstrates the elusive forms through which women narrated experience. It argues that careful and flexible attention is required to hear the complexities of testimonies.

Any telling is produced of silences and erasures. Human rights reportage is no different in this respect. The categories used to understand violence, the transformation of experience to data, and the collation of these has the effect of homogenising complex social relations (Wilson 1997; Taylor 1994). The

Commission found that 'women' were at risk of diverse bodily harms. One effect of the homogenisation of women is to obscure power's work in shaping identity under apartheid. By focusing on women who defined themselves as politically active and examining testimonies about detention, Chapter 3 traces the force of violence on subjectivity as representatives of the State attempted to 'unmake' the self and women tried to maintain a sense of coherence and community in the face of cruelty.

The remaining chapters explore the Commission's work in relation to Zwelethemba. Chapter 4 examines one woman's testimony as it was elicited in a public hearing and then repeated, interpreted and reconsidered in media reports, the Commission Report, academic studies and her hometown. Much of the rhetoric surrounding testimony suggests that 'stories' of violation are intact, awaiting only the opportunity to be told, whereupon they offer release and catharsis. Interrogating the claim that 'the truth heals', and demonstrating that the frameworks within which people's truth claims are interpreted shape ideas about victimhood, blame and accountability and the reception of testimonies in testifiers' hometowns, the chapter offers methodological insight into considerations of recovery.

Chapter 5 assesses conventional measurements of harm in relation to young women. Drawing from my work with women in Zwelethemba who were students in the 1980s, the chapter traces the difficulties of recording their experiences. It describes the variety of harms to which young people were exposed and illustrates the need for close attention to their activities, experiences and the meanings that are given to these. The chapter proposes that telling of pain is an act of intimacy. Harm is not easily expressed and attempts to probe deeply may jeopardise strategies to cope, often tentative and fragile, that may already be in place.

Finally, I explore ideas about social reconstitution through efforts to construct an ordinary daily life different from that possible under apartheid. Drawing on Njabulo Ndebele's (1994) ideas about the revolutionary potential of a focus on the everyday, the chapter explores women's past political mobilisation in Zwelethemba, their reluctance in the present to identify themselves as the site of harm, and their use of particular tropes to position themselves as powerful in their descriptions of past political activities. Their strategies suggest ways of examining violence that differ from the Commission's focus on gross violations of human rights.

Writing performs an odd alienation: for some testifiers, seeing the self as though from the outside can be disconcerting, even painful.[5] Some have been angry at the ways in which, once uttered in public, their words circulate beyond their control, reported and repeated in the media, on the internet, reproduced and analysed by scholars and others. Frequently, discomfort stems from a sense that the products of these processes do not do justice to the self. Where people struggle to re-establish 'authorship' over 'stories' (Das and Kleinman 2000: 12), the separation of voice from self may be experienced as detrimental, even violent. The arrogation or loss of voice may then be haunted by abjection. Yet, as I argue in Chapter 4, if social reconstitution has partly to do with efforts to rest experience in social recognition, scholarly work may assist. I have tried to write in ways that do not injure. Where I fail, the fault is my own.

The study has been a long time in coming to fruition. The research and writing processes have been emotionally, intellectually and physically taxing. It is extremely painful to listen attentively to stories of pain and to tarry with them in order to identify and reflect on patterns in testimonies, narrative forms and silences. The experiences of 'gross violations of human rights' described in hearings, conversations and interviews were cruel, the more so when set against the backdrop of apartheid's racial discrimination, its violent interpolation into everyday life, and the poverty and other forms of violence that colonial and apartheid rule entrenched and that still endure.

Some of those with whom I worked have found it difficult to revisit and admit painful experiences, especially where these have not been recognised, or where new forms of acknowledgement rebut local idioms of distress and agency. In the excitement of a formal end to apartheid and the 'transition' to democracy, it is too often easy to forget the duration of harm's consequences. Apartheid's devastating effects on family life and sociality continue to render individuals and groups vulnerable in the face of change. Grief and loss and suffering remain. The struggle to make ends meet endures. Notwithstanding efforts to create new and vibrant forms of sociality, social institutions are fragile. It is asking a great deal to expect of people that they reflect with a stranger on the conditions that shape the intimacies of their lives. I am grateful to those who set aside justified anger and mistrust, who allowed my intrusion, and who have been so generous with their time.

1   MAKING THE SUBJECT

SINCE the Constitution of the Republic of South Africa, 1993 (Act No. 200 of 1993), provides a historic bridge between the past of a deeply divided society characterized by strife, conflict, untold suffering and injustice, and a future founded on the recognition of human rights, democracy and peaceful co-existence for all South Africans, irrespective of colour, race, class, belief or sex;

AND SINCE it is deemed necessary to establish the truth in relation to past events as well as the motives for and circumstances in which gross violations of human rights have occurred, and to make the findings known in order to prevent a repetition of such acts in future;

AND SINCE the Constitution states that the pursuit of national unity, the well-being of all South African citizens and peace require reconciliation between the people of South Africa and the reconstruction of society;

AND SINCE the Constitution states that there is a need for understanding but not for vengeance, a need for reparation but not for retaliation, a need for ubuntu[1] but not for victimization;

AND SINCE the Constitution states that in order to advance such reconciliation and reconstruction amnesty shall be granted in respect of acts, omissions and offences associated with political objectives committed in the course of the conflicts of the past;

AND SINCE the Constitution provides that Parliament shall under the Constitution adopt a law which determines a firm cut-off date, which shall be a date after 8 October 1990 and before the cut-off date envisaged in the Constitution, and providing for the mechanisms, criteria and procedures, including tribunals, if any, through which such amnesty shall be dealt with;

Be it therefore enacted by the Parliament of the Republic of South Africa as follows; [that] There is hereby established a juristic person to be known as the Truth and Reconciliation Commission. (Promotion of National Unity and Reconciliation Act No. 34 of 1995)

TRUTH BE TOLD

Michel-Rolph Trouillot writes of power in relation to history: 'The naming of the "fact" is itself a narrative of power disguised as innocence', and that 'Naming the fact ... already imposes a reading and many historical controversies boil down to who has the power to name what' (1995: 114). In the discussion that follows, I explore the effects of naming apartheid as a particular form of violence and injury amenable to examination by a Commission.[2] The subjects and objects of the Commission's enquiry were made through at least three moments of translation. As I show in the remainder of the book, the categories these produced have important consequences in relation to recognising harm and constituting new social formations.

The Commission was an innovative and imaginative social intervention, one of several designed to redress some of the effects of colonialism and apartheid.[3] It originated from the agreement on amnesty reached between representatives of the South African State, political parties and some liberation organisations in 1993, during negotiations to end apartheid and institute democratic governance in South Africa. The negotiations faltered over questions of amnesty, and the negotiating parties agreed that after the first elections the new government would establish a mechanism to facilitate the granting of amnesty to individuals.[4] The amnesty agreement was incorporated into the Interim Constitution, whose 'post-amble' describes the Constitution as an 'historic bridge' between the apartheid past and a democratic future based on non-discrimination and a respect for human rights. It continues by pledging the new government to create a law through which to deal with amnesty, in the interests of 'understanding but not ... vengeance', 'reparation but not ... retaliation', and '*ubuntu* but not ... victimisation'.

The Interim Constitution did not oblige the new state to conduct a truth commission. Depicting the options as a choice between political prosecutions (the so-called 'Nuremberg' option) and 'amnesia' characterised by blanket amnesty, a Commission was posited as a third option that bypassed the complexities of legal trials while still meeting the state's constitutional obligations and acknowledging some of the harms inflicted by the system of apartheid (see Boraine and Levy 1995; Boraine, Levy and Scheffer 1994; Asmal, Asmal and Roberts 1996; Minow 1998; Boraine 2000; Hayner 2001). The proposal for a Commission drew impetus from the work of similar Commissions elsewhere, particularly in Chile and Argentina (Rosenberg 1992; Weschler 1990; Zalaquett 1994), and from two Commissions of Enquiry conducted by the ANC into abuses in its training camps outside South Africa (Skweyiya 1992 and Motsuenyane Commission Report 1993). The Commission was contentious; opponents on the right of the political spectrum argued that it would be a 'witch-hunt', while those on the left argued that in offering amnesty from civil and criminal prosecution, a Commission compromised justice[5] for those most affected by apartheid.

After a lengthy consultative process, the Promotion of National Unity and Reconciliation Act No. 35 of 1994 (henceforth, the Act) was tabled and passed in Parliament. It passed into law on 16 December 1995. The Act's preamble recognises apartheid as having comprised more than one form of violence and imagines a future founded on peaceful co-existence, human rights and democracy. To achieve its aim 'to promote national unity and reconciliation in a spirit of understanding which transcends the conflicts and divisions of the past', the Act created three committees: one on amnesty, one on human rights violations (the focus of the first part of this book) and one on reparation and rehabilitation.[6] It also provided for an investigative unit, a research unit and a limited witness protection programme, and granted the Commission considerable powers, including rights of search, seizure and subpoena.

The Commission established four regional offices, based in Cape Town (covering the Western and Northern Cape Provinces), Gauteng (dealing with Gauteng, Mpumulanga, the Northern and Northwest Provinces), Durban (focusing on KwaZulu-Natal and Free State) and East London (for the Eastern Cape), staffed by 438 people, including 17 Commissioners, selected and appointed on the basis that they were 'fit and proper persons who are impartial and who do not have a high political profile' (the Act). Commissioners were drawn from a narrow range of professions: Archbishop Tutu, Alex Boraine, Reverend Bongani Finca and Reverend Khoza Magojo were at the time, or had been, practising Christian theologians and Yasmin Sooka was President of the South African Chapter of the World Council on Religion and Peace. Eight Commissioners – Dumisa Ntsebeza, Fazel Randera, Wynand Malan, Denzil Potgieter, Richard Lyster, Sisi Khampepe, Chris De Jager and Yasmin Sooka – had legal training, four were medical professionals (Mapule Ramashala, Wendy Orr, Hlengiwe Mkhize and Glenda Wildschutt), one, Mary Burton, was a civil society activist. Two – Alex Boraine and Wynand Malan – had been politicians. In accordance with a stipulation in the Act, a judge, Hassan Mall, was appointed to the position of chairperson of the Amnesty Committee. Once established, the Commission appointed additional members to its three committees: investigators, researchers, data processing and data capture staff, media liaison staff, and administrative personnel.[7]

Chapter Three of the Act describes the Commission's objectives as:

(a) establishing as complete a picture as possible of the causes, nature and extent of the gross violations of human rights which were committed during the period from 1 March 1960 to the cut-off date, including the antecedents, circumstances, factors and context of such violations, as well as the perspectives of the victims and the motives and perspectives of the persons responsible for the commission of the violations, by conducting investigations and holding hearings;
(b) facilitating the granting of amnesty to persons who make full disclosure of all the relevant facts relating to acts associated with a political objective and comply with the requirements of this Act;
(c) establishing and making known the fate or whereabouts of victims and by restoring the human and civil dignity of such victims by granting them an opportunity to relate their own accounts of the violations of which they are the victims, and by recommending reparation measures in respect of them;
(d) compiling a report providing as comprehensive an account as possible of the activities and findings of the Commission contemplated in paragraphs (a), (b) and (c), and which contains recommendations of measures to prevent the future violations of human rights.

Multiple forms of social destruction described in the founding statement – deep divisions, strife, conflict, untold suffering and injustice – are here reformulated in the Act's concern with 'gross violations of human rights'. Two transitions are involved in this formulation of injury: from 'apartheid' to different manifestations of 'violence'; and from 'violence' to 'gross violations of human rights'.

The definitions of violence and violation laid down in the Act were narrow. They did not address forms of structural violence or the racial discrimination that characterised apartheid. The Act defines 'gross violations of human rights' as killing, torture, abduction (often referred to in the Commission's work as 'disappearance') and/or severe ill treatment, or the conspiracy or attempt to commit such acts. Severe ill treatment is not clearly defined in either the Act or the Commission's Report (Truth and Reconciliation Commission 1998: Volume One: 80; see discussion in Chapter 3 and in Ross 2001b; all subsequent references to the Truth and Reconciliation Commission Report 1998 will denote simply volume and page number). Notwithstanding provisions in the Act for recognition of pecuniary harm and other forms of damage, the Commission's focus was, for the most part, body-bound. Resolving that 'its mandate was to give attention to human rights violations committed as specific acts, resulting in severe physical and/or mental injury, in the course of past political conflict', it focused its attention on what the Report describes as 'bodily integrity rights': '... rights that are enshrined in the new South African Constitution and under international law. These include the right to life ... the right to be free from torture ... the right to be free from cruel, inhuman, or degrading treatment or punishment ... and the right to freedom and security of the person, including freedom from abduction and arbitrary and prolonged detention' (Volume One: 64). Here is a third moment in translation; a narrowing to focus on violations of bodily integrity.

The translations described above not only affected the object of enquiry but also identified and shaped its subjects. The Act bifurcated violence into a concern with 'perpetrators' who committed or commissioned acts of violence, or who failed to intervene to prevent them, and 'victims' who suffered their consequences. The dichotomy obscured the roles of 'beneficiaries', prompting Mahmood Mamdani (1996) to ask at what point reconciliation becomes an embrace of evil. It drew attention away from structures and structural violence that maintain oppression (see Asmal, Asmal and Roberts 1996; NGO Coalition 1997). Rather than commencing from the historical grounds of the constitution of the subject under apartheid, then, the Commission considered its subject in terms of injury – the violation of particular rights. According to the Act, victims are:

(a) persons who, individually or together with one or more persons, suffered harm in the form of physical or mental injury, emotional suffering, pecuniary loss or a substantial impairment of human rights (i) as a result of a gross violation of human rights; or (ii) as a result of an act associated with a political objective for which amnesty has been granted; (b) persons who, individually or together with one or more persons, suffered harm in the form of physical or mental injury, emotional suffering, pecuniary loss or a substantial impairment of human rights, as a result of such person intervening to assist persons contemplated in paragraph (a) who were in distress or to prevent victimization of such persons; and (c) such relatives or dependants of victims as may be prescribed.

Using a notion of 'even-handedness' that presumed that 'violation' necessarily produced 'victims', the Commission's work stripped away context[8] and the effects of power by condensing suffering to its traces on the body. The resultant legal person, 'the victim', produced through occupation of the signs of injury, has a different relationship to the state and legal systems from other citizens, not least in the abrogation of recourse to the law for redress for criminal and civil wrongs (Ross 2001b).

The Act that established a Commission on *Truth* and *Reconciliation* gave no definition of either term. In the debates concerning the formation of a commission, in the Commission's early work and in public discourse, truth was viewed as singular, uncompromisingly objective, neutral and its revelation empowering: 'the Truth'. It was presumed to be amenable to discovery through scientific method and quantification, and to be accessible through individuals' memories and the material remainders of apartheid. The link between truth and reconciliation was considered self-evident and consequential: that disclosing the truth would result in reconciliation. Indeed, the Commission's slogan was explicit: 'Truth – the road to reconciliation'. Reconciliation was viewed as paramount in nation-building, itself assumed to be necessary to democracy (Wilson 2001: 13–17).

Although a direct result of a constitutional provision for amnesty, the Commission was depicted in the popular imagination as a healing intervention, ideas about which drew from three models of damage. Commissioners and social commentators frequently metaphorically likened South Africa and South Africans to wounded bodies. They compared truth-telling with the opening and cleansing of unhealed wounds caused by gross violations of human rights, or, more frequently, by the system of apartheid itself, and used words like 'wound', 'fester', 'cleanse' and 'operation' to describe aspects of the Commission's work. In the second model, society was depicted as a psyche. In the corresponding healing matrix, people's memories and experiences were to be the subject of 'analysis' in which the past was to be revealed in all its pain and ugliness. After due acknowledgement, it was assumed that the process of daily life could begin afresh. Drawing heavily from a simplified model of psychoanalysis, 'recollection' was presumed to ensure 'non-repetition'. Alongside these two models circulated a third, that of spiritual, Christian healing generated through the process of contrition, confession and acknowledgement. The model was emphasised through use of words like 'martyr', 'sacrifice', 'confession', and 'forgiveness'. The models were established early: explanatory notes to the draft of the Promotion of

National Unity and Reconciliation Bill describe the Commission as originating from the principle that:

> [R]econciliation depends on *forgiveness* and that forgiveness can only take place if gross violations of human rights are fully *disclosed*. What is therefore envisaged is reconciliation through a process of *national healing*.
> The Promotion of National Unity and Reconciliation Bill, 1995, seeks to find a balance between the process of *national healing and forgiveness*, as well as the granting of amnesty as required by the interim Constitution. [TRC CD-Rom 1998: Notes to the Bill 1995: 1, emphasis added]

Implicit in these models lies an underlying assumption about the constitution of the subject in the post-apartheid era. In terms of the Act, 'victims' were entitled in law 'to relate their own accounts of the violations of which they are victims', an intervention designed to 'restor[e] the human and civil dignity of such victims'. This innovative intervention explicitly linked 'voice' ('relating their own accounts', 'testifying' or 'telling one's story') with the restoration of dignity and thence with the subject. In addition, the work of the HRVC made an explicit link between 'experience' ('gross violation of human rights') and the resultant subject-position ('victim').

The Act did not provide measures by which the Commission might ascertain its success. There are no absolute indicators of the number of people who suffered violations of the order the Commission was required to investigate, and its sample was not probabilistic. People whose experiences of harm fitted the Commission's definitions of gross violations of human rights were invited to make statements to designated HRVC officials, 'statement takers', and were recorded on specially devised forms, 'protocols', the format of which was standardised and altered several times during the Commission's process to accommodate the complexity and variety of harm reported to the Commission (Buur, 1999; Report, Volume One: 139). By December 1997, the closing date for the submission of statements concerning gross violations of human rights to the Commission, 21,298 statements concerning 37,672 violations had been received (Volume One: 166).[9]

Much of the work of data collection and analysis remained 'behind the scenes', hidden within the bureaucratic workings of the HRVC and the data collection and capture units (Buur 1999 and 2000). The HRVC's most visible work, and that which drew the most public attention, was 76 public hearings lasting between two and five days, held in towns throughout South Africa between April 1996 and June 1997.[10] Approximately 10 per cent of deponents testified before 'Victim Hearings', which were quickly standardised and, in some ways, ritualised (Bozzoli 1999). At each hearing, audiences were seated in rows in a hall decorated with Commission slogans and a national flag, facing a stage decked with flowers and plants and laid out in such a way that the testifier, seated at a 'witness stand', faced a panel of Commission members. The panel, ranging from 3 to 17 Commissioners and Committee members, heard approximately 10 testifiers every day of the public hearings. Audiences were not allowed to participate in the testimonial process, were frequently warned that noise in hearings would not be tolerated, and on occasion, proceedings were halted when panellists felt that audiences behaved disrespectfully.

Prior to the hearing, each testifier was allocated a committee member whose task was to assist the testifier to 'tell their stories' in public. Before the hearings, testifiers were briefed about what to expect from the hearing process. When giving testimony, testifiers were usually accompanied by a 'briefer', a designated official whose tasks were to brief testifiers prior to hearings, 'debrief' them afterwards and provide psychological support during the testimonial process. Attending to the expression of pain was considered traumatising, or perhaps polluting, and briefers were 'debriefed' by a consultant psychologist after each hearing. Later in the Commission's process, Commissioners and journalists were also offered debriefing to deal with 'secondary traumatisation'.

Kinsfolk or friends or eyewitnesses frequently accompanied testifiers. Each testifier was called to the stage, sworn in, asked to describe his or her family background by way of introduction and then to describe the violation about which they had made a statement. The testimonies were the culmination of a series of steps: individual experiences of violence were narrated, distilled, recorded, translated from narratives of pain into 'data' about human rights violations (Buur 1999; see Chapter 4). On several occasions, testifiers were told by Commissioners to address only the violations that they had described in their statements. In the initial hearings, testimonies lasted from between 15 minutes to more than an hour-and-a-half. Towards the end of the Commission's work, most testimonies lasted approximately 30 minutes.

Testimony was given in the testifier's language of choice (there are eleven official languages in South Africa) and was simultaneously translated into English, Afrikaans and one other major language spoken in the region. Translation, undertaken by specially appointed translators, some of whom had previously worked in the courts, was an emotionally demanding task. Many translators commented on the psychological difficulties they experienced in having to use the first person in translating other peoples' pain. One young man explained, 'It is difficult to interpret victim hearings ... because you use the first person all the time. I have no distance when I say "I" ... it runs through me with I' (quoted in Krog 1998: 129). Another, a woman, likened translation of victim hearings to the pain of childbirth (Buur, personal communication, 5 March 2000). If a testifier stumbled or halted during testimony, the designated committee member asked 'probing questions'. Briefers comforted testifiers who wept at the memory of loss or harm; a box of tissues, placed at hand on the witness stand, became a potent symbol of the hearings. On a few occasions, when a witness cried, Archbishop Tutu led the audience in a hymn. One hearing I attended was adjourned while a testifier wept. Once a woman was deeply disturbed by the process of testifying and chose not to continue with her testimony. Usually however, a silence was preserved in the hall until the testifier's equilibrium was restored, then the testimonial process began once more.

When each testifier finished describing the event(s) of violation to the Commission, the chairperson solicited additional questions (usually of clarification) from the Commission panellists, whose responses were often formulaic. In the early hearings, testifiers were frequently asked what they desired the Commission to do for them. In media briefings, Commissioners professed themselves astonished at the limited nature of the requests: usually for assistance in caring for the children of those who had died, or for educational assistance, tombstones or reburial ceremonies. Very few testifiers asked for monetary compensation, partly because the public nature of hearings mitigated against the expression of such requests, and only a small number demanded the prosecution of those who had committed crimes.

Testifiers were not cross-examined. People named as perpetrators in testimonies were notified by the Commission and were allowed to make representation to the Commission in defence, but their legal representatives were not permitted to address questions to testifiers. (This was in stark contrast with public hearings of amnesty applications, where detailed cross-examinations were conducted.) When no further questions were forthcoming from the Commission panellists, the testifier was thanked, dismissed from the stage and taken for 'debriefing'. The next testifier was called and the process repeated.

Emotional events, the hearings were a public performance of memory, loss and grief. Testifiers described the full range of violations that the Commission's operational definitions admitted, including terrible torture, injuries and death. They also described the everyday humiliations of apartheid and a diversity of harms that the Commission did not consider gross violations of human rights. Representatives of the state committed most of the violations to which testifiers referred (Volume Five: 212). Testifiers spoke quietly, furiously, with passion, fearfully, with humour. Some were elliptical in their descriptions of horror, some spoke directly of violence. A large number of testifiers wept as they spoke; sometimes audience members did too. Commissioners were less likely to display emotion, though once Archbishop Tutu wept when a man described the torture he had endured; and, as I show in Chapter 4, a close emotional attachment sometimes developed between a particular committee member and a testifier during the testimonial process.

Public hearings were widely broadcast: daily updates on the hearings and the Commission's work were carried in the print and electronic media and the proceedings were broadcast live on television and radio. The hearings may be likened to a mnemonic device. The audiences at hearings and those following them through the media were tacitly asked to envisage testifiers as people with unique experiences and, simultaneously, as representatives of those who had suffered similarly.

Different explanations have been given for the selection of deponents, among them that 'the hearing should reflect accounts from all sides of the political conflicts of the past'; 'the entire thirty-four year mandate period should be covered'; 'women as well as men should be heard, and the experiences of youth should also be considered' and that 'there should be an attempt at least to provide an overall picture of the experience of the region' (Report, Volume Five 1998: 5–6). Notwithstanding efforts at representivity, the sample was not probabilistic:

Section 4(b) of the Act required that the Commission accept statements from all South Africans who wished to make them. Hence, the Commission did not carry out a 'survey' of violations in the sense of drawing a probabilistic sample of victims. Those who chose to come forward defined the universe of people from whom the Commission received information.

Human rights data are almost never taken from probabilistic samples. Instead, people decide for themselves if they will make statements. [Report, Volume One: 163]

The Report adds that the Commission's sample probably excludes those who lived at a distance from Commission Offices and had limited access to the media; those who were traumatised, ill or elderly; or those who belonged to constituencies antagonistic to the Commission. My data suggest that the sample excluded a large number of women who were eligible to make statements and a large number of activists who chose not to see themselves as victims. I explore these claims in more detail in Chapters 5 and 6.

Thus far, I have described the ways that the Act progressively reduced and reified the understanding of apartheid to violence and its effects on the body. Formulated in the Interim Constitution and the inaugural statements of the Act as multiple forms of social disruption, apartheid was reformulated in the Act as the violation of particular rights; those of rights of bodily integrity. Breaches of the latter – 'gross violations of human rights' – produced 'victims', distinct from those who suffered under apartheid. While, as Murray Last (2000: 330) argues, it is important to recognise victims, the terms in which this is done have implications for our understanding of sociality and the measures necessary to enable social reconstruction. Understanding violence in terms of gross violations of human rights flattens the complex social terrain instituted by colonialism, apartheid and various resistances, and eliminates an investigation of the subjects produced by these processes. (I pursue these arguments further in Chapters 3 and 5.) In effect then, the Commission's work effaced certain of power's historical dimensions. One such was apartheid's differentiated effects on the constitution of gender.[11] The author of the chapter on Women's Hearings in the Commission's Report (Volume Four: 282–316) recognises a bias inherent in the Commission's definitions of gross violations:

The Commission's relative neglect of the effects of the 'ordinary' workings of Apartheid has a gender bias, as well as a racial one. A large number of statistics can be produced to substantiate the fact that women were subject to more restrictions and suffered more in economic terms than did men during the Apartheid years. The most direct measure of disadvantage is poverty, and there is a clear link between the distribution of poverty and Apartheid policies. Black women, in particular, are disadvantaged, and black women living in former homelands remain the most disadvantaged of all. It is also true that this type of abuse affected a far larger number of people, and usually with much longer-term consequences, than the types of violations on which the Commission was mandated to focus its attention. [Volume 4: 288]

WHOSE VOICES?

Commissioners were concerned that the Commission might not obtain the 'whole story' of gross violations of human rights committed in the period under review. Their concerns grew as two distinctive patterns in testimonial practices became evident early in the public hearings and were sustained throughout the process of the Commission's work. The first was that although approximately equal proportions of men and women made statements, for the most part women described the suffering of men whereas men testified about their own experiences of violation. The second was that women who had been active in opposing the Apartheid State seldom gave public testimony.

In hearings I attended, women accounted for 54 per cent of testifiers but made scant mention of their own experiences of human rights violations.[12] Seventy-nine per cent of women testified about violations committed against men. By comparison, only 8 per cent of men's testimonies concerned violations committed against women. Women were more likely than men to testify about women.

Forty per cent of the victims about whom women testified were their sons, while husbands account for a further 16 per cent. Seventeen per cent of testimonies concerned other male kin, 6 per cent, unrelated men, and 14 per cent of women's testimonies concerned their own experiences of gross violations of human rights. Six and a half per cent of testimonies concerned women kin and a further half per cent concerned unrelated women.

Men testified about their own experiences of gross violations of human rights in 62 per cent of cases. Twenty-two per cent of the remainder concerned male kin, and 7 per cent, unrelated men. Nine per cent of men's testimonies concerned women kin and 2 per cent, unrelated women. Men's reporting of their own experiences of brutal treatment was almost four times that made by women.

As a result of these patterns, Commissioners and the media frequently referred to women as 'secondary witnesses'.

Table 1.1 disaggregates the data by describing the relationship of testifiers to those for whom they testified. The table enables a comparison of the frequency of men and women's testimonies in each category of relationship described. It also provides a percentage of total victims identified in each category.

Table 1.1. Relationship of testifiers to those about whom they testified

Testimony concerning:	No. of victims identified by women	No. of victims identified by men	total number of victims	Total percentage of all victims
Self	29	113	142	36
Sons	83	14	97	25
Brothers	18	16	34	9
Husbands	34	0	34	9
Unrelated men	13	13	26	7
Male kin	14	4	18	5
Daughters	5	3	8	2
Fathers	3	5	8	2
Sisters	7	0	7	2
Wives	0	5	5	1
Female kin	2	2	4	1
Unrelated women	1	3	4	1
Mothers	1	2	3	1
TOTAL	210	180	390	101

(Figures are rounded up and do not add up to 100 per cent.)

Commission Data

The Commission's data, drawn from statements about gross violations of human rights and presented in the Report, confirmed the patterns reflected in public hearings I attended. Volume One (p. 166) reports that a total of 21,298 statements concerning 37,672 violations were received by the Commission. Africans made 89 per cent of statements (Volume One: 168).[13] No data pertaining to income or other class differentials are given in the Report, but given the intersection of race and class in South Africa, it is likely that most deponents were poor.

Women made approximately half of the statements and 60 per cent of women deponents were African women (Volume One: 169). Of the reported violations, 23,020 (61 per cent) were committed against men. In 5,458 cases of violation (approximately 14 per cent), the sex of the victim was not reported. The authors of the Commission Report argue that 'the violence of the past resulted in the deaths mainly of men' (Volume One: 169). They continue 'Men were the most common victims of violations. Six times as many men died as women and twice as many survivors of violations were men ... Hence, although most people who told the Commission about violations were women [*sic*], most of the testimony was about men' (p. 171).

Volume Four of the Report confirms that women's statements mainly concerned human rights violations committed against men. Approximately 44 per cent of female deponents were victims of gross violations of human rights (Volume Four: 285), although the data presented show marked differences by region with more than half the female deponents in the Durban regional office reporting violations committed against themselves. (No regional data regarding 'racial classification' of deponents are provided.) By comparison, in the Cape Town regional office, which solicited statements from deponents in the Western and Northern Cape, 39 per cent of cases reported concerned gross violations of human rights committed against women. Of these, approximately 24 per cent concerned violations suffered by the women deponents themselves.[14] A gender researcher, Beth Goldblatt, is quoted in the Commission's Report as stating that the data

... reflect the reality that women were less of a direct threat to the Apartheid State and were thus less often the victims of murder, abduction and torture. This was due to the nature of the society that was, and is, structured along traditional patriarchal lines. Men were expected to engage with the state in active struggle while women were denied 'active citizenship' because of their location within the private sphere. [Volume Four: 290]

The statement implies that the 'private sphere' was somehow less political than the public sphere, an implication that I challenge in Chapters 4 and 6.

The most frequently reported gross violation of human rights suffered by women deponents recorded by the Commission falls into the category of 'severe ill-treatment' (Volume Four: 286), a category that came under considerable debate and scrutiny within the Commission (Volume One: 64–5 and Volume Five: 12–13; Ross 2001b). The definition of severe ill-treatment is circuitous[15] but the following violations were considered to fall into the category of severe ill-treatment: rape and punitive solitary confinement, sexual assault, abuse or harassment; physical beating resulting in serious injuries; injuries incurred as a result of police action during demonstrations; 'burnings'; injury by poisoning, drugs or other chemicals; mutilation; detention without charge or trial; banishment or banning; deliberate withholding of food or water to someone in custody; failure to provide medical attention to someone in custody; destruction of a house through arson or other attacks (Volume One: 81–2). These categories suggest the range and materiality of violence but do not consider other forms, such as forced removals, structural violence, or symbolic violence. Submissions to the Commission suggested that 'severe ill-treatment' could be interpreted more broadly to include forced removals, economic inequity and racial classification (NGO Coalition 1997; Goldblatt and Meintjes 1996), but the Commission retained its focus on violations of rights to bodily integrity.

Women deponents were older than male deponents: most were between the ages of 37 and 60, while the largest proportion of male deponents were aged between 25 and 48 years at the time of making the statement (Volume One: 170). Most reported victims were young men (Volume One: 171; see also Volume Four: 258ff), many of whom were aged between 13 and 24 years at the time of the violation they reported (Volume Four: 258). It is likely that the age differences of victims reflects the fact that men aged 13 to 24 in the 1980s (the period for which most statements were received) testified about their own experiences of gross violations of human rights whereas women testified about their children (usually sons) injured in the 1980s. The Report states that the data reflect 'the perceived threat posed by males to the state' (Volume Four: 259), but also acknowledges a systematic patterning of women's testimonies concerning their own experiences of violation.

'WOMEN' – A CATEGORY WITH A HISTORY

The patterns of women's testimonies described in the data above were striking from the outset of the HRVC's public hearings. For example, Christina Stuckey, a journalist, reported of the first week of hearings in April 1996 in East London:

> Throughout the first hearings of the Truth and Reconciliation Commission this week, the words 'witness' and 'victim' were alternately used to describe those giving testimony. Neither description does justice to those who came forward to tell their stories.
>
> These people – the majority of the testifiers were women[16] – were neither broken victims nor detached witnesses. Their courage in the face of indescribable adversity was breath-taking, their strength and grace exemplary ...
>
> It is indeed women like them and the many others who faced the Commission to recount their stories who are the key to the success of the country's healing process. Some of the women are illiterate, others educated. Some of them had been forbidden by their husbands to work and most followed the tradition of standing by their husbands and not asking too many questions about their activities outside the home ...
>
> Their husbands' deaths forced them to take over the traditional duties of the man and to play the dual role of father and mother to their children.
>
> The deaths also pulled them into the midst of the struggle, some willingly, some less so. As policemen continued to harass them ... the women drew from a well of strength which many didn't know they possessed ...
>
> [*Sunday Weekend Argus*, 21 April 1996: 6; reproduced in part in the *Sunday Independent*, 21 April 1996: 4]

Stuckey's account of the hearings was the subject of a letter of congratulation to the editor of the *Sunday Independent* (5 May 1996) written by Beth Goldblatt and Dr Sheila Meintjes, academics and gender specialists at the University of the Witwatersrand. They applaud the fact that 'The article is at pains to show that women were not simply victims of our Apartheid past but were active agents in the resistance to injustice. This characterisation of women is very important since it would be quite easy for our history to ascribe its struggle as one of men fighting and women remaining invisible and uninvolved.' They do not state why women might be excluded from an historical lexicon of resistance, adding only that: 'In their resistance to this system, women were tortured, imprisoned and horribly abused. They [suffered] not only as mothers, wives and daughters, but were also leaders and sources of strength in their families and communities. Women were also perpetrators of injustice and cruelty.'[17]

Goldblatt and Meintjes had some months earlier predicted that women would not speak easily of the harms inflicted on them, a prediction that was to hold true in many of the later hearings. On 19 March 1996, a month before the Commission's public hearings began, the Centre for Applied Legal Studies at the University of the Witwatersrand hosted a workshop entitled 'Gender and the Truth and Reconciliation Commission' in Johannesburg. Workshop participants were drawn from a range of professions and organisations, including psychologists, lawyers, representatives of non-governmental organisations (NGOs), members of the Provincial Legislature, and, perhaps most importantly, some Commissioners and members of the Commission. Participants examined the gender dimensions of violence in South Africa. Goldblatt and Meintjes prepared a submission based on the discussions and their research and submitted it to the Commission in May 1996. Ostensibly a position paper on 'gender', the submission dealt unashamedly with 'women'. It drew on interviews conducted with eight women who had been actively involved in resistance to the Apartheid State inside South Africa and in exile, on testimonies given before the Commission in earlier hearings, and on secondary materials. The submission begins with an explanation of the importance of 'gender' in an understanding of past violence, stating,

The purpose of emphasising gender relationships is to highlight the particular manner in which women have been subordinated and oppressed through socially constructed differences. Indeed, gender differences have meant that South African men and women have often experienced our history in different ways. In South Africa, as in most societies in the world, women have been accorded identities [that] cast them in particular social roles [that] have restricted their civil and political status. Intersecting with gender are also race, class and other identities, such as ethnic and religious allegiances. These form the basis of the 'public-private' divide, which has given to men the role of civil and political representative of the household, to the exclusion of women. [Goldblatt and Meintjes 1996: 5]

The submission described the escalation and intensification of violence inflicted on women in South Africa between 1960 and 1990 and documented the range of violations they suffered. Stating that apartheid laws had a differential impact on men and women and that racial classifications and class intersected with gender to limit women's positions in society, it argued that women were 'indirectly affected' by apartheid laws and by the violence inflicted on their children and husbands. The submission proposed that the Commission extend the definition of 'severe ill-treatment':

... to include a wide range of abuses which took place under Apartheid. Detention without trial itself is severe ill-treatment. Imprisonment for treason against an unjust system is severe ill-treatment. Forced removals, pass arrests, confiscation of land, breaking up of families and even forcing people to undergo racially formulated education are all forms of severe ill-treatment. [Goldblatt and Meintjes 1996: 21]

The submission continued:

Whilst it is important to emphasise the killing and torture in our past and the extraordinary suffering of opponents of Apartheid, we need also to pause and recognise that
the Apartheid system itself violated the basic rights of human beings in ways that systematically destroyed their capacity to survive. In addition, the gendered dimensions
of this system had an added dehumanising effect on many people's lives. [p. 22]

The authors urged the Commission to examine the multiple sites of violence
and recognise that violence against women is a political and not a private
act. Twenty-one recommendations concerned making the Commission's
work, decisions and Report 'gender sensitive'. These made it clear that the
contexts within which women might be prepared to testify differed from the
hearing format already in place. The authors argued that it would be difficult
for women to overcome the stigma attached to speaking publicly of harm,
particularly sexual violation.[18] Five recommendations pertained directly to
the statement-making and testimonial process (Goldblatt and Meintjes 1996:
63–4). One was that the Commission should make it clear that statements
could be made confidentially. Another, that women need not testify in public.
A third was that women deponents be permitted to request that their
statements be taken by women, and a fourth, that women testify in closed
hearings to women Commissioners. A fifth proposal was that the
Commission arrange for women supported by social workers and psychologists to testify in groups.

Ilse Olkers, a legal consultant on gender affairs, reported through the
journal *AGENDA* that the submission had little effect on shaping the Commission's initial process or its response to deponents (Olkers 1996; see also
Owens 1996). She castigated the Commission for its assumption of a 'gender
neutral truth', calling its failure to recognise gender as a powerful feature in
determining violation 'a shameful distortion' of reality (1996: 61) and
accusing the Commission of rendering women 'invisible' except in
stereotyped roles as victims and mothers of victims.

Some Commissioners were sympathetic but the Commission took no
public action to identify 'women' as a special category until the patterning
of testimonial practices was marked. Then, concerned about the emergent
patterns in testimonial practices, the Commission called two public meetings
to which it invited representatives of the media and women's organisations
in order to consider how the Commission could better elicit statements about
women's experiences of harm (Volume Four: 282–3), particularly those of
sexual harm. (The Commission's archive is not yet publicly accessible and I
am unable to trace its internal deliberations.) At a meeting in Cape Town on
14 June 1996, at which the Commission sought to elicit assistance from
NGOs and academics in supporting and extending its work, Commissioner
Mapule Ramashala expressed her disquiet about the limited number of
women who testified about their own experiences of violation. She said,

Now, having had the first round [of hearings in East London, Cape Town, Johannes-burg and Durban], I've been very disturbed that women witness stories about other people, and are totally removing themselves. Part of this has to do with the male-dominated structure of the Truth Commission, and the lack of probing questions ... Women are articulate about describing their men's experiences but are hesitant about themselves ... The pain expressed has been the pain of others, not of themselves. Are we colluding by not providing space for women to talk? ... *If women do not talk then the story we produce will not be complete* ... Culturally, we think we understand. For example, people may not have told their spouses. We should have special *in camera* hearings, but then do men learn from these? [emphasis added]

Clearly, the Commission was concerned that it might not gather 'the whole truth' and that hearings might fail in their didactic intent.

By the end of June 1996, the Commission had decided to hold 'Special Hearings on Women', that took place in Cape Town (8 August 1996), Durban (24 October 1996) and Johannesburg (29 July 1997). No Women's Hearing was held in the Eastern Cape region, a fact to which the author of the Report's chapter on women (Volume Four: 283) draws attention, stating, 'It should be noted that the absence of a special hearing in the Eastern Cape could, in itself, distort the picture as the Eastern Cape is known as an area in which treatment in prison was particularly brutal.' No reason for the decision is given in the Report.

The Commission undertook other measures to secure statements about violations suffered by women, including training statement-takers to ask 'probing questions' of deponents and modifying the human rights violations protocol so that by April 1997 it included a cautionary note to women deponents: 'IMPORTANT: Some women testify about violations of human rights that happened to family members or friends, but they have also suffered abuses. Don't forget to tell us what happened to you yourself if you were the victim of a gross human rights abuse' (Statement Concerning Gross Violations of Human Rights, Version 5, 1997: 3).

The Commission and gender activists were particularly concerned that women testify about *sexual* violation. At the Special Event Hearing for Women held in Johannesburg in July 1997, Sheila Meintjes said:

Indeed, we know that very few women have, in fact, come forward to recount their experience of sexual abuse in the context of political violence. Of nearly 9000 cases of violations only about nine have claimed they have been raped. Yet, in our research we came across many cases of violations [that] could be described as rape or where women knew of others who had been raped.

Researchers attributed women's 'silence' about sexual violation to a 'general stigma' that attaches to women in a society that regards rape as 'private' (Goldblatt 1997: 10). Yet, in the context of political violence or detention, rape may be deliberately public. What is at stake is not the privacy or otherwise of the act but how society acknowledges it as a form of violence and makes provision for its recognition as injury.

Addressing the Commission's Women's Hearing held in Johannesburg on 28 July 1997, Thenjiwe Mtintso,[19] previously a commander in *Umkhonto weSizwe* (MK), and at the time of the hearing the chairperson of the Gender Commission, commented on the difficulty of testifying:

When today they [testifiers] make their sobs, they must know that there's a flood of tears from those who did not even dare to come here today. They must know that when they make their sighs when they remember, that many of us are groaning inwardly, because we are not yet ready to make those outward sighs of pain. As they try to free themselves today of the burden, they must know that they are freeing some of us who are not yet ready, Chairperson. I speak as one of those ... I could not sleep last night, because I sat with myself, I sat with my conscience. I sat with the refusal to open those wounds.

She suggested that violation of women was also an indirect attack on men, driving home their failure to protect women in their care, and accused men of using women's bodies as a terrain for male struggle (see also Turshen and Twagiramariya 1998; Das 1995).

Sexual violence was represented in the hearings and in public discourse as a defining feature of women's experiences of gross violations of human rights. It was identified as an experience about which women *could* and *should* testify, and about which they *would* testify under certain conditions. It was considered incumbent upon *women* to describe in public the kinds of sexual harms to which they were subjected. It is disturbing that men were not called to testify about sexual violation. Sexual violence and threats thereof mark brutal incursions that were not restricted to women or to the apartheid past. Rape and sexual violation of women and children are widespread in South Africa, and remain institutionalised forms of violence in prisons. Although men also made statements to the Commission about their experiences of sexual violence, their disclosure of rape and/or sexual violation was seldom public. The focus on women's experiences of sexual violation, while important, precludes a wider understanding of the ways in which power may work in gendered ways. Diana Taylor (1997), for example, argues that, in the Argentinian case, state power works by feminising and infantilising political opponents.

The Report contains a chapter on the Special Hearings on women and one on children (Volume Four, Chapters 9 and 10). It also contains a specific set of findings in relation to women (Report, Volume Five 1998: 256):[20]

The State was responsible for the severe ill treatment of women in custody in the form of harassment and the deliberate withholding of medical attention, food and water.

Women were abused by the security forces in ways which specifically exploited their vulnerabilities as women, for example, rape or the threat of rape and other forms of sexual abuse, threats against family and children, removal of children from their care, false stories about illness and/or death of family members and children, and humiliation and abuse around biological functions such as menstruation and childbirth.

Women in exile, particularly in the camps, were subjected to various forms of sexual abuse and harassment, including rape.

The Report did not make comparable findings about men.

'Women', then, was a category with a particular history in the Commission's work. It emerged after specific interventions: patterns in testimonies given before public hearings (themselves patterned by distinctions between public and private realms and the conventions of speech and behaviour considered appropriate to each – see Chapter 2), and interventions by a variety of social specialists. The Commission's response was to modify its methodological approach, thereby transforming women's experiences of harm into a category that could be investigated and about which findings could be made. Such interventions succeeded in drawing attention to particular forms of violation characterised as specifically gendered. Simultaneously, however, diverse identities, activities and experiences were obscured through the emphasis on sexual difference and harm. The effect of essentialising suffering and gender in this way is to displace questions of resistance, class, race, age and cultural difference in the making of apartheid's subjects and their re-making in the post-apartheid era. An emphasis on the similarity of women's bodily experience comes at the expense of an historical understanding of the constitution of the subject. As a result, the subject of violence is construed as naturally gendered, and the sociological problem to be explained becomes women's experiences of violence, rather than violence and its links to gender and power.

The instantiation of 'women' as a category in the Commission's work matters, not only because it influences how the apartheid past is understood, but also because it has come to shape general ideas about transitional justice and its use in democratising states. For example, Martha Minow (1998) writes that truth commissions need to take specific account of women. Priscilla Hayner comments that women's experiences, especially of sexual abuse and rape, are underreported (2001: 77) and warns, 'If a truth commission does not take special care in addressing this issue, it is likely that it will remain largely shrouded in silence and hidden from the history books' (p. 79). Here, naming absence as failure leaves intact the model of rights and their violation that transforms injustice and suffering into injury.

The history of the category 'women' in the Commission's work suggests that its interventions were supplementary. Feminist historians, political philosophers and scholars of law will be better positioned than I am to trace the long-term effects of such a project. However, Joan Scott offers an apposite warning about the limitations of undertakings that work by the 'addition' of other knowledge to existing wisdom. Criticising feminist historians for adding 'women's experiences' to existent histories in an attempt to 'render historical what has hitherto been hidden from history' (1991: 775), she argues that their efforts run the risk of precluding critical analysis of the conditions within which discourses are produced, thereby replicating or legitimating the power structures that had excluded 'women's experiences' in the first place. Scott expressly recognises that a supplementary project poses difficulties in authorising new knowledge. One way in which feminist historians have dealt with the difficulty has been by 'appealing to experience' (p. 786), resting on the assumption that a subject's own account of personal experience must be true (p. 777). Experience becomes the bedrock for political claims but at the same time may have the effect of naturalising categories and obviating the historical processes through which people are constituted as subjects. Scott proposes:

[W]e need to attend to the historical processes that, through discourse, position subjects and produce their experiences. It is not individuals who have experiences, but subjects who are constituted through experience. Experience ... then becomes not the origin of our explanation, not the authoritative (because seen or felt) evidence that grounds what is known, but rather that which we seek to explain, that about which knowledge is produced. [pp. 779–80]

She calls for analysis of the conditions that produce and legitimate particular forms of knowledge at the expense of others.

Deborah Battaglia draws from theories of deconstruction to argue that supplementation does not *necessarily* replicate existent frames of knowledge: in her view it is 'a process of new knowledge acting upon prior (never total or sufficient) knowledge, and in consequence destabilizing it' (1999: 120). Destabilisation of this order is, she claims, the task of ethnography. Seeking a methodological approach that recognises 'the open subject', she proposes that

Persons, their subjectivities and identities (selves) are shaped by and shape relations to others, under the press of historical and cultural contingency. From this it follows that selves are 'not given to us' by natural law (Foucault 1984: 341), nor fixed and unchanging. And certainly they are not ontologically prior to relations of power ... Rather, selves are from the start an open question. [1999: 115]

The descriptions of the subject offered by these scholars differ considerably from that of the Commission, with its emphasis on the sovereign subject. I have found them useful in thinking about violence and social suffering: their destabilisation of taken-for-granted categories offers a conceptual space to consider how some interventions in social life may create different qualities of speech and diverse forms of silence. I begin to probe these claims through a study of women's testimonies.

2 TESTIMONIAL PRACTICES

I, the survivor, I wrap you in words so that the future inherits you. I snatch you from the death of forgetfulness ... I have translated you from the dead. (Krog 1998: 27–8)

'The saying' is born of ... fracture, separation, and exile: separation from the beloved, exile from oneself. It is born of an impasse, a stricture and constriction, an eclipse of language and thought ... Yet that speechlessness, the impasse of that fracturing, is also a passage into another scene. There, like an angel, appears the poetical word ... [F]or a poet, the loss of the object, its disappearance into a distance beyond reach, is the condition of poetical speech. (Pandolfo 1997: 11)

Testimonial interventions, long customary in courts, have become important in a variety of other social arenas including as part of counselling for political exiles and increasingly as components in 'political transitions' through mechanisms such as truth commissions and commissions of enquiry. They fall into the ambit of what Richard Werbner has described as 'rights of recountability' – 'the right, especially in the face of state violence and oppression, to make a citizen's memory known and acknowledged in the public sphere' (1998: 1). The coming-to-voice in a public sphere that testimony frequently represents may hold the promise of new subjectivities in the aftermath of disrupted social formations or in establishing fresh forms of sociality. Yet, as demonstrated in a growing literature on testimony, a large portion of which is impelled by and drawn from memories of Holocaust survivors,[1] pain and horror puzzle both language and memory. Elaine Scarry (1985), writing of the horrifying effects of torture, and Lawrence Langer (1991, 1995), whose work examines Holocaust survivors' testimonies, describe the devastating effects of these extremes: showing that such experiences or conditions cannot easily be recalled into language, they propose that some kinds of experience stand outside of language's redemptive possibilities. The disruption of language thus occasioned has been interpreted as rendering certain forms of experience unsayable (for example, Felman and Laub 1992; Bar-On 1999; Hayner 2001).

Philosopher Giorgio Agamben, writing in relation to human extermination at Auschwitz, is critical of this claim, not least because it may confer 'the prestige of the mystical' (1999:32). For Agamben, it is not the spoken word's inadequacy that is at stake, but language's interpolation of subjects.

He argues that testimony 'contains a lacuna' (p. 33) that calls into question the identity and reliability of witnesses. Proposing that 'every testimony is a field of forces incessantly traversed by currents of subjectification and desubjectification' (p. 121), and that it occurs at the point where there is no possibility of 'conjoining the living being with language' (p. 130), he sees testimony as 'the disjunction between two impossibilities of bearing witness ... If there is no articulation between the living being and language, if the "I" stands suspended in this disjunction, then there can be testimony. The intimacy that betrays our non-coincidence with ourselves is the place of testimony. *Testimony takes place in the non-place of articulation*' (p. 130: emphasis in the original). Testimony then implicates the subject in particular ways: for Agamben, the only true witness to Auschwitz is one who cannot be a subject in language – the *Muselmann* – one who has been dead and can testify to that state.

While the problems of language and the subject positions it makes possible may be particular, they raise important questions to consider in relation to testimonial interventions. Where violence ruptures the range of voice and the articulation of experience, it raises anew the problem of how to acknowledge suffering. The problem has to do with listening.

Describing the faculties with which one may mourn a lost lover, novelist Jeanette Winterson speaks of hearing thus:

Hearing and the Ear:

The auricle is the expanded portion which projects from the side of the head. It is composed of fibro-elastic cartilage covered with skin and fine hairs. It is deeply grooved and ridged. The prominent outer ridge is known as the helix. The lobule is the soft, pliable part at the outer extremity.

Sound travels at about 335 metres per second. [1933: 135]

The starkness of Winterson's description of the physical characteristics of the ear, a description which is followed by a deeply personal account of loss and grieving, make it an appropriate way to commence a chapter on stories of loss. The description of the physical ear acts as a counterpoise to my argument about the difficulties involved in listening and attending to stories of pain and loss.

SPEAKING TRUTH

Notwithstanding the patterning of testimonies described in Chapter 1, testimonial forms were diverse. I consider this in relation to the ways that women testified about men, beginning with the testimony given on 17 April 1996 in East London's ornate red brick City Hall by Nyameka Goniwe about the death of her husband, Matthew. The story has been told many times: her husband was a well-known activist and news of his death in June 1985 was carried in national and international media. Nyameka Goniwe had spoken frequently to the media and before the courts at two inquests held into his death. Her testimony to the Commission was clear and direct. Events were given in sequence and were chronologically ordered. The focus of attention was Matthew. The story as I tell it is distilled from her words to the Commission that day.

Nyameka Goniwe began her testimony at 9:30 am, in a hall full of people silent in expectation. She sat with the widows of three other activists who had been killed with her husband, on a podium facing the semicircle of Commissioners and panellists. National flags flew from the corners of the stage behind the Commissioners, and a large banner bearing the words: 'Truth and Reconciliation Commission: Healing our Past. First Hearing, East London, 15–18 April 1996', lined the wall at the back of the stage. A lighted altar candle burned at the edge of the stage, flanked by tasselled maroon velvet curtains and potted palm trees. Mrs Goniwe read her prepared statement in English, commencing, 'To talk of Matthew Goniwe and my life is a daunting task. I'll try to bring together the events that led to his death.' She then told one of the most famous stories of a man's resistance against the state in South Africa.

Matthew Goniwe was a teacher and an anti-apartheid activist. His life with Nyameka Goniwe was marked by his frequent arrests and imprisonment, the first of which occurred in 1976, shortly after their marriage the previous year. Arrested in terms of the Suppression of Communism Act No. 44 of 1950, for setting up a 'political discussion group' in Transkei,[2] he spent 15 months as an awaiting-trial prisoner before being sentenced to four years' imprisonment, a sentence that he served in Umtata. Mrs Goniwe had meanwhile enrolled at the University of Fort Hare, which meant living some 100 kilometres away, far from her child who was cared for by Matthew's mother in the rural town of Cradock. As she described that time to the Commission panel, she remembered the hardships she faced:

My biggest challenge at the time was to be available to my baby as often as possible, to attend to my studies and also give support to my husband in prison. I remember that year being one of the toughest years I have faced in my life. I was short of money and had to rely on my brothers-in-law for assistance, and the small grant I used to get from the Dependants Conference of the SACC [South African Council of Churches].

Goniwe was released from prison in 1981. Shortly afterwards, he was transferred by the Department of Education and Training (DET, the department responsible for the education of Africans) to the small town of Graaff-Reinet. The following year he was moved to Cradock, where he became principal of the High School, and one of the founders of the Cradock Residents Association and of CRADOYA, the Cradock Youth Association. In 1983, both organisations were affiliated to the newly launched United Democratic Front (UDF – an association launched in 1983). Prior to being banned by the Apartheid State in 1988, it comprised more than five hundred affiliated organisations in a broad front against apartheid. It was formally disbanded in 1991 after the ANC and PAC had been unbanned. Goniwe became involved in 'rekindling the politics of resistance' locally, his widow told the Commission.

In December 1983, Goniwe was transferred to Graaff-Reinet once more. However, seeing it as an attempt to curtail his political activity, he refused to go. The community and youth of Cradock supported him in his decision. Youths boycotted schools, demanding his reinstatement. In March 1984, he and three others were detained under Section 28 of the wide-ranging provisions of the Internal Security Act, which provided for 'preventative detention' for an indefinite period. He spent six months in detention.

Nyameka Goniwe recalled that the situation in Cradock had deteriorated as protests against State action increased and the State responded with ever harsher repression: 'The situation in the township worsened in their absence and violence escalated on a scale never experienced before. All school committees resigned. The pressure forced the Security Police to release Matthew and his colleagues. They were released on the 10 October 1984 and were given a hero's welcome by the community.'

Matthew Goniwe immediately returned to his political work, creating street committees and rallying youth leadership. He was elected as regional rural organiser for the UDF. On 27 May 1985, the South African Defence Force (SADF) sealed off the township. Helicopters dropped pamphlets denouncing Goniwe. Police searched the houses of known activists. Goniwe's movements were closely monitored by the Security Branch, the branch of the South African Police tasked with matters of internal security. Nyameka Goniwe described for the Commission the ways that the family was harassed by police: 'The whole family bore the wrath of the Security Police which took the form of harassment, early morning house raids, constant surveillance, death threats, phone bugging, short-term detentions for questioning, mysterious phone calls, tampering with cars, and so on.' Later, when tapes and transcripts of his telephone calls were produced during the inquest into his death, she learned of the extraordinary extent to which the Security Branch had monitored Goniwe's movements and actions.

The last time that Nyameka Goniwe saw her husband was when he left home with Fort Calata, Sparrow Mkhonto and Sicelo Mhlawuli to attend a UDF meeting. She told the Commission that she had warned him to be careful, prompting him to consider his safety and saying, 'Please don't travel at night! Rather sleep over!' She recalled sorrowfully, 'They laughed at me, of course: they didn't take me seriously. I don't know why, perhaps they never thought that they would be killed.'

She told the Commission that when Matthew had not returned that night she knew that something had happened. The next day she telephoned friends and anti-apartheid activists and organisations. She sought information, and, not finding it, decided to look for him by travelling the route he usually used when he drove home. She and her brother-in-law, accompanied by political activists, went in search of him. They stopped at two police stations to ask if the police had seen Matthew. She told the Commission that the police behaved suspiciously when she had asked about him, renewing her fears about his safety. The searchers returned home where they received a message that the police had left with a child. It said that the remains of Matthew's burnt-out car had been found near the Port Elizabeth Race Course. She recalled, 'Immediately we knew that something serious had happened. Of course we had pointers because in May, you know, the PEPCO Three had disappeared without a trace.'[3] Alarmed, Nyameka alerted the international and local media. The community embarked on boycotts of shops and schools, a common protest tactic throughout the country at the time.

In her matter-of-fact reading before the Commission, Nyameka Goniwe described how the bodies of her husband and his comrades were found: 'On Saturday the 29th of June 1985, the bodies of Sparrow Mkhonto and Sicelo Mhlawuli were found and those of Matthew and Fort were found on the 2nd of July 1985. All the bodies had multiple stab wounds and were badly burned.' Nyameka Goniwe presented the Commission with her analysis of the likelihood of police complicity in the deaths: 'He couldn't have slipped [past] the police monitoring networks. Whatever befell him on that night of the 27th was known to the police and they killed him.' She pointed out that the state 'hated him for raising rural awareness', and considered him 'a dangerous man, a threat to the state'.

She described the first inquest into his death as 'a circus', and told the Commission that the second inquest made a finding that the State Security Forces were responsible for Matthew's death but that no person could be named as culpable. When asked by a Commissioner who she thought had killed her husband and his comrades, she said, 'We have a picture of what happened, although we can't prove it to the courts', and went on to describe the similarities between the deaths of the 'Cradock Four' and the 'PEBCO Three', implicating the state in the deaths.

Nyameka Goniwe's testimony was spare, lucid, ordered and presented in chronological fashion. The testimony implicated the state in sustained and sanctioned violence and horror, emphasised through relational clauses that mark a radically divided social order.[4] She appeared to hold emotion carefully at bay as she read from her prepared statement in a tempo that varied little from its measured pace. At times her tone and words were distanced from the events described, as in the quotation above. It was clear that she had a detailed knowledge of the connections between the SADF, the police, Security Branch, State Security Council and 'hit squads'.[5] Her statement focused on Matthew and the family's attempts to locate his killers, and she carefully edited herself from the catalogue of events she described. Other than a brief comment on the harassment of the family, she did not address the question of her own experiences or those of her family until expressly asked to do so by committee member, John Smith, who asked how she would feel if someone were to apply for amnesty for the death of Goniwe. She replied, 'Well I look forward to that. I mean I know it's difficult after suffering such pain and trauma. But we need to know what happened and who they are, and also ... they have to show some remorse.' He pressed her to elaborate and she replied, 'They have to show us remorse, [show us] that they're sorry for what they did. I don't say that it would immediately make us happy: it's a challenge; we're going to be challenged in that kind of way, and grapple with that, and it will take a long time. Healing takes a long time.'

*   *   *

Several women testified in a similarly concise and chronological fashion. Elizabeth Floyd, for example, spoke in Johannesburg (2 May 1996) of the death in detention of Neil Aggett – unionist, medical doctor and conscientious objector to compulsory military conscription. Aggett had been detained on 27 November 1981 in terms of the General Law Amendment Act No. 37 of 1963 that allowed for detention for up to 90 days without access to a lawyer. He had been held in Pretoria Prison and then transferred to John Vorster Square on 11 December 1981, where he had remained until his death. On 5 February 1982, he had been found hanging from the grille across the window in his cell. The inquest into his death found that he had committed suicide and that no person could be held responsible for his death.

Elizabeth Floyd described his activities as a unionist, commenting that his activities had been monitored by the police and adding, 'We were well aware of what we were up against: a cruel, a dirty and an unjust system.' She gave a summary of his death and said that even if Aggett had chosen to kill himself, the state was still responsible for having pushed him to the point where suicide may have seemed to be his only option. She did not describe Aggett's political activities or her own in detail. She focused her attention on describing both the effects of his death on the activist community inside South Africa and the effects of torture on detainees: 'With his death our worst fears about detention were confirmed. He was the first white to die in detention. For the black people involved, this was very significant; he had not held back in the struggle and had paid the price ... When I was released from detention, our community was shattered. Neil's death was a watershed, as was David Webster's death.'[6]

Elizabeth Floyd told the Commission that at the inquest into Aggett's death, evidence had been presented that showed that he had been tortured with electric shocks. He had also told a co-detainee that he had been tortured. Floyd described the torture practices commonly used against detainees: sleep deprivation, solitary confinement, suffocation and electric shocks. She explained that the combination of torture and solitary confinement was devastating to people with few defences left after the shock of capture. She argued that 'The fine line between life and death in those situations becomes a very fine line and death is clearly behind the detention system and it's not by chance that we regularly have death in detention.' She described a chronology of violence and traced changes in torture practices over the 34 years that the Commission investigated, making a clear and precise connection between Aggett's death and the systems that underpinned apartheid, and linking the violent treatment of detainees to similar torture in other parts of the world. She claimed that the security services still harboured people accused of abuse.

Testifying with pedagogic intent, she said she felt it important for people who had taken little notice of the violence in the country, particularly white people, 'to understand that ... while they may not have taken specific responsibility, they can't pretend that it didn't happen.' She added, 'I think it's critical that people do know – and not just about the events of 1981 or 1982.'

Like Nyameka Goniwe, Elizabeth Floyd presented her understanding of the state's persistent attempts to halt activism, indicating, through her familiarity with state processes, a kind of political literacy. Elizabeth Floyd's testimony was similar to many other women's in that she testified about a man. Yet her testimony differed from many others in that she did not identify herself as a victim but as someone imparting expert knowledge. Her credibility as a witness seemed predicated on her knowledge and the authoritative way she was able to present it to the Commission. Neil Aggett is named as a victim in the Commission's Report; Elizabeth Floyd is not.

* * *

In the two cases described above, the attention of the audience is focused on the stories of Matthew Goniwe and Neil Aggett, rather than on Nyameka Goniwe and Elizabeth Floyd. Their testimonies presented a coherent chronology of the state's attempts to control opposition, presented in accord with a detailed understanding of state structures and personal awareness of violence and its effects. The information was starkly given, presented linearly and with emotion carefully controlled. There are parallels between the testimonies described here and those of women who described themselves as political activists (see Chapter 3), most notably in the intimacy with state power implicit in the testimonies.

Elizabeth Floyd's testimony is, perhaps, more difficult to characterise than Nyameka Goniwe's in that she did not describe her relationship to Aggett (she was his partner and herself an activist) and presented herself as an expert witness. Testimony of this kind presented the speaker as someone who 'knows' and who has valuable information to impart. Nyameka Goniwe spoke from a single position of authority in this context, as the widow of a well-known political activist.

In much African convention, widowhood is an ambiguous if not dangerous status. Widows embody dichotomies between female and male, sacred and profane, personal and political, and public and private (Ramphele 1996). The discomforts of widowhood were described by Sepati Mlangeni, who, on 2 May 1996, told the Commission of the death of her husband, Bheki Mlangeni, a human rights lawyer killed by a parcel bomb he received in 1990. Weeping, she said, 'Today I am a widow. I'm an outcast in our society because I'm a widow. In our community and our society you are associated with all sorts of things when you are a widow.' Her words begin to suggest the sense of unease that may result from speaking from a 'difficult' subject position: one in which convention – which Judith Butler (1997a: 25) describes as that 'inherited set of voices, an echo of others who speak as the "I"' – cannot necessarily be relied upon to endorse current action. Testifying from and about such a subject position may feel both liberating and compromising in its deviation from custom.

Occupying a social position that imputes them to be ritually polluted and potentially polluting, widows (unlike widowers) are, for the duration of mourning, liminal figures, dangerous. The position occupied by women whose deceased husbands had been well-known figures in anti-apartheid resistance is still more complex. Describing such women as 'political widows', Mamphela Ramphele (1996) demonstrates that they are simultaneously the reminder of loss and are also transformed in the public arena into 'political capital'. The position of women who occupy the zones of political widowhood is precarious. Ramphele writes:

> The political role of the political widow derives from her relationship with her husband; she is not seen as a woman but as someone standing in for a fallen man. She becomes the ultimate honorary man ... her agency is not completely eliminated, but constrained. To the extent that she can renegotiate the terms of her engagement, she is able to enlarge her socio-political space as a public figure. It is a tough balancing act, fraught with danger. [1996: 112]

Widowhood implies a state of ritual danger and liminality. In their testimonies, few political widows directly imputed victimhood to self. Rather, as Ramphele shows, such women exemplify social memory, embodying the brutality of the state and the struggle of their menfolk.

HEROES AS MODELS: TIME AND THE DOMESTIC

The testimonies I now present differ from those described above in that they drew on narrative forms and tropes common to Southern African oral traditions. Writing about oral performances in Southern Africa, Harold Scheub (1975,[7] 1996 and 1998) suggests that, like culture, genres of oration shift and flow. He says, 'The oral tradition is never simply a spoken art: it is an enactment, an event, a ritual, a set of symbols, a performance' (1998: 126). Its conventions are flexible: as Scheub points out, 'Story is routinely recast in contemporary frames' (p. 296), and, 'history is constantly being revisited and retold' (p. 21). In relation to the latter point, he describes the Commission as a new forum within which stories were performed (p. 292, endnote 5). (I elaborate on the notion of 'story' in the Commission's work in Chapter 4.)

A successful performance is dependent on location (Hofmeyr 1994; Benjamin 1992), audience imagination (Zenani and Scheub 1992) and on emotion elicited through the patterning of performance's structural components – image, narrative, rhythm and trope (Scheub 1998: 6–15). These evoke emotional responses by drawing from three emotional sources: the life experiences and emotions of each member of the audience; the experience of past 'conjurations' of stories; and the storyteller's own emotional history (Scheub 1998: 185). Scheub compares the resultant layering of meaning to palimpsest (p. 240–2), a delicate 'tracery of biography' (p. 242).

Testimonies that drew from oral tradition had deep cultural echoes, even as the contexts in which the forms were used were new. Audiences in Human Rights Violations hearings responded visibly and audibly. On occasion, they were warned to be silent. In their telling, women who used these forms invited audiences to participate with them in performances of memory and meaning, and drew audiences with them in the testimonial process. The performances did not rest solely on words to convey experience but drew on what Veena Das calls 'an aesthetic of gestures', a phrase that describes how utterances 'are bristling with unstated words, performative gestures and a whole repertoire of culturally dense notions that surround them' (2000: 211). There was a taken-for-granted character to many of the testimonies offered before the Commission: given before audiences who were often familiar with the context described in testimonies, if not the instance being described, testimonies were coloured with local knowledge and idiom and fixed to local and national events.[8] They were often explicitly located within the domestic sphere. Some women were consummate tellers. They used rich metaphor, tone and gesture and drew on poetic language and performative convention to carry their meanings. Other women found it less easy to convey the complex stories they told: the setting, so unlike traditional spaces of telling, was intimidating and the harm of which they spoke too great to bear easily in words.[9]

There is perhaps an ease of empathy, a suspension of critical judgement, in listening and watching that is not present in the same way when reading testimonies. Priscilla Hayner, for example, comments on the confusion of trying to understand what she calls the non-chronological 'strangeness' of testimonies (2001: 148–9). Gaps in information, poetic language, emphases, diversions, fluctuations in narrative's time flow create a rhythm in what Coplan (1995) describes as 'aural'[10] processes that may seem peculiar or limited when subjected to writing's linear rigour. Transcribed testimonies sometimes jar: events do not follow one another clearly, the narrative may seem incoherent, and the taken-for-granted nature of information and idiom does not easily survive transliteration. In places I have intervened in the flow of testimonies in order to make clear the sequence of events. Some testimonies required little intervention; where women have told the stories before, narrative forms have crystallised. In other cases, I have rendered into words what was implicit in the performance.

Three testimonies by Nonceba Zokwe, Eunice Miya and Sylvia Dlomo-Jele tell about the deaths of their sons. I draw from their accounts themes that are reflected in other women's testimonies, and narrative forms that embed experience firmly in a domestic world marked by daily struggle.

*   *   *

On 17 April 1996, shortly after Nyameka Goniwe had spoken of Matthew's death, Nonceba Zokwe testified about the death of her son, Sithembile. She introduced herself to the Commission by her clan name and place of origin: 'I am Nonceba Zokwe, a daughter from the Nogaka Family at Inymakwe. I went to school from Sub A to higher primary until up to a teacher's certificate at Blyspoed. That is the certificate I got. As time went on I went to work only at two places, and I met an activist there called Siphabalala Zokwe.' She told the Commissioners of how she had met the man who was to become her husband, describing him as 'a propagandist of human rights'. At this point her story took on the lyric and rhythmic style that was to characterise it throughout the telling.[11]

I went to work and I met the activist Siphabalala Zokwe. I met him there during the difficult times of struggle and oppression, when the government was removing people from place to place ...

He would ride his horse every day, morning till night. My husband was fighting for human rights. We had children, the first one was Thobela, the second born was Sibongile, Sithembile was the third and Sibusiso, the last one.

Nonceba Zokwe continued with an account of her children's political activities. One son, Thobela, had escaped the illegal cross-border raid made by the SADF on Maseru, Lesotho in 1982, and had gone into exile, first to Zimbabwe and then to Austria. He returned to South Africa after the 1994 elections. Another son, Sithembile, had died. It was his story that she had come to tell.

As a schoolchild, Sithembile was involved in the struggle against the apartheid regime, and, after taking his school-leaving examinations, he had left to join the liberation forces in Botswana.[12] He returned briefly to South Africa to tell his mother that he had joined 'the struggle' and then he left again for Lesotho, Angola and East Germany. The family received scant news of him. Mrs Zokwe was told he had disappeared and later she learned from human rights lawyers that he had been arrested in Bophuthatswana, an 'independent homeland'. She was told he was being held in a prison in Soweto. Mrs Zokwe sought her son. She wrote to the Commissioner of Police, and was told that Sithembile had been sent to Transkei (another of the 'independent homelands') to serve a prison sentence.

In 1988, after two years in prison, he returned to his mother's home at Butterworth. He told his mother about the taunts he levelled at the guards, whom he had addressed as 'oppressors', and she recounted them for the Commission: 'And he said, "Mum I was arrested in Bophuthatswana, and I was put into prison here in Soweto. [I told them] ... They must either charge me or release me." He just stood by that fact. He went further to say, "I was raised up, every morning, every afternoon, my family was fighting for their human rights, I want to destroy Apartheid."'

He found work at a liquor store, 'carrying beer up and down, in and out. He was in and out of jail also, accused of being a communist born of a communist mother ... It became clear that something would happen to him', his mother recalled. Sithembile had told his mother that the police would kill him and warned her to accept what would happen to him. She told the Commission that the police made three attempts on her son's life. On one of the three occasions he had been shot in the head and dumped into a river. Mrs Zokwe said that he had been rescued by 'God and the birds'. She did not elaborate on the attack or his survival but continued, telling the Commission that her son had carried on with his work as a political activist: 'Then this youth would sit without doing anything. He did not want to do anything but the struggle.'

She had had dreams that she read as premonitory: 'I dreamed that this child of mine was looking into death's eyes, and I think this was the second premonition on a Tuesday because I dreamed the same dream again.'

In June 1988, Sithembile was killed. Mrs Zokwe related how she learned of his death. 'On that day I was [returning] from the wholesalers', said Mrs Zokwe. 'I met him on his way to town with my grandchildren on his shoulders ... He saw me and hugged me.' She told him to go home and wait for her. She went to Chicken Licken (a fast-food outlet) where she was stopped and told that her son and his friend had been arrested.[13] Stopping at a salon, she was told the story again by passers-by, in more detail. She described to the Commission her return home where she saw a policeman silhouetted against the house, and where she was greeted by 'the leader of the Apartheid regime, a policeman, the head of the Security Branch, who said, "Here's that communist mother".' She had responded angrily: 'On these premises *I* am the government', and, when he threatened to kill her, she said, 'The only pain I know is the pain of giving birth.' She told the Commission that she had attempted to attack him and had been restrained by neighbours. She described trying to leap over the wall surrounding her property to reach her son near the police van in the street, and recalled: 'A few minutes later I heard the sound of a revolver. I knew I had to close my son's eyes, but I could not.' Amid threats from the police, the van reversed into the yard, breaking the gate and wall and destroying the flowers.

In response to questions from a panellist she explained, 'I was hopeful that he was still alive, that he was just being arrested but I had this feeling that something terrible was happening to my son.' She did not describe how he came to be in the van, nor how she later discovered he was dead and his body in the state morgue. Instead, she continued her story with the search for her son, whom she feared dead. She visited the police station and hospital and a relative, a policeman, who promised to try to find out what had happened. She did not describe the complexities and ironies of asking her kinsman to assist her when he was employed as a policeman by the same government that her son – and, it seemed, she – was working against. She told the Commissioners that when she returned home without having found him, she saw signs of struggle everywhere. She listed them carefully: they included a burnt passage, bullet holes in walls, wardrobes and suitcases scattered on the floor, a patch of blood between the wardrobe and the bed, a jacket still hanging in the burned cupboard, and torn curtains. Her children were crying.

Then she moved to the identification of her son in the mortuary: 'He was on a stretcher, smiling in death. He would tell us to be strong ... He was dead but smiling ... I was proud because I *knew* why my child had died.' Later she described the return of the policeman who had promised to find out about her child. He had not performed the appropriate rituals to cleanse himself after her son's burial.[14] He came to the house but would not enter. He bore news that the policemen who had killed her child had been imprisoned but had escaped from prison. She greeted him and told him that her son had been buried and that he should wash his hands in a ritual to remove the polluting traces of contact with death.

Mrs Zokwe's story was about her own experiences in relation to her child's death. In her story she described herself as protector of the child, as boss in her home, as mother. Later, when a Commissioner asked her about the source of her strength, she replied:

It depends on your upbringing ... My home was a traditional home ... Nobody was regarded as a stranger in this house ... We had the examples of heroes as models. They gave strength. I saw they could survive and therefore said I could survive, too. I *know* my struggle. I am proud of womanhood. It is womanhood which brought me this strength ... You have to decide for yourself who you are and what you'd like to be tomorrow.

Her testimony was elliptical; it used repetition and pause, gesture and silence, conventions drawn from oral culture that resonated strongly with audience members. Nonceba Zokwe saw her strength as being based on traditional values, and her narration gave form to these ideas. The largely black audience responded audibly to her narrative. Nods and repetition of well-known names punctuated her testimony. Some Commissioners nodded in response to her testimony. Others listened with impassive faces.

*   *   *

Women used the metaphor of the domestic world differently. Eunice Miya, testifying on 23 April 1996 in Cape Town, used domesticity and chronological time to fasten her experience of the death of her 23-year-old son, Jabulani, one of seven young men killed in what became known as the case of 'the Gugulethu Seven'. They were killed by police who claimed that the seven men were members of an MK cell and that they planned to ambush a police vehicle. In fact, the youths had been trained in weapons handling by *askaris* (informants)[15] who had been briefed by the police to assist them and to report back on their activities to their 'handlers'. It appears that the youths had been tricked into a police ambush (Report, Volume Five: 451).

Eunice Miya told the Commission about how she learned of the death of her son:

On the 3rd of March 1986 I was working in offices in town. I left the house at half-past-four in the morning as usual, to be at work at six o'clock. Just before I left, my son [who lived in a room in the back yard] knocked on the door. I opened it – it was about quarter-past four or twenty-past – and he came and got bread and cold water and asked for two Rand. I said that I only had five Rand and would be short if I gave it to him. But I gave it to him because I wanted him to work. He said he wanted to accompany me to the station. I said 'This is the first time!', but he insisted.

He left to go to his bedroom and I closed and bolted the door. The garage is next to the house and he came through the garage and insisted on accompanying me. I was suspicious and I said 'Turn back', but he accompanied me to NY59 [a nearby street]. I told him to turn back. That was the last time I saw him. I went to work on the quarter-to-five train.

Her story is precisely located and framed: at a given time in the morning of a specific day, as she was preparing to go to work. It is placed squarely within the domestic domain that then introduces her position within the economy as she prepares for a double shift as a char, and her encouragement of her son's search for a job. The story is framed in space; the scene moves from the kitchen, now locked and bolted and secured from the dangers outside, to the garage, and outside into the street; from the relative security of domesticity into the unknown of the world at large. The story about her son's death is thus not simply the recall of an event, but of the conditions of life that characterised and shaped it.

The beginning of the day was marked in her mind because her son's behaviour was unusual; his insistence that he accompany her transformed it from an ordinary day into an extraordinary one. Her memory of the day indicates, retrospectively, a prescience of violent change. It points also to the ebb and flow of violence: although she locked up carefully, Mrs Miya did not expect the intrusion of violence and death into her home, notwithstanding the contexts of violence, fear and repression that marked both that time (mid-1980s) and the place (a black township).

The way in which the story was placed in daily experience was sustained in the next part of her testimony in which she described hearing about the violence in Gugulethu that day. As usual, she went to clean offices and then went to work in a private home:

I worked as usual, but at about half-past ten my boss, Mrs __ came to me and said, 'Eunice.' I said, 'Madam.' She said, 'I heard on the news there are Russians [slang term for members of liberation organisation members, some of whom were trained in and received support from the USSR] in Gugulethu who were killed. Is your son in politics?' 'No', and I continued working.

At about two o'clock I went home. On the way I did the shopping, and caught the five o'clock train. [I arrived home] and put on the TV for the news. My daughter put it on.

[Pause while she cries. The panellists and audience are silent, waiting for her tears to subside.]

When the music started for the news, then I was told that seven children were killed by Russian guerrillas.[16] One was shown on TV with a gun on his chest and I saw it was my son. My daughter said, 'It's him!' I said, 'No. I saw him this morning and he was dressed warmly.' I prayed that the news would rewind.

Again, her testimony drew from her daily experiences; at work with the 'Madam', shopping, then the return home, watching the news with her daughter, and recalling what her child had worn that day. In her testimony, the mundane provides horrid counterpoint to the violence of loss.

*   *   *

Many of the women spoke explicitly about the loss of loved ones and how it changed their expectations of time and of ageing. Sylvia Dlomo-Jele, testifying on 30 April 1996 at a hearing in Johannesburg, explained to the Commission that the death of her son, Sicelo, had altered her expectations of the future, and that his activism had affected her life. She explained,

The harassment and pain [we experienced] did not start when my child died. It started in 1985, when he began to be harassed by police as a student activist. He was harassed at school; the police and Defence Force went to the school and the headmaster would hide him with other children ... The house was petrol-bombed. I suffered a lot and my mother nearly died ... The police used to come in and out of my house and told me to tell my son not to be political.

In response to their warnings she said that she did not know what they were talking about, and that she knew nothing about politics. She passed on their warnings to her son, but he would not desist from his activities. Instead, concerned at the harassment of his family, he stopped sleeping at home and her expectations of family life, that, at least, children should sleep under the same roofs as their parents, were disrupted. She continued,

On the Wednesday before his death he came to me and said 'Mother, Father, I've come to sleep at home.' I was relieved because he had been sleeping with other people or outside. He looked tired and had a headache. I used to give him my nerve tablets. A child, he knew what he was fighting for. He told us to be strong if he died; 'Pick up my spear and continue my struggle', he said.

I told him to sleep at home. He refused, saying that it would not be nice for his parents to see the police killing him. He left. He did not like to be followed, but I did so. I think he slept in the passage [the strip of ground separating houses].

On Saturday he phoned his aunt and told her to cook for him. He did not return on Saturday to fetch his food. We were worried, but prayed. On Sunday, while still preparing new food for him, at about ten o'clock, the phone rang. It was Sicelo who asked if I was okay, then kept quiet. I thought he did not have money for the phone. That was the last time I spoke to him. The next day the police arrived with his [Sicelo's] pocketbook. I said, 'Have you killed my son?' and he [the policeman] denied it.

The failure of her son to collect his meal was an indication that something was amiss, a further breach in a social order already shaped by apartheid's intrusion. His mother had no means to ensure his well-being: she could not even provide him with food and shelter. Prayer was her only remaining intervention but her prayers were to no avail. Sicelo's body was found under a tree in the bushlands. When the policeman who had identified the boy from his pocketbook and reported to his mother offered her a police escort, she refused and instead went to the site with a neighbour. There she found her dead son.

'The pain did not end there', Mrs Dlomo-Jele told the Commission. After identifying Sicelo's body, she went to the Pretoria police station to report his death. The policemen on duty accused her of having a 'big mouth' yet of being unable to control her own child. When her other son grew angry at their taunts he was detained. Later, at Sicelo's funeral, police threw teargas at the mourners and her niece almost suffocated as a result. Family members were harassed even after Sicelo's death. Mrs Dlomo-Jele suspected members of the police of having killed her son. The murderers were not found. During a public hearing into violations committed by the 'Mandela United Football Club', a lead article in the *Mail and Guardian* (21–27 November 1997) stated that new evidence would emerge that would link Winnie Mandela-Madikizela (Nelson Mandela's ex-wife) to Sicelo Dlomo's death. On 31 January 1999, the *Sunday Times* ran a short front-page article that claimed that four men had applied for amnesty for killing Sicelo Dlomo. They were MK members. They claimed that Sicelo was killed because he was suspected of being a police informer. At the time of writing, the amnesty applications have not yet been heard in public. Sicelo Dlomo is not reported as a victim of gross violations of human rights in the Commission's report, nor is his mother.

Mrs Dlomo-Jele's health suffered as a result of Sicelo's activism and death. At the Commission hearing, she spoke of the change in the shape of her future, saying that Sicelo had been a good student who would have found work and supported her. Her husband's mental health was unstable and he had not worked for three years. Her own state of health prohibited her from regular work, and her expectations of support from Sicelo had been dashed. Her future was no longer predictable and the way she had envisaged time, prompted by cultural expectations that emphasise the obligations of children to parents, could not be fulfilled.

At the funeral, Mrs Dlomo-Jele said, she was unable to mourn her child as her own (personal communication, November 1995). He had become a child of the community, a symbol of resistance. In the outpouring of public grieving that accompanied his funeral, she felt unable to acknowledge to herself the loss of her son. His death and burial became a public opportunity to make political statements that were otherwise impossible, a common occurrence at funerals of those killed by the police at the time. The children in the community had given her their lunch monies on that day in com-memoration of the loss of her son. She explained to me that they did so because they recognised that her child would not be able to fulfil his obligations to her. For that day, at least, collectively, they took symbolic responsibility for her.

On 13 March 1999, Mrs Dlomo-Jele died. The Centre for the Study of Violence and Reconciliation in Johannesburg, with which she had worked in establishing the Khulumani Support Group, a survivor support and lobby group, notified those of us who knew or had met her. The message, sent by email, stated:

Her son, Sicelo Dlomo, lost his life on the path to freedom in South Africa. Sylvia not only completed his journey while carrying the heavy burden of his death, but took many with her. Ironically, in the end, it was the stress of his death and the partial truths about him being killed by his fellow comrades that were too much for her. In this regard she symbolises the plight of so many in South Africa who have only been left with half-truths about the past. Her death reminds us that it is people like Sylvia who ultimately paid the price for the democracy we now enjoy ...

THE LAYERING OF EXPERIENCE

Many women seemed to testify to *layers* of experience entwined in wide sets of social relations. Hidden in the discourses of domesticity are powerful forms of knowledge and agency that need to be recognised and sensitively heard. Four themes emerge from the testimonies of Nyameka Goniwe, Elizabeth Floyd, Nonceba Zokwe, Eunice Miya and Sylvia Dlomo-Jele as resonant with the testimonies of most women who spoke before the Commission. These have to do with experiences of family life; with expectations of time; with silence and secrecy; and the location of self in stories. Each weaves through the others.

Family and the domestic

Many women testified about their losses using metaphors drawn from their domestic roles. It seems that women used domesticity, a space over which women usually have more control than other spheres, to map the interpolations of violence in their lives. Perhaps domesticity is used to mark a world that is relatively ordered and predictable, in which kinship relations have a degree of coherence, and time, too, flows predictably – 'as usual'. The domestic metaphor encompasses family life. Stories told using domestic tropes were not concerned only with an event but with the contexts of daily life, in which women are linchpins as they seek to make and maintain homes, to work and raise children. Women's testimonies, largely about the loss of men, explicitly and implicitly indicated male absences. Women testified about the death and disappearance of men, yet were silent on the subject of men as actors in their domestic worlds.[17] Indeed, it is this silence about the presence of men in family life that draws attention to the contingencies of the domestic in South Africa: women told of the disruption of family life at many levels by the state and by the political activities of loved ones. They spoke of the ways that families were separated and of their efforts to secure families under the harsh conditions imposed by apartheid.

Women's efforts were not confined to the immediate locales of home, neighbourhood or community. In their testimonies they described the distances they travelled in order to find lost kin or to obtain news of them. They sought lost ones in police stations and mortuaries, in hospitals and prisons. They travelled to nearby towns and across borders to Lesotho, Botswana, Zambia, Angola and Tanzania. The search as motif is diffuse, spanning huge geographical spaces and long periods of time. Women testifying before the Commission still sought a proper end to their quest: the return of a body, its correct burial, appropriate reparations, and, sometimes, retributive justice.

Women described their attempts to protect family members. Frequently they were violent in their responses to state incursions into the domestic realm: Nonceba Zokwe shouted that on her property she was boss, even as a policeman was aiming a gun at her and trying to arrest her son. Eliza Adonis told the Commission that she hit a policeman on the head with a chair when he came to arrest her son (Kimberley hearing, 10 June 1996). Sometimes, as in Mrs Zokwe's case, they confronted harm-doers with strength drawn from personal conviction and sanctified by the spirit and actions of resistance within a family or community.

At other times their efforts to avert violence and hold it at a distance were less successful. It is important to recognise the points at which efforts to secure families were unsuccessful and the pain that might endure in the recognition of a failure to keep harm at bay. The 'trace' (Werbner 1998:76) left by violence may wound in its recall. For example, Maria Mthembu recalled that her brother had been killed 'by accident' by police who were seeking her (Gauteng, 29 April, 1996). The death of one child in lieu of another points to the ways in which the body was not necessarily a signifier of individuality to the state (a discussion I continue in Chapters 4 and 5).

The testimonies point to the contingencies of home and of domesticity. Locked doors could not protect families from either random or directed violence; individual activism brought harassment and death to kin. The emphasis on domestic context in women's speech highlights the failures of home to protect and contain. The care with which women detailed their domestic worlds and time points to the depths of state irruption in them.

Time and continuity

Time is implicated in testimonies in intricate ways.[18] It is clear that the experience of temporality is more complex than linear chronologies of events would suggest, and its instantiation in testimonies has not yet received the attention it deserves. The historical, cultural and mythical resonance of testimonies needs close attention: my analysis here is based on the simultaneous translations of testimonies into English that lack the detail and form of their originals, and cannot do justice to their complexity. Nevertheless, it is clear that where past events are told in relation to testifiers' lives in the present and in relation to the narrower immediacy of hearings, the simple present is confounded. The past is complicated by shifting temporalities and interjections, and testifiers forecast their futures on the basis of the changes wrought in their expectations by violence and loss.

Where violence ruptures the conventions, rituals and expectations that tradition enjoins, the effect may be a sense of temporal disorientation that hinders recuperation. Earlier, I described Sylvia Dlomo-Jele's expectations of a time when her child would provide for her, and how these were changed by her child's death. Her expectations are paralleled in the story that Nokiki Gwedla told to the Commission in Cape Town, on 24 April 1996. She explained that she had been brought from her rural home by her son Zongesile Kopolo, who had built a shack for her in Crossroads. Three weeks after she arrived in the city he was shot by police during the *witdoek* violence of the mid-1980s.[19] He was badly injured: Mrs Gwedla told the Commission that he still has difficulty in speaking, that his arm is lame and that 'bullets' remain lodged in his skull. Their roles are now reversed: instead of being cared for in her old age, she looks after her disabled son, abandoned by her husband 'because he could not stay with an abnormal son', afraid to sleep because her son roams the streets. In response to a question about her feelings posed by a Commissioner, she said bitterly, 'There are many things about my child that are affecting me ... I told myself that I wished that he was dead, I would be happy if he was dead, but now I have to work and I have to take care of such an old man. But sometimes when I am alone it becomes too much for me.'

By tradition, Nokiki Gwedla's son should care for her in her old age. Instead, living in an unconventional script in which she cares for her son rather than being cared for, scrutinised by neighbours who humiliate her, she reported feeling vulnerable. Her son was even more so: he refused to testify and sat silently at his mother's side as she wept.

Her story is echoed in the words of women, who spoke of the expectations they had held of their (male) children, spouses and kin. Frequently prefaced with 'He was a good boy', or 'He was good in school, and would have supported me', or in Mrs de Bruin's words, 'My son was like a daughter to me' (Worcester hearing, 25 June, 1996), the women's requests of the Commission were oblique. Yet implicit in their testimonies and requests were commentaries about the ideal shape of social relationships, the role of the family, the kinds of support that should be available to the aged. Sindiswa Mkhonto, speaking about the death of her husband, Sparrow, at the hands of the Security Forces, said, 'Because I have no husband, my child has no father ... Today I don't have a husband and my son has no father. The family is lost' (East London, 16 April, 1996).

Sometimes change was predicted. Many testifiers reported dreams and portents that marked an expectation of horror. Nonceba Zokwe told the Commission that on two occasions before the death of her son Sithembile, she had dreamt that her child was looking into death's eyes. Nonthuthuzelo

Mphelo testified to the HRVC on 18 April 1996 about the death of her husband, who was accused by his neighbours of having betrayed Black Consciousness leader Steve Biko to the police. Nonthuthuzelo reported that her husband had told her, 'A person dies only once. Take this as an indication that I will die.' Mary Mabilo, who testified in Kimberley on 11 June 1996 about the death of her son, told the Commission that she had lain abed the night of his death and wondered, 'Whose child is being killed at this moment?' She had gone outdoors, troubled, and, feeling that 'God was sending a message', she had knelt and prayed. Monica Qaba, a resident in Zwelethemba who made a statement but did not testify about her son's death in exile, dreamt that she was walking alone in a desert. A river of blood ran across her path and as she waded in the blood a woman's voice told her to go no further. Mrs Qaba was deeply distressed by the dream and sought advice from neighbours who told her to go to church. While she was in church, the rumour of her son's death was brought to neighbours.

In African custom, dreams and premonitions are experiences that lie within ordinary registers and are widely held to be offerings from the ancestors who frequently require ritual intervention in response. Dreams may guide or warn. Yet in the context of apartheid South Africa, forewarned did not necessarily mean forearmed. The dreams and premonitions were recalled retrospectively in women's testimonies as markers of beginnings of drastic change, markers, in a sense, of endings. They touched time and expectations of its usual flow with dread and the grotesque, the unimaginable and the unspeakable.

Silence and secrecy

Women spoke about secrecy and the multiple levels at which activism and violence created silences within family life. Some women claimed not to know that children, husbands, kinsfolk were politically involved. Sylvia Dlomo-Jele, for example, used the claims of ignorance to resist police demands for information about her kinsmen. Nqabakazi Godolozi said that she and her husband used passwords to identify themselves before they entered their own house. Secrecy shaped conversation, too; information about activism was hidden from parents and children, sometimes even from spouses. Silences and secrecy played themselves out in gender struggles, and in conflict over roles. 'We are not allowed to ask our husbands about politics in my culture', was Feziwa Mfeti's wry comment (East London, 16 April 1996), a comment that was greeted with nods and laughter from the audience, and later confirmed by Govan Mbeki's commentary to the Commission. A stalwart of the struggle against apartheid both in South Africa and in exile, Mbeki told the Commission of the difficulties that family life had generated in the early days of the struggle:

After work we went into the township to educate. The police were looking for meetings. So when you left you did not tell your wife where you were going, and when you returned, at twelve or one in the morning, they were asleep and your food was on the stove ... Women created problems for the [liberation] movement because they wanted to know. [Cape Town hearings, 28 April 1996]

Women's efforts to secure families and the safety of loved ones was sometimes read by men as interference. Sheila Masote, who testified before the Commission's special hearing on women in Johannesburg in July 1997, told the Commission that the PAC, of which her father, Zeph Mathopeng, had been president, had discouraged women's political involvement. Describing herself as a member of 'a family that had been through the struggle', she detailed the effects of her father's activism on herself and her family. She spoke about his absences, her mother's illness, police harassment and arrests, and her anger with her mother for not confronting her father and demanding that he cease his political activities. She explained to the Commission, 'Then, the PAC's policy was that women should stay home, should not participate. That is why ... even when the *toyi-toyi*[20] ... was for us ... the policy was looked after [that is, adhered to]. It was all by way of trying to say, "when we [that is, men] go to jail, when we go out to be killed, you look after the children" .... The husbands would not share much.'

Her words point to the stresses between generations around gender models: men's efforts to secure safety differed from women's and the differences created tensions within households and sometimes even within the individual, as Sheila Masote pointed out: 'I've always said I don't seem to [have] an identity that [belongs] to me. I'm always Zeph's daughter, Mathopeng's daughter or Mike Masote's wife. Or no ... Zef Masote's mother. But no, I feel I am me.' Her claim, 'I feel I am me', speaks to the difficulties of maintaining a coherent sense of self in conditions of violence, oppression and resistance, a point to which I return in Chapter 3.

The location of self

Although the Commission instituted Special Hearings on Women because of the 'failure' of women to testify about themselves, personal suffering was not lacking from women's reports in public hearings. Submerged, but structuring the form and cadence of their narratives, women spoke of the effects on their own lives of the ruptured lives of others. Most testimony began with an event in which the speaker was firmly located as witness in space and time. Sometimes Commissioners sought this information but even when it was not requested, women prefaced their stories by placing themselves firmly in the plot. Yet one is required to listen carefully to hear precisely where it is that they are placed. For example, when speaking to the Commission about Neil Aggett, Elizabeth Floyd did not state that she had been a political activist. Her political consciousness and its price were implicit in the way she framed her statements, prefacing them with comments such as 'When I was released from detention'. Other women positioned themselves differently, but notwithstanding the differences, the testimonies they gave to the Commission implicated self almost immediately. They did so through explicit reference to the effects of loss on women's well-being and through allusion. Sylvia Mabija, for example, speaking in Kimberley on 10 June 1996, commenced her testimony about the death of her brother in 1977 while in detention; 'On the 7th of June, the police came. *We were all in the dining room.* They came with Phaki who was haggard ...'. Nonceba Zokwe's political consciousness was evident in her statements about her son, whom the police sought for being 'a communist born of *a communist mother*'. Sylvia Molekeli, testifying in Kimberley on 10 June 1996, framed her statement in time; 'It was the 16th of June 1993, in the morning, between nine and ten. *We were toyi-toyiing,* just a small group of people.' (The framing is significant to a wider community: 16 June is a day of mourning and protest throughout the country in memory of the young people who were killed when police opened fire on protesting students in Soweto in 1976. The event is now remembered in a public holiday on 16 June, Youth Day. The words, '16 June' immediately evoke a particular context of violence and located her position within it, for the day was commemorated by many opposed to apartheid but was not recognised as significant by the state.) Mabu Makhumane said: 'When Christopher died, *I was with my younger daughter.* I was very ill' (10 June 1996). Busiswe Kewana's testimony opened with a comment on the separation of families: '*While I was in Grahamstown* [at school], I received a telegram from my grandmother to say my mother had died [in Colesburg]. She was burned'[21] (Cape Town hearings, 24 April, 1996. All emphasis in this paragraph has been added).

The harm wrought on others changed women's lifestyles and expectations. In their testimonies, women explicitly identified their health as having suffered as a consequence of the harm done to those about whom they testified. Drawing from testimonies made by women during hearings held in the Eastern Cape, Ruth Smithyman and Glynnis Lawrence argue that women 'were ... more likely than men to talk about the psychosomatic and psychological problems experienced' (1999: 3). Many women attributed ill health, particularly 'high-blood' or 'low-blood' (pressure), diabetes, stress and dizziness to the losses and anxieties they suffered. The objective correlates for these conditions are not clear, although the Commission records that, 'There is ... evidence that people exposed to trauma, even indirectly, are more likely to develop stress-related illnesses such as heart disease and high blood pressure' (Volume Five: 141). This is confirmed in material drawn from elsewhere. Arthur Kleinman and Joan Kleinman (1994) have suggested that in conditions of state-sponsored violence, bodily symptoms can be read as forms of circumspect social criticism (see also Desjarlais and Kleinman 1994; Scheper-Hughes 1992).

In describing and analysing the somatic components of loss, Smithyman and Lawrence argue that another's pain can indeed be shared – a point to which I return below. What is clear from their work is that even expectations of health and security were affected in the aftermath of loss and damage.

TESTIFYING AND LISTENING

Writing of violence in Sri Lanka, E. Valentine Daniel argues that 'Words are symbols that, even at the edges, pull one toward culture's centre. Deeds, even when culturally centred – "habitus" notwithstanding – threaten to push against culture's limits' (1996: 199). As words, testimony pulls towards culture's centre, reshaping language, drawing on and adapting convention and gesture to convey meaning. As practice, testifying threatens culture's limits, remaking the everyday by uncovering silenced domains of experience that underpin habitual ways of being. Testimony and its performance are paradoxical, compounded by the strictures of language and memory in the face of suffering.

These factors, combined with the subtlety of the testimonies described here, raise problems to do with listening. The forms through which violence is reported are delicate, often oblique. Some women represented their experiences in narratives that appeared on the surface to mark silence and absence, but in their testimonies about others, women told of their own experiences. Their telling was couched in metaphor and allusion, and implied in the narrative structure of stories and their performance. Some women drew from oral tradition while others spoke in clipped speech. Some spoke using forms rounded with rhetoric and gesture, others in words bleached by pain. Part of what women described to the Commission concerned the disruption of the communal, the social, cultural expectations of time and place. Women described the absences of men, the diffusion of family over extended spaces, the silences that activism wrought, and the effects of these silences on the ways that their political consciousness and personal identities could be shaped and expressed both at the time and in the present. They told about the ways that daily life was shaped by apartheid and of their attempts to oppose the ordinariness of oppression, to maintain families in the face of great odds: aspects of experience that need to be acknowledged.

It is, perhaps, in these kinds of stories rather than those which speak more directly to the experience of violation, that the breadth of apartheid's degradation is revealed. The laments over violence and destruction offered in testimonies bear the weight of pain that go beyond the individual. Hidden within women's words are narratives of the destruction of kinship, of the alteration of time's expected flow, of the power of economies in shaping experience, of the intrusion of the state, and of women's determined attempts to create and maintain families. Read together, the accounts describe the penetration of violence into everyday life. The fact that the contexts of violence were so little elucidated – their taken-for-granted presence in testimonies – is evidence of the power of apartheid in shaping the quotidian world.

Scholars need ways of hearing the effects of the dissolution of the everyday, the taken-for-granted nature of time and relationships that are implicit in many women's testimonies. We need ways to map the reverberations of violence and horror outwards from the individual to kin and friends and communities. The physical experience of pain is but a part of a far wider destruction. By focusing too closely on bodily experience, we run the danger of failing to attend to the experiences of which women speak. A focus solely on the body and its violation fixes experience in time, in an event, and draws attention away from ways of understanding of that experience as a process that endures across bodies and through time.

It is easy not to recognise the layered effects of violence and pain. Veena Das argues that, 'Denial of the other's pain is not about the failings of the intellect but the failings of the spirit. In the register of the imaginary, the pain of the other not only asks for a home in language but also seeks a home in the body' (1996: 88). Das argues that failure to recognise an affirmation of pain ('I am in pain') is to participate in and perpetuate violence. She suggests that pain be considered 'as asking for acknowledgement and recognition'. Quoting Wittgenstein, she asks whether it is not possible to experience another's pain in one's own body (1996: 69–71). For her, the question begins to provide a philosophical grammar for the exploration and experience of pain; pain becomes amenable to expression and sharing, rather than being that point at which language fails, thereby demarcating the self most distinctly from the world, as Elaine Scarry (1985) has it. In Das's formulation, pain is not confined to the individual body but is shared and possibly transformed by the relationships between people.

The communication of pain rests on words, gesture and silences. Pain's recognition requires imaginative engagement: acknowledgement of the limitations of language and the validity of silence or the apparent erasure of self as a means of communicating particular kinds of experience. Das proposes that some horror is not and cannot be articulated: silence marks particular kinds of knowing, and, further, silence may be gendered. In other words, silence is a legitimate discourse on pain and there is an ethical responsibility to recognise it as such. As she comments in another context, 'in reading history we must learn how to read silences, for the victim rarely gets an opportunity to record his or her point of view' (1987: 13; see also Das 1997). She is insistent that the silence of Indian women about the violations they experienced during the Partition that divided Pakistan from India is an act of conscious agency. Showing how some women *create* silence out of their experiences of violation, Das points to constructions of agency that do not lie in linguistic competency but in the refusal to allow it; in the ability to *do* something with the experience, namely to hold it inside, silent.

Examining the production of historical knowledge in and about Haiti, Michel-Rolph Trouillot argues that, 'Silences enter the process of historical production at four crucial moments: the moment of fact creation (the making of *sources*), the moment of fact assembly (the making of *archives*), the moment of fact retrieval (the making of *narratives*), and the moment of retrospective significance (the making of *history* in the final instance)' (1995: 26, emphasis in the original). He adds, 'Any historical narrative is a particular bundle of silences, the result of a unique process, and the operation required to deconstruct these silences will vary accordingly' (p. 27). His argument offers a critique of positivistic methodologies that do not recognise that power traverses the unsaid. It alerts us to the need for care: diverse ways of telling have different qualities, and silences are not neutral or homogenous or uniform in their effects.

These issues raise further questions about how those who listen – whether the audiences of the public hearings, or of television and radio – are to attend to stories both told and untold, taking into account the historical, social and cultural conditions that may mould patterns of speech and forms of silence. Different ways of telling require that attention be differently focused. Conventional genres may not neatly mesh with the forms of speech required in public interventions. Socially and culturally defined subject positions may narrow the scope for speaking about painful memories; vocalising suffering may involve speaking from a position that does not necessarily do justice to the self. Speakers may be situated within intersecting and conflicting conventions. Recognising these, their effects, and the process of their production matters.

The Commission's work relied on giving words to experience. Yet, women's 'silence' can be recognised as meaningful. To do so requires carefully probing the cadences of silences, the gaps between fragile words, in order to hear what it is that women say. Words can be weapons; giving voice to the voiceless, the specific aim of the Commission, assumes, perhaps patronisingly, that the world is knowable only through words and that to have no voice is to be without language, unable to communicate. The testimonies reported here suggest otherwise.

3   THE SELF IN EXTREMITY

*In this world of frailty at the edge of the battlefield, the line between **I** and **not** **I** has a dangerous tremor. (Griffin 1992: 210)*

The previous chapter considered the nature of women's testimonies, tracing their experiences of daily life under apartheid through their words about the harms inflicted on others. These testimonies are perhaps best described as lamentations, forms of sorrowing and grieving.[1] Although predominant in testimonial patterns, they were not the only ways of describing the violence of the apartheid past. Women members of liberation and anti-apartheid organisations seldom testified before the HRVC, but when they did, as I describe below, they testified in ways that differed in important respects from women who were not activists. Their testimonies shed light on the Commission's ideological effects, the sites of cruelty, and cruelty's effects on the constitution of the self.

Neither the HRVC nor the Commission Report distinguishes between activists and others, considering that gross violations of human rights produced victims, irrespective of context,[2] political commitment or affiliation. For reasons sketched above and elaborated in the chapter, I have drawn a distinction between 'activists' and others. While taking seriously Lila Abu-Lughod's caution against succumbing to 'the romance of resistance' (1990), I caution that to fall short of recognising resistance where it exists is both an ethical failure and a failure of the anthropological imagination. Later chapters develop these ideas against the backdrop of the material presented here.

My definition of activists differs from that of the post-Apartheid State which, for the purposes of providing pensions to political activists, instituted the Special Pensions Act No. 69 of 1996. It recognises 'persons who made sacrifices or served the public interest in the cause of establishing a democratic constitutional order' and lays down stringent eligibility criteria for prospective pensioners, predicated on age and sustained engagement with either a liberation organisation or against the Apartheid State. The applicant must have been over 35 years of age in 1996. She or he must have served for at least five years as an active member of a political organisation that, before 2 February 1990 (the date that a number of political parties were unbanned), was restricted or unlawful, and that had a permanent governing body. Or she or he must have been banned, banished, imprisoned or detained for political activities.[3] The definition does not recognise the key role played by young people in 'the struggle' and favours those in exile or operating 'underground' at the expense of those engaged in or organising mass protest and resistance. The eligibility criteria that shape access to the Special Pension posit a particular interpretation of the past: that 'the struggle' was fought and won by commissars and military people and not through mass popular protest. In this respect, the criteria elide the roles of women and youths in bringing about social and political change in South Africa.

I have defined as activists those people who were members of and actively involved in sustained anti-apartheid protest or clandestine anti-apartheid activities. I include the United Democratic Front (UDF) and its affiliated organisations in this definition.

Table 3.1 describes the political affiliations of women who testified about their own experiences of violation during selected hearings.[4] The representation is based on information available from the testimonies and may be incomplete, as testifiers did not necessarily offer their political affiliations and Commission representatives did not always ask for them. In Table 3.1, under the column 'Organisation Affiliation', 'PE' represents women whose affiliations with anti-apartheid organisations were explicitly stated in their testimonies, 'PI' identifies women whose claims to particular political identities were implicit, and 'SE', those employed by the state. 'PD' indicates testifiers who presented themselves as politically disengaged. The remainder of this chapter focuses on testimonies offered by women whose political activism was clear.

Fifty-five women came before the Commission to testify about their own experiences of human rights violations at the hearings I have selected. Thirty-four of the testimonies concerned events that occurred between 1980 and 1990. Nine concerned events between 1991 and the first democratic elections in 1994. Four were concerned with events that took place in the 1970s and the remainder described violations that were inflicted in the 1960s. Sixteen of the testifiers (29 per cent) were not affiliated with political or mass movements. One woman, Marina Geldenhuys, worked as a secretary for the South African Air Force and was injured in a bomb blast. In several cases, political identification is unclear. Ivolyn de Bruin, who was tried in connection with what has come to be known as the 'Upington 26' case, found 'guilty by association' and incarcerated, did not state a political affiliation, claiming that her arrest, trial and imprisonment were wrongful.[5] Ntobeko Feni appeared briefly before the HRVC hearing in Cape Town in April 1996 where she provided supporting evidence for Lucas Sikwepere who described being injured in a confrontation with the police in Cape Town in 1985; Mrs Feni was also injured in the attack. The political affiliations of some women who testified about rape in the Durban Women's Hearings are also unclear.

Using elliptical language, five women implied that they had been engaged in protest activities. For example, Ellen Moshweu said she was detained 'at the *toyi-toyi*', and Nomatise Tsobileyo said that she was 'with the comrades' at a 'protest' against forced removals when she was injured with birdshot. Dee Dicks, who described her detention, spoke about joining youth protests. Sylvia Moleleki was at '*umzabalazo*' (Zulu – 'the struggle'), '*toyi-toyiing*' when she was shot by police.

   Table 3.2 describes the political affiliations of the 27 testifiers who unambiguously described themselves as engaged in political activities against the Apartheid State. As is clear from Table 3.1, a number of women were members of more than one organisation, but for ease of analysis, Table 3.2 categorises on the basis of stipulated primary political affiliations. The 27 women are of all races. Most claimed allegiance to the ANC or to organisations linked with the UDF. There were no representatives of AZAPO or the PAC, although Sheila Masote described how the activities of her father, Zeph Mathopeng, who was the president of the PAC between 1986 and 1990, impacted on her life. In addition to police harassment, she was detained in connection with his activities. Part of her testimony is quoted in Chapter 2. No woman identified herself as politically engaged on behalf of Inkatha (now the Inkatha Freedom Party, IFP). Two women, Stephanie Kemp and Jean Middleton, were members of the Communist Party. Six women – Mamgotle Mohale, Zanele Zingxondo, Joyce Marubini, Deborah Matshoba, Nozibonela Mxathule and Thandi Shezi – described their political activities in youth or student organisations. Lizzy Phike and Marie Magwaza were members of organisations affiliated to the UDF and Virginia Mkhwanazi and Sylvia Dlamini said they were members of the UDF. Two, Deborah Jokazi and Jubie Mayet, were trade unionists. Rosie Hugo and Nomakula Zweni were representatives of civic associations established in the 1980s in opposition to the state-sponsored councillor systems.

   Five of the 27 women identified themselves as members of armed resistance movements: Shirley Gunn, Litha Mazibukho and Zahrah Narkedien were members of MK; Sandra Adonis was a member of the Bonteheuwel Military Wing (BMW), an organisation affiliated with MK that operated out of the Cape Town suburb of Bonteheuwel. Stephanie Kemp was a member of both the Communist Party and of the Armed Revolutionary Movement (ARM).[6] In addition to the five, Tryphina Jokweni was an ANC member whose testimony and its introduction by Hugh Lewin, a member of the HRVC, implied that she was an MK operative. (Lewin said, 'I'd like to welcome you as one of the first, and I am not sure, possibly the first, person to come as a woman combatant to appear before the Commission.' Tryphina Jokweni's testimony sketched her task of assisting young people cross the borders into exile and infiltrating MK soldiers back into South Africa. She did not say that she was a combatant and her testimony does not offer such evidence.)

   All the women who described themselves as political activists spoke about experiences of violence visited upon them as a consequence of their interpolation as subjects in opposition to the state. Lita Mazibuko described the ill-treatment, including rape, of women by ANC comrades in the training camps outside South Africa, and in Durban, young women testified about

Table 3.1 Women's political identities as declared in specified public hearings

Date, place and type of hearing	Name of testifier	Human Rights Violations (HRV)	Date	Age at HRV	Organisation affiliation	Activities	Victim status
April 1996 – East London. HRV	Beth Savage	Injured in bombing by PAC	1992	Not given	PD		Yes
April 1996 – Cape Town. HRV	Nomakula Zweni	Detained/assaulted by police	1960, 1977, 1978	Not given	PE: ANC? – Civic	Organised pass protest,1960. Exile?	No
	Nomatise Tsobileyo	Injured in forced removal	1985	Not given	PI: Indirect association of self with 'comrades'	Protest	Yes
	Nontobeko Feni	Injured by police	1985	Not given	PD		No
April–May 1996 – Johannesburg. HRV	Marina Geldenhuys	Injured in bomb blast	1983	± 20	SE: SADF		Yes
	Mamgotle Mohale	Detained, torture	1976	26	PE: Student Christian Movement	Help people cross border into exile	Yes
	Shanti Naidoo	Torture	???	28	PE: Indian Congress		Yes
May 1996 – Durban. HRV	Helen Kearney (& clients)	Injured in bombing by ANC	1985	Not given	PD		Yes
	Tryphina Jokweni	Detention, torture	1987	63	PE: ANC – (MK?)	Help people cross border into exile	Yes
June 1996 – Kimberley. HRV	Ellen Moshweu	Injured at funeral by police	1990	Not given	PI: Indirect association of self with 'comrades'	'toyi-toyi'	Yes
	Sylvia Moleleki	Injured by police	1993	Not given	PI	'toyi-toyi'	Yes
July 1996 – Worcester, HRV	Yvonne Khutwane	Detained, torture, sexual assault by police	1985	45	PE: ANC – Civic		Yes
	Mina Day	Injured by police, possible sexual violation	1986	Pensioner	PD		Yes
	Nowowo Tsenze	Injured by police	1985	Not given	PD		Yes
	Annaleen Abrahams	Injured by police	1990	Not given	PD		Yes
August 1996 – Cape Town. HRV/Women's Hearing	Shirley Gunn	Detention, arrest, torture, wrongful accusation and imprisonment	1990	± mid-30s	PE: ANC-MK	'Underground activities'	Yes

Hearing	Name	Circumstances	Year	Age	Organisation	Role/Notes	
	Monica Daniels	Injured by police	1985	Teenager	PD		Yes
	Zubeida Jaffer	Detained, torture	1980, 1985	± mid-20s	PE: ANC	Journalist, trade union organiser	Yes
August 1996 – Beaufort West, HRV	Zanele Zingxondo	Detained, torture	1986	± mid-20s	PE: Youth organisations		Yes
	Rosi Hugo	Detained, torture	1986	Not given	PE: Civic		Yes
	Nonight Qayi	Detained, torture	1985	Not given	PE: ANC?		Yes
October 1996 – Upington, HRV	Ivolyn de Bruin	Detained, arrested, tried	1985	54	PD: ?		Yes
October 1996 – Paarl, HRV	Lizzy Phike	Detained	1985	Not given	PE: Women's organisation		Yes
	Maria Segrys	Injured by police	1990	Not given	PD		Yes
October 1996, Durban, Women's Hearing, HRV	Sophia Liphoko	Injured by police	1986	Not given	PD		Yes
	Sylvia Dlamini	Detention without trial, torture	1986?	15	PE: UDF, 'comrade'	Political education	Yes
	Unnamed by request	Assault and rape by Inkatha member or vigilantes (not clear from testimony)	1992	Not given	PD		Yes
	Unnamed by request	Abduction and rape by 'comrades'	1992	16	PD		Yes
	Marie Magwaza	Police harassment, detention, solitary confinement	1985?	Not given	PE: Links to various organisations, including NUSAS and ECC		No
	Virginia Mkhwanazi (Mbatha)	Police harassment, detention, torture, solitary confinement	1986	Not given	PE: UDF	Assisted people cross border	Yes
	Ntombenkulu Ngubane	Police harassment, banning orders, detention, solitary confinement	1963	23	PE: ANC		Yes
	Dorah Mkhize	Rape (by Inkatha members? Testimony unclear)	1990	35	PD		Yes

Table 3.1 continued

Date, place and type of hearing	Name of testifier	Human Rights Violations (HRV)	Date	Age at HRV	Organisation affiliation	Activities	Victim status
	Stephanie Kemp	Solitary confinement, torture	1964	23	PE: Communist Party, ARM		Yes
	Phyllis Naidoo	Arrest, detention, restriction and banning orders, exile	1960–76, 1977	Not given	ANC?	'underground operative'	Yes
	Fatima Meer	Detention, banning orders, arson, assassination attempt	1952–85	Not given	PE: Natal Indian Congress, ANC, Black Women's Federation		No
November 1996 – 'Pollsmoor hearing', Cape Town, HRV	Amina van Dyk	Injured by police	1985	30	PD		Yes
May 1997 – 'Children's hearing', Cape Town, HRV	Dee Dicks	Detained, imprisoned	1985	17	PI: Youth organisation?		Yes
	Sandra Adonis	Detained	1987	15	PE: Bonteheuwel Military Wing		Yes
May 1997 – 'Trojan Horse hearing', Cape Town, HRV	Zainab Ryklief	Injured by police	1985	Not given	PD		Yes
July 1997 – Johannesburg. Prison Hearing (special event hearing)	Deborah Marakalala	Detention, assault (while pregnant), solitary confinement	1986	Not given	PI: Church organisation/Advice Office	'helping the youth and comrades'	No
	Jean Middleton	Imprisonment	1964	Not given	PE: Communist Party		Yes
	Zahrah Narkedien	Detention, torture, solitary confinement	1986	Not given	PE: ANC - MK		Yes
	Theresa Ramashamola	Death row	1984	24	PD	–	?+

July 1997– Women's Hearing, Johannesburg, HRV						
Kedibone Dube	Rape by 'comrade'	1992	?	PD		Yes
Deborah Jokazi	Injured in grenade attack (by rival unionists?)	1992	Not given	PE: Food and Allied Worker's Union		Yes
Winnie Makhubela	Rape by hostel residents	1993	14	PE	-	Yes
Joyce Marubini	Detention, assault	1986	Not given	PE: Youth Congress, Phalaborwa	Executive member of youth organisation (Father was PAC head)	Yes
Sheila Masote	Detention, torture	1977	Not given	PD		Yes
Deborah Matshoba	Detention, torture	1976	Not given	PE: South African Students Organisation	Organise student protest	No
Thandi Mavuso	Arson, shot (not clear by whom)	1992	Not given	PE: ANC		No
Jubi Mayet	Detention, banning	1977, 1978	Not given	PE: Union of Black Journalists		?+
Lita Mazibuko	Detention by ANC, Rape by 'comrades'	1988, 1993	Not given	PE: ANC – MK	Assist people cross into exile (Swaziland) and infiltrate MK soldiers into South Africa	Yes
Nozibonela Mxathule	Attempted rape by informer, Assault by police	1991	Teenager	PE: Youth Congress		Yes
Joyce Sikhakhane Ranken	Detention, torture	1969	± mid-20s	PE: ANC? DPSC	Investigative journalist	No
Thandi Shezi	Assault, detention, torture, rape	1988	± mid-20s	PE: Youth Congress and women's organisations	Transporting arms	Yes

Source: transcripts of hearings and Commission Report, 1998, Volume Five.

+ = In two instances women may have been identified in the Report by different names to those they used when testifying. The Report identifies only one victim with the surname Ramashomola. The first name given is Machabane and not Theresa. The Report shows Zubeida (not Jubie) Mayet to be a victim.

Note: In the 'Organisation Affiliation' column, 'PE' indicates politically explicit affiliation with anti-apartheid organisations, 'PI' politically implicit affiliation, 'PD' politically disengaged, and 'SE' those employed by the state.

sexual violations committed by neighbours with opposing political views. All the other women activists described acts of violence committed by state representatives. It is on the content of the latter testimonies that the chapter mainly focuses.

Table 3.2: Women's primary political affiliations

Organisation	Number of members
ANC	6
Youth	6
UDF	4
Armed wings of Liberation Organisations	4
Communist Party	2
Union	2
Civic	2
Indian Congress	1

With the exception of ten women,[7] all of those whose testimonies are presented here have been declared by the Commission to be victims.

The discussion of Nyameka Goniwe and Elizabeth Floyd's testimonies in Chapter 2 hint at the differences between the testimonies of activists and others. Testimonies of the former indicate a chilling intimacy with the state and its apparatus of power. Activists tended to speak more directly of pain, its agents and its consequences than did women who were not politically active, who, as I have shown, frequently used frames drawn from domestic life as markers for experiences of suffering. Most women activists testified about detention, describing it as a site of cruelty's enactment. Some descriptions were explicit. Fearing that repetition may repeat injury, I have chosen not to give descriptions of torture here in the same detail as testifiers offered them. Activists frequently framed their experience in terms of a coherent and enduring commitment to political ideologies in opposition to the state. They often named those responsible for their pain and that of others, and demanded accountability and particular action from the Commission. Some offered lists of people who they believed should be subpoenaed to answer questions. Others, less explicit about their expectations from the Commission, spoke powerfully about the consequences of their encounters with state power. Few women activists described the complexities of their political positioning in relation to cultural convention. Similarly, few spoke about patriarchal conventions that structure everyday life or about forms of violence less closely identified with the formal sphere of politics. Their testimonies identify the state as the locus of blame, and distinguish resistance to apartheid as a moral good. Despite this, a striking absence in their testimonies is direct reference to political activities, which remain rough sketches implied through statements such as Mamagotle Mohale's reference to assisting students to cross the borders into exile, or Zubeida Jaffer's comments that she became involved in organising trade unions. Even if, as in Zahrah Narkedien's case,[8] testifiers had applied for amnesty, they did not describe their political activities in hearings of the HRVC. It may be that through their silence, women testifiers continue to resist an incursion of the state, perhaps now benevolent, but an incursion nevertheless.[9]

Three important analytic themes that crosscut the testimonies, here set against the backdrop of a description of detention, have to do with gender-specific violence and vulnerabilities, with the fracture of social relationships and efforts at solidarity, and with activists' senses of self. The themes emerge at the point where cruelty makes subjection visible. Feeding into and implicit in one another, when read together in the light of post-structuralist theories of the subject, they point to forms of harm wider than those anticipated by methodologies that focus on embodied injury or those reported by the Commission.

DETENTION

Detention can be characterised as a space of violent potential, frequently actualised. Sanctioned in law (see Appendix A), along with its most cruel legal forms, such as detention without trial and solitary confinement, it was also a space into which were inserted forms of cruelty that were not officially sanctioned but which the state frequently ignored (Orr 1999). Detention figures in testimonies as a space of ugly intimacy, a zone where particular violence and its resultant pain challenged women's identities and senses of self. Subjected to many of the same kinds of treatment as men, women were beaten, held in solitary confinement, verbally abused, threatened, shocked, raped, sexually violated and variously tortured. With the exception of solitary confinement, most violence took place after detention but before formal charging. In part this may have had to do with the explicit ending of detention's liminality: sentencing and imprisonment mark an increased formalisation, legitimacy and visibility of state power over its subjects. This is not to suggest that incarceration of opponents was legitimate or that prisoners were not ill-treated but rather that the nature of ill-treatment changed after sentencing.

Detention's liminality was ensured in law. For example, under laws enacted as part of the successive States of Emergency, detainees could be held for up to 180 days without being charged.[10] In terms of Section 29 of the Internal Security Act (ISA), detainees could be held indefinitely in solitary confinement. In law, detainees were entitled to medical assistance from a district surgeon and to make their complaints known to a magistrate. In practice, neither of these mechanisms was strictly adhered to (see Foster et al. 1987; Rayner 1990; van Heerden 1996, 1997; Commission hearings on Legal and Medical Professions, 1997, and the findings of these reported in Volume Four: 93–164). Many detainees were released only to be detained again as they left prisons. They were not necessarily always held in the same place but were shifted about. They were not always held in state prisons or police cells (Reynolds 1995a; see Chapter 4). Testifiers reported that police lied about the whereabouts and well-being of detainees. Laws and the local interpretation of these created a space of formal 'not-being' into which violence in many forms could be and was inserted – and one that was largely invisible to the world outside the prison or cell walls.

It is unclear how many women were detained in the period under review. The Commission Report does not differentiate between women who were politically engaged and those who were caught in violence inadvertently. It does not provide data pertaining to the numbers of women arrested or detained by the state, who may therefore have experienced the kinds of harm that women described in public hearings. State statistics are notoriously unreliable, and NGO estimates vary considerably. The state's figures were not usually disaggregated by gender (House of Assembly, 1960–90), so it is not always clear what number of detainees at any one time were women or young girls.

Take for example the years 1960, 1976 and 1985–87, years that were marked by extremes of violence and resistance. In 1960, the issuing of Proclamation 91 followed the protests that took place at Sharpeville and Langa against the passes that Africans in urban areas were obliged to carry. Proclamation 91 declared a State of Emergency that came into effect on 30 March and remained in force until 31 August 1960. The ANC and PAC were banned that year and operated in exile and clandestinely until their unbanning in 1994; 1976 marked the Soweto Uprising by young people who protested against Afrikaans as the medium of instruction in schools. No State of Emergency was declared but many children were detained and all questions about detentions were referred to the Cillie Commission, established to investigate the Uprising. 1985 marked the onset of an extended State of Emergency that remained in force until 1990.

In these three periods of considerable 'Unrest', detention figures were at their height and one might anticipate that most women were detained during this time. Drawing from Parliamentary question-and-answer sessions, as reported in Hansard's House of Assembly documents (1960–95), from the South African Institute of Race Relations (SAIRR) Race Relations Handbook (1960–94), and from academic publications, the following picture emerges for the three periods. In 1960, the state acknowledged that it held 11,503 political detainees, but the figures are not disaggregated by gender. In the same year, the SAIRR reported only 35 women detainees. In 1976, the state refused to divulge data on the number of detainees. Citing 'the interests of national security' as the reason for its refusal, all questions asked in Parliament about detention were referred to the Cillie Commission. The SAIRR reported 2,403 detainees in that year, but did not state how many were women. In 1985, the state did not disclose the numbers of people detained under the Emergency Regulations or the ISA, although the SAIRR publicised a figure of 11,750 detainees. Again, it is not stipulated how many of the detainees were women or girls. The Minister of Law and Order stated that 2,016 children under 16 years were detained under the Emergency Regulations but did not stipulate the age ranges or gender of those detained. In 1986, the state indicated that 3,989 people were held in terms of Emergency Regulations, and that 48 of these were women. The SAIRR recorded a total of 25,000 detainees in the same period. Other sources suggest a higher proportion of female detainees than either the State or SAIRR figures indicate. For example, the Detainees' Parents Support Committee estimated that women comprised 12 per cent of detainees held by the State in 1986–87 under the State of Emergency laws (DPSC 1988), and Coleman (in Russell, 1990: 15) estimated that 14 per cent of children detained in the same period were girls. Coleman (1998: xi) states that between 1960 and 1990, 80,000 opponents of apartheid were detained for up to three years without trial. Ten thousand were women and 15,000 were children under the age of 18.

It is possible that a considerably larger number of women and children were detained than available figures suggest. Many people were detained only briefly. Often shifted between police stations during interrogation, they were not necessarily recorded as arrested or detained, no charges were laid, and they were released from police 'custody' after a relatively short period of holding or interrogation. The length of time they were held does not, of course, bear any necessary relation to the treatment endured during that time.

Detention as both a space and a practice of 'not-being' was marked by counter-tendencies. The first was to 'hide' detainees from visible gaze while at the same time making detention a visible category of policing, of govern-mentality. The second, practices of violence inflicted in detention, had the effect of rendering visible traces of ordered (albeit often illegal) state power on detainees while at the same time, through the inaccuracies, elisions, evasions and refusals to reply, rendering the extent of the state's involvement in cruelty less visible.

VIOLENCE AND VULNERABILITY: THE EMBODIMENT OF HARM

Rape and Sexual Violation

As I have described in Chapter 1, the Commission and gender activists were concerned that women testify about sexual violence. The few women who did so described sexual tortures that were viciously enacted. Zanele Zingxondo, testifying in Beaufort West in August 1996, told the Commission that she had been detained ten years previously in the small coastal town of Knysna in connection with the burning of a man named Africa in the neigh-bouring town of George. She denied having been part of his death but was held in detention, interrogated at length and severely tortured. Later, a man she presumed to be a policeman entered the cell where she was kept in solitary confinement. He tried to rape her. She screamed. When inmates of the adjoining cell added their shouts to hers, he left without molesting her further. She was moved to another prison and again interrogated. Later, transferred to 'Rooihel', a prison in George, she shared a cell with other women she knew. She recalled, 'There were quite a lot of woman inside, people I knew and we told each other experiences. But mine at the time were too difficult to tell.' On 17 June 1987, she was released, only to be immediately detained again by detectives who drove her to Knysna where she was held on charges of public violence. She was released on bail and eventually charges against her were dropped. Her anguish remains:

People in George still believe that I was part and parcel of the murder of Africa, the man who was burnt to death. I was not. I cannot, until today [that is, to this day], tell where I was, and I am quite sure that the person who I was with can also confirm that I was not there during the evening of the scene, during the evening of his death.

His parents are also putting the blame on me, yet I was not [there]. My late mamma died, not knowing if I was innocent or guilty. She died having a question mark whether her daughter was a murderer or not. I was not.

Thandi Shezi testified at the Johannesburg Women's Hearing about being gang-raped by four policemen when she refused to succumb to their demands for information under torture.[11] At a HRVC in Worcester, Yvonne Khutwane (see Chapter 4) told the panel that she and her comrades knew that the police raped detained women. Nomvula Mokonyane, who made a submission on behalf of FEDTRAW (the now-defunct Federation of Transvaal Women), commented that 'Young girls at the age of twelve, coming from Kagiso, coming from Alexandria, were victims of detention without trial ... [and] ... victims of abuse, victims of rape during interrogation, victims of unwanted pregnancies from security forces who were taking them in and out of detention' (Johannesburg Women's Hearing, 29 July 1997).

Despite these alerts, the violence visited upon young women and girls was seldom given focused attention save for a series of testimonies offered by anonymous women in Durban. They testified from behind screens and, to protect their privacy, their names were not released to the public during the hearings (although their names are given on the transcripts released on the Commission's official website and on the CD-ROM that was produced from the website). These women spoke of the ways in which men from opposing sides of the political spectrum in KwaZulu and Natal (the ANC and Inkatha) abducted them and subjected them to rape. On occasions where women spoke about the complexities of political and sexual identities outside of prison, their testimonies illustrate the interpenetration of public and private spheres, and the ways that the personal and the political interweave. One woman, for example, spoke of how she was raped by her neighbour, a member of an opposing political party. Neighbourliness was negatively redefined twice over, once by a violent act and then by the political motivation she envisaged as having initiated it. In addition to physical violence, the result is to disrupt community, disorienting accustomed directions of sociality.

Rape is common in South Africa. The Special Hearings on Women took place during a period when the frequency of violence enacted against women was headline news. Statistics offered by Rape Crisis, an NGO, project that one woman is raped every 36 seconds in South Africa, usually by men they know (Shifman, Madlala-Routledge and Smith 1997). Very few cases are reported and still fewer are successfully prosecuted. The need for anonymity, or at least concealment of some testifiers, suggests that neither the threat of violence nor the stigma attached to rape has abated.

Kate Millett remarks that detention is marked by violation of both privacy and taboo: that is, power strips away cultural convention (1994: 174). From women's testimonies before the Commission, it is clear that their bodies were turned into the sources of their humiliation. Women were exposed to the gaze of interrogators and wardresses when forced to strip for searches on entering and leaving prison for the courtrooms. Many were not allowed changes of clothes for extensive periods and some reported embarrassment when menstruation became public. Most women who testified about detention or imprisonment spoke about indignities and humiliations visited upon them in interrogation rooms and cells. Their testimonies in this regard suggest that where women's bodies become sites of the visible enactment of power, shame is produced as residue.

Agnes Heller's 'general theory of shame' proposes that shame is the primary, socialised affect that ensures conformity to a given cultural environment and suggests that, externally imposed and internally generated, it operates from the level of the taken-for-granted in the world. Shame is neither rational nor irrational, but is a response to the rupture of social and cultural norms (1985: 13). Shame and pain are linked: 'Bodily pain, the other main "socialiser" is mostly effectual only if accompanied by shame' (p. 6). A powerful tool of conformity, as Tzvetan Todorov (1996: 263–5) points out in relation to concentration camp survivors, its effects endure (see also Levi 1989; Agamben 1999). Yet, Heller points out, while shaming is an important mechanism in legitimating systems of domination, shame cannot regulate 'out-group relations' (1985: 40). That is, where people reject the legitimacy of a form of domination, then shame is not likely to be a regulatory mechanism in ensuring *compliance* with that domination.

While important, her argument does not explain why women whose bodies have become sites for cruelty's enactment feel shame even where their torturers are defined as enemies, or why, under such circumstances, sexual violence is seldom discussed. Georgio Agamben offers an alternative explanation that links subjectivity and shame (1999: 112). For him, subjectivity rests on 'the fundamental sentiment of being *a subject*, in the two apparently opposed senses of this phrase: to be subjected and to be sovereign … [Shame is] produced in the absolute concomitance of subjectification and desubjectification' (p. 107) so that the subject in shame 'becomes witness to its own disorder, its own oblivion as a subject' (p. 106). Shame then is produced in the moment of reflexivity where a being recognises itself and that the power that constitutes it is not innate.[12] Agamben argues that this produces a complex interaction with language so that shame and selfhood are linked and inversely related with speech (p. 125). The 'I' produced by shame is precluded from speech of certain kinds, which sheds light on why it is so difficult to talk about events or experiences that are considered shameful.

Haunting and Hauntedness

Power did not operate solely at the level of bodily transformation. Indignities and humiliations added to the physical pain of detainees and political prisoners. Compounded, these had the effect of foreclosing relationships and the forms of identity that rest on relational links. An example: testifiers explained that criminal prisoners were frequently told not to talk to political prisoners. Theresa Ramashamola, who spent seven years on death row for a political crime she says she did not commit, spoke of the devastation of being 'estranged from others while still alive'. She explained, 'I was not supposed to meet ... other prisoners at all. If a prison [were to be] constructed because of me there would be a place designated alone for me, so as not to meet others.' Prisoners were told not to have eye contact with her when passing her or bringing her food. Joyce Sikhakhane Ranken described similar experiences: 'Within the prison yards any awaiting-trial or convicted women prisoners who crossed the path of my heavily armed Special Branch brigades would automatically hide their faces to avoid being whiplashed or booted, with the accompanying vulgar command, "Do not look at the terrorist".'

The word 'terrorist' and the violence with which commands could be enforced had the effect of estranging prisoners from the 'politicals' in certain cases, almost as though political prisoners might somehow contaminate other prisoners.[13] The effect was to produce self-doubt. Yet at other times within the prison or detention context, corporeality was overemphasised. Torture, imprisonment and solitary confinement rendered the body an object, emphasising the ease with which pain could be inflicted at the same time as demonstrating the fragility of life and the contingency of sociality. While in interrogation rooms and cells, political prisoners were treated as little more than recalcitrant bodies. Outside of them, political prisoners were often treated as ghosts. Alongside the lowered gaze of prisoners not allowed to meet the eyes of political prisoners, the state's medical and legal systems, too, did not always 'see' detainees.

Ideologies of Womanhood

Warders and policemen taunted women about their failures to be 'women'. Prison authorities made women's political choices seem aberrant, inappropriate. It is as though an ideal of womanhood existed against which all women were measured. Underlying the model is a notion of the correct occupation of space that finds its echoes elsewhere in the world, particularly in Latin America, where women were punished for taking to the streets in political protest (see Fischer 1989, 1993; Schirmer 1993; Taylor 1997). Implicitly, an ideal woman was one who was acquiescent to the state, a woman who remained in the confines of the domestic realm.

Sheila Meintjes commented on the humiliation caused by the taunts and the damage done to women's sense of security in their identities and political choices. At the Women's Hearing on 29 July 1997 held in Johannesburg, she quoted an anonymous woman detainee: '[The police] may try many ways to make you feel that you should not be here, a woman should not be here. You are here because you are not the right kind of woman. Constantly undermining women, saying you are the equivalent of a whore to be doing this. You are irresponsible, you are an unnatural woman, an unnatural mother. They say all sorts of things to you.'

The taunt of unnaturalness marks a model of womanhood that political activists contravened. At the same hearing, Thenjiwe Mtintso said,

I am sure that women will confirm that when you come into the clutches of the security police, [they make] statements like, 'you have joined these men, because you have failed as a woman, you have failed to find a husband, you have failed to look after your children, you are a failure. This is why you have joined. You are not a proper woman.'

Another favourite statement would be, 'you are with these men, because you are a whore, you are an unpaid prostitute, you have come to service these men.'

This consistency of drawing away from your own activism, from your own commitment as an actor, was perhaps worse than torture, was worse than the physical assault ...

Physical violence, aversion and acts of verbal injury reduce the possibilities of recognising the body as a site of selfhood – a point I return to below. In addition, detention and torture reduce the possibilities for maintaining and creating identities that build on social relationships, further isolating the subject in relation to state power.

DANGERS POSED TO RELATIONAL IDENTITIES

Ex-detainees frequently reported threats of violence against others, usually family members, especially children. Described by those who made them as being a result of detainees' own intransigence, the threats undermined activists' sense of self and called into question the consequences for others of their political engagement.

For example, Zahrah Narkedien explained that when her interrogators realised that the physical abuse to which they subjected her was not having the desired effect of 'breaking' her, the police resorted to 'psychological treatment'. This included threatening to collect her nephew from the house she and her sister shared, taking him to the building in which she was being tortured and dropping him from the thirteenth floor. She believed the Security Police were capable of carrying out their threats and felt, 'I could risk my life and I could let my body ... be handed over to these men to do what they liked but I couldn't hand over someone else's body, so at that point I fully cooperated.'

Mamagotla Mohale told the Commission that the police threatened to kill her mother unless she cooperated. Zubeida Jaffer, speaking at the Cape Town Women's Hearing in August 1996, expanded on the diverse threats faced by women detainees, particularly rape and threats of pain inflicted on family members. She described the emergence of her political consciousness when, as a young reporter, she covered stories of the violence that wracked the Cape Flats in 1980. She was detained and interrogated for five days in different police offices. She was not allowed to sleep in that time. The police did not accept the life story they forced her to write because it carried no mention of the ANC, for which they held she worked. She fell ill during the interrogation, was dizzy with palpitations. Later, a doctor told her that he suspected she had been poisoned. When she still did not tell the police what they wished to know, the captain in charge of the interrogation turned to a policeman and told him to rape her. The man did not do so, but the threat of rape was so real that Ms Jaffer recalled feeling that she would die at that point. After days of interrogation she signed what she thought was a confession of ANC membership but was actually a statement that incriminated a student in showing her banned literature. The Security Branch representatives also tried to make her disclose the name of a journalist who had covered a story on the military. She resisted. Then,

[T]hey said that later in the morning after they continued questioning me ... 'Zubeida if you ... don't cooperate with us and tell us – give us the answers – then we are going to detain your father.' And I thought that they were ... just trying to trick me again or something, but then in the course of the morning they made a phone call and then they called me to the phone and they handed me the phone and it was my father on the phone. And they had detained him in Cape Town ... I was shattered at that point. I just felt, it's fine if they involve me, it's okay, but why involve my family to this extent, and why involve my father? And so ... after they put the phone down, I signed the statement ...

In 1985, Zubeida Jaffer, by then a member of the ANC and a trade union organiser, and her husband were arrested. Captain Frans Mostert, a police officer with an evil reputation among activists in the Western Cape, interrogated her. She was newly pregnant and, learning this, he attempted to use the unborn child as a lever against her to elicit a confession. Saying that he had prepared a chemical that would force her to miscarry, he told her that he 'was going to burn the baby from my body'. Her previous experience of being drugged was warning enough. She was faced with the choice of either giving the police the information they wanted and in doing so, betraying her comrades but possibly saving her child, or refusing to divulge the information and possibly losing the baby. Faced with an impossible choice, for ethical reasons she decided on the latter course:

I felt that I didn't want my child to grow up with that burden on her, because I felt that ... she is not even brought into this world yet and if she is brought into this world thinking that ... her mother gave this information so that she could live, that, that's a heavy burden for a child to carry. So I think that that unborn baby inside of me, made it possible for me to be strong enough to tell them or not to give in to their threats. So ... eventually he didn't ... actually give me the chemical to drink, when I said I didn't want to give them any information, and I was a step past him [in] that there was nothing that he could really do.

Nomvula Mokonyane told the Commission that people like her, pregnant when detained, faced not only the humiliations inflicted by prison warders but also the medical interventions of district surgeons. She accused the latter of attempting forcibly to abort pregnancies:

The district surgeon in collaboration with the security forces as well as the prison warders would insist that, 'your fallopian tube is blocked' and they had to make sure they unblocked them so then you can begin to [menstruate] and if you begin to resist that then torture will take its own course. You will be subjected to electrical shock, you will be subjected to solitary confinement without a meal and all that you would only be served with is a jug full of salted water.

The close ties between women and children, presumed to shape women's identities, were frequently played upon by interrogators. Joyce Sikhakhane Ranken, an investigative journalist who also worked with political prisoners and their families, was detained at dawn on 12 May 1969. She described to the panel at the Johannesburg Women's Hearing her anguish at leaving her son, Nkosinathi, a toddler, when she was detained. She explained how solitary confinement, deprivation and the interrogators' manipulation of maternal sentiments by the introduction of reminders of children during interrogation were used to break people's intellectual and emotional stability: 'It is not only your intellect which is important in your life, it is also emotions, your relationships with other people, how to deal with those people. So, when they brought that child [a toddler] they knew how much I was in love with my son. They knew that I would break down immediately. So this is part of the warfare, part of the game. They put the child there.'

Shirley Gunn, too, described the ways that her child was used against her. She was an MK cadre at the time she was arrested and detained in connection with the bomb that exploded in 1988 at Khotso House, head-quarters of the South African Council of Churches and a place long associated with resistance. Her arrest and incarceration were part of a larger disinformation campaign: it later emerged that the state had been responsible for the bomb and had blamed it on the liberation organisations.[14] Gunn was detained under Section 29 of the ISA. Her infant son, Haroon, was held with

her. They were taken first to a police cell near Cape Town and then to the
Security Branch headquarters, Culemborg, in the city centre. She was
interrogated and tortured but resisted betraying her comrades. During the
interrogations a recording of her son's cries was played to her. She was
constantly afraid both for her own safety and that of her child. The interrogating policemen taunted her, calling her a bad mother. She reported that
they said, 'I am a very terrible person, that I can put my son through this
episode ... That I am subjecting my child to these conditions in a prison and
to gruelling interrogation sessions. And that if I had any heart, I would hand
him over to my family or I would hand him over to them and they would ...
put him in a place of safety...'

She refused. Trained as a social worker, she believed that conditions in
places of safety were not always optimal, and she believed that her son was
safest with her. Then, in July, two social workers came with a warrant for
Haroon's arrest. Gunn argued, pleading that he be allowed to remain with
her. She showed the two women that she managed to keep him clean and
cared for in spite of the foul conditions in the cell, but they took him away,
despite her pleas and his screams. He was held in a place of safety for children.
Gunn decided to embark on a hunger strike until her child was returned to
her.[15] During her strike, her interrogation intensified. Spyker van Wyk, a
policeman notorious for his brutality, was called in to question her. 'I named
my son after Imam Haroun,[16] and here was his murderer in front of me',
commented Gunn in a moment of awful irony.

She decided to continue to breastfeed her son. She stopped her hunger
strike and demanded that the police take the milk she expressed to the child,
wherever he was. The police refused to deliver it. Haroon was returned to
her eight days later, sick and thin. He had not been eating.

Gunn and Haroon were taken from Cape Town to the Caledon Women's
Prison, more than a hundred kilometres from the city centre, and held
together in a cell. One day, Haroon fell ill. Eventually the commanding
officer of the prison allowed Haroon to see a doctor, who told her that the
problem lay less with the child than with his mother. Gunn felt that he
treated her as 'the bomber' and not as the mother of a sick child or as a
patient in her own right.

Shirley Gunn was released after 'sixty-four days of hell and fear'. She
described to the Commission's panellists her consequent post-traumatic
stress disorder and her attempts to cope with the fear that Haroon might be
stolen. The Commission found both Shirley Gunn and Haroon to be victims.

At the end of her testimony to the Commission, Gunn requested
permission to tell a story. It was a humorous story directed at women in the
audience.

I want to explain something to you. At Culemborg when I was interrogated ... I used
to say to these men, these big white men, that they must clear out of the room because
I wanted to express my milk now, I was in agony. And that I needed hot water, and
only the woman could be present, naturally, and I was brought big container, a big

container of warm water, which cooled down very quickly because it was a wide ... pan, and as soon as it was cold I could no longer really express milk very easily, so I asked for more. But I want to show you something: that if you pour a little bit of water in a litre of water, a little bit of milk in a litre of water, it [the water] goes milky white. [She demonstrated as she spoke, using a water jug on the witness stand and some milk that she had brought with her from an earlier tea break to illustrate her point.] And these buckets of water – of 'milk' – were coming out of the interrogation room ... and the men were hopelessly intimidated by this.

She added, 'Sometimes we have to seize being a woman and take advantage of that.'

Her intervention with humour mapped a particular language of pain, its acknowledgement and its distancing that had wider currency outside of the Commission hearings and is described in more detail in Chapter 6. Her testimony pointed to the power of imagination in confronting the state's officials and in sustaining a coherent identity. It also implies possibilities for solidarity that exist among women. Here, Gunn suggests that women share in common the potential for motherhood, and that this can be mobilised to form solidarities and a united front against the abuses of state power. Her argument is both reminiscent and subversive of that offered by Sarah Ruddick (1989), who proposes that women's biological attributes and the innate characteristics of nurture that accompany them fit women for pacifism in the face of state power. The intervention described in the story above, made by a trained soldier, presents a different possibility.

The small acts of resistance Gunn described occurred in a context in which the state and its functionaries ultimately had the upper hand, where cruelty was incipient and where patriarchal assumptions were flagrantly paraded and frequently violently enacted. In such contexts, the possibilities of maintaining relational identities were limited both by the state's threats of violence against others and by activists' own attempts to care for others by limiting the dangers to which they were exposed.

FORGING RELATIONSHIPS

Nevertheless, women's testimonies indicate that even in harsh conditions they attempted to forge relationships with those at hand. They were resourceful in doing so, although relationships were fragile under detention and imprisonment's conditions. Testifying in Worcester in July 1996, Yvonne Khutwane told the panel that she had used the time held in detention with criminal prisoners to 'conscientise' them about politics, but had also been afraid that a female cell-mate was a spy. Some women managed to create relationships with wardresses, a few of whom would assist women detainees but some of whom appeared to go out of their way to express cruelty. Gender did not forge automatic ties: race, class, gender and political ideology were important in structuring daily life in South Africa and life in the prisons was no different.

Opportunities to generate solidarity were not available to all political prisoners or detainees. A number were held in solitary confinement. Not all women were automatically held as political prisoners, and women recounted their pleasure when they were incarcerated with other 'politicals'. Testifiers recited the names of those with whom they shared cells, or whom they knew to have been detained, bringing them through memory into a public space. By implication, their testimonies extended beyond their own experience to include the experiences of others. Nomvula Mokonyane's statement on behalf of FEDTRAW at the Johannesburg Women's Hearing is peppered with examples of hardship and suffering inflicted on women, each example of pain illustrated with the name of a woman who had experienced it. Drawing together names of those who suffered harm creates a remembered community. A list of women detainees offered by Joyce Sikhakhane Ranken during her testimony is comprised of women whose roles as political activists have become well known: 'I listed here the names of women detainees I knew: Lillian Ngoyi, Helen Joseph, Ruth First, Dorothy Nyembi, Winnie Mandela, Rita Mzana, Martha Dlamini, Tobozile Ngomo, Shanti Naidoo, Albertina Sisulu, Thandi Modise, Barbara Hogan, Thenjiwe Mtintso and Jenny Schreiner.'

The women she named were engaged in different anti-apartheid activities between the 1950s and 1994. Although of different political persuasions, they were united in their general opposition to apartheid across its racial divides. Some belonged to women's organisations they had been instrumental in creating, some to the Communist Party, others to the ANC. One had been a member of the Black Consciousness movement, some were MK soldiers, and one was active in parliamentary politics as a member of the Opposition. In calling to mind these names, Joyce Ranken's testimony bears witness to a kind of community of women opposed to apartheid, linking their activities at different times to generate inclusivity. The implied solidarity might be a form of symbolic resistance to state practices that tried to dissolve social relationships and networks of support, or markers of attempts to generate a sense of ontological security and political commitment in a context marked by danger. The names may bring to life again the relationships wrought in prison. Sometimes such interventions have an almost nostalgic tone: temporal distance blurs ideological divisions that were powerful at the time.

SUSTAINING A SENSE OF SELF

If, as Susan Griffin argues, unmitigated terror has the effect of 'stripping away ... every extraneous layer ... every role we play in life' (1992:13), then in dread contexts, identity itself is at stake. Elaine Scarry (1985) has characterised torture as unmaking: for her, pain's dissolution of language sunders the possibility of sociality. Suggesting that Scarry's model is too rigid in opposing violence and language, Judith Butler (1997a: 9) draws on Austin's distinction between illocutionary and perlocutionary acts to propose that language itself may perform injury. The descriptions above – of bodily violation, humiliation, verbal threat and 'percepticide' (Taylor 1997: 124) – show that physical violence, gesture and language can work to unmake the self through instituting radical doubt. Nawal El Sa'adawi, scholar and activist, writes that 'doubt is the most certain of tortures. It is doubt that kills the intellect and body – not doubt in others, but doubt in oneself ...' (1991: 136).

Testimonies indicate that where sociality was limited, where relationships became contingent and were threatened by cruelty, and where doubt was profound, detainees and prisoners were cast upon their own ingenuity in sustaining their senses of self. In the following discussion, I use the latter phrase in the sense of efforts to create a continuity of subjectivity: a 'fiction' told to the self about its coherence over time. In extremity, political commitments were important in surviving violence and sustaining a sense of self. They enabled activists both to withstand extreme hardship and to return to protest or resistance activities on their release. External factors should not be underestimated here: to fail to return to political activities after release may have been read as a marker of betrayal. Few women admitted to doubt in their political beliefs. Jean Middleton's report to the Commission at a Special Hearing on Prisons offers an illustration. Having joined the Communist Party in the early 1960s after the ANC and PAC had been banned, she was arrested in 1964 and incarcerated, first in The Fort in Johannesburg and later, for the duration of her three-year sentence, in Barberton Prison. She explained, 'I think they [the wardresses] used to get annoyed about the political prisoners because it's not easy to humiliate a political prisoner, you know. You're proud of what you've done: you're not ashamed of it ... .'

Her sentiments were reiterated by other witnesses. Zahrah Narkedien told the Commission that after she was arrested when trying to cross the border into exile in Botswana: 'For the first seven days they did torture me quite a bit because I felt that I didn't have to co-operate ... I was proud of who I was as an MK comrade and I was proud of the fact that I joined the struggle, that I was a revolutionary and I was willing to just suffer the consequences.'[17]

Here, pride, marking the interpolation of the resistant subject, marks also an inward movement towards reliance on the self. That movement's effects are clearly illustrated in Narkedien's description of 'transporting' herself away from the scene of pain so that she became 'like a person who was physically there' but 'spiritually and mentally I wasn't there.' In so doing she claimed to have been able to endure torture so extreme that, with a peculiar sensibility, the policemen would ask the policewoman usually present during torture if she would care to leave as 'they were going to intensify the treatment.'

An ability to make oneself bodily present yet mentally absent is, perhaps, an ironic inversion of the state's techniques of invisibility described above.

Detention and cruelty impel closeness to madness and death. Asked by a Commissioner to describe the effects of solitary confinement, Jean Middleton said, 'I can't describe its effects to you very well because you go slightly crazy and it's very difficult to describe your own craziness.' Zahrah Narkedien's description of her experiences of abjection in solitary confinement gave metaphoric form to death's closeness. After an argument between herself and two political prisoners with whom she was incarcerated, Narkedien was sent into an isolation cell in the basement of the prison, where she spent seven months. The isolation units made her feel like one of the living dead: 'I became so psychologically damaged that I used to feel that all these cells are all like coffins and there were all dead people in there because they were not there, no one was there, it was as if I was alive and all these people were dead. I was so disturbed but I would never, never let the warders know.' She added, 'I felt as the months went by that I was going deeper and deeper into the ground. Physically I wasn't but psychologically I was.' As a consequence, 'I had to accept that I was damaged, a part of my soul was eaten away as if by maggots, horrible as it sounds, and I will never get it back again.'

Cruelty's Effects

Zahrah Narkedien's description crystallises cruelty's stakes. Given violence's dissolving effects on the sense of self, why was political belief so important in sustaining coherence? In thinking about this, I have found Judith Butler's model of the relationship between subjection and subjectivity helpful. She proposes that 'the subject is the effect of power in recoil' (1997b: 6), and is therefore both 'the *effect of* a prior power and the *condition of possibility* for a radically conditioned form of agency' (p. 15, emphasis in the original). Elsewhere she argues that resistance is implicit in the power it opposes (1997a: 40),[18] a point echoed in Etienne Balibar's (1998) formulation of violence and ideality as dialectically implicated. Butler argues that the power that 'initiates' the subject – 'a power exerted on' – precedes, produces and positions subjects: without it, there can be no subject (1997b: 12). But initiating power is not continuous with 'the power that is the subject's agency' (ibid.). The latter power is more open-ended and contains the possibility for agency and resistance through 'the assumption of a purpose *unintended* by power' (p. 15, emphasis in the original). This is given graphic illustration in women activists' testimonies: where cruel conditions, ostensibly devised to limit and punish resistance, do not 'break' the subject, they seem to reinforce that which they seek to punish.

The extremes of torture and deprivation described above, and their effects in forcing the attention inward, have echoes in Butler's description (1997b: 39ff) of the Hegelian subject in its early stoic guise. Analysing Hegel's lord–bondsman relationship, Butler describes the emergence of the subject and its 'unhappy consciousness' as a result of forms of reflexivity 'achieved through the experience of *absolute fear*' (p. 39, emphasis in the original). That fear is 'conditioned by the finite character of the body' (p. 52). It effects a split between body and consciousness, resulting in an unhappy consciousness that 'emerges here in the movement by which terror is allayed through a resolution of stubbornness or rather through the action by which terror of bodily death is displaced by a ... stubbornness ...' (p. 42).

For Butler, 'stubbornness' is 'self-will' in servitude. She continues: 'Consciousness clings or attaches to itself, and this clinging to consciousness is at the same time a disavowal of the body, which appears to signify the terror of death' (1997b: 43). This form closely fits the descriptions given in testimonies, where, recognising death's closeness, detained and imprisoned activists consistently reported having retained faith in the sustaining ideologies of resistance. The act returns them to the same structures of power through which subjectivity was instantiated, suggesting that cruelty performs power's circle.

This is not to deny the effort required to create a coherent sense of self but rather to draw attention to the effort and costs of this exertion in the face of the state's raw power, brutally wielded. The weight of consequences is suggested in the testimonies. Take for example the intervention offered by Tokyo Sexwale, who on 27 July 1997, addressed the Women's Hearing in Johannesburg, and described the extremities of the 'treatment' to which women were subjected in detention.[19] He told the Commission panellists that he and his comrades were amazed at the power of women to withstand the extremes of torture visited on them. He began:

It has been said that a nation that does not accord a human status to its womenfolk is a nation that lacks integrity and that does not belong to a future. Such an assertion can never be more true than in a country such as South Africa where the pain that has been felt by a whole nation has been felt even more by our mothers, our sisters, our aunts, our daughters, our women ...

The frame of reference, the collective male self, moves outwards to encompass female kinsfolk and other women then narrows to one woman, Paulina Mohale, to whom Sexwale paid tribute and who stands in his representation as emblematic of the unsung heroine:

I was on trial in 1977, 1978 ... One of us was a woman. She is hardly known by many people. We were tortured, we were electrified, we were beaten ... [When the trial resumed] we learnt with horror what one of us, Paulina Mohale, went through. It will be difficult for me here to speak for her, but the kind of pain that even we, as men, could not withstand, was doubly inflicted upon her. She was humiliated, her dignity was violated, her values were questioned, alone resisting ... and when the whole [case of the] 'Pretoria Twelve', as we were known at the time, resumed, Paulina Mohale stood tall. She nearly lost her mind, but she stood tall. To us that represented a focal point of admiration. We often thought that it is only the men who were supposed to [that is, able to] withstand the kind of pain ...

[T]hat name – Paulina Mohale – I thought I should invoke here to indicate that in the chambers of torture many such unsung heroines also stand to be counted ...

Mamagotla Paulina Mohale had testified a year earlier, in April 1996. She told the Commission that she had worked for the Student Christian Movement, mobilising and supporting student protest. In 1976, she and her brother were detained at the Swaziland border while trying to help young people cross the border into exile. Appallingly treated, tortured, after three days she collapsed and was taken to the district surgeon, who, she said, examined her and said that there nothing wrong with her despite the blood that seeped from her body. The police continued to interrogate her throughout the period of her pre-trial imprisonment. They accused her of having hidden guns and demanded that she tell them where the arms were. Once they threatened to kill her mother if Mamagotla did not cooperate. They threatened to make her 'fly like a bird' from the window of the interrogation room. She described the policemen as being 'like cannibals', with huge, luminous eyes. She spent six months in prison without even a change of clothes before being moved to The Fort in Johannesburg where she stood trial as the only woman in the case of the 'Pretoria Twelve'. In total, she spent 18 months in prison.

In her telling, detention had the trappings of nightmare. Her survival, celebrated by her comrades, came at considerable cost to her own sense of sanity. She briefly described to the Commission panellists her 'nervous breakdown', the irritability and tension she suffered for a long time after her detention and imprisonment: 'It really made me feel bad. At times I would dream. I couldn't adjust to the situation, to the normal situation of the family. I got quickly irritated, even by music, because where I was I couldn't listen to music. Even if a child was crying, I felt this cry in my nerves.'[20] Eventually she consulted a neurologist, and currently takes medication for a condition she did not name.

Of the 27 women who identified themselves as political activists, three – Shirley Gunn, Zubeida Jaffer and Virginia Mkhwanazi – explicitly described themselves as having suffered from post-traumatic stress disorders (PTSD). Sandra Adonis and Marie Magwaza said that their efforts to cope with having been detained had been complicated by the fact that their husbands, both political activists, had suffered from PTSD after being released from prison. Zahrah Narkedien stated, 'I'm out of prison now for more than seven or ten years but I haven't recovered and I will never recover. I know I won't: I have tried to. The first two years after my release I tried to be normal again and the more I struggle to be normal, the more disturbed I become.'

Their descriptions demonstrate the difficulties of maintaining coherence as a consequence of cruelty's circular effects. Nevertheless, the Commission report seems to confirm that activists were able to maintain that sense of self.

While finding that 'Exposure to violence is considered to lead to sleep disorders, sexual dysfunction, chronic irritability, physical illness and a disruption of interpersonal relations and occupational, family and social functioning' (Volume Five: 129), the report also finds that 'Political activists were less prone to post-traumatic stress disorder.' Note however that these findings are drawn from sources other than its own data: 'it was not possible to diagnose actual disorders or problems based on the statements and testimony at hearings' (Volume Five: 130). While local and international studies[21] are cited to argue that 'non-activists, even if subjected to lower levels of torture, display significantly more severe symptoms of post-traumatic stress disorder' (Volume Five: 133), the chapter's author also notes that in South Africa stressors such as gross violations of human rights may be confounded by other stressors such as 'dire social circumstances' (Volume Five: 136). I return to these arguments in Chapter 5.

The Commission's findings lack temporal depth and do not consider the effects of changing historical conditions on the experience of self as subject. The effect of detention is to impose limits on social relationships. As I have argued above, power's excess – the possibility for agency – is recirculated, narrowing the range of possibilities for the recognition, exercise and endurance of a sense of self. Such singularity may be effective in the short term but may not necessarily remain so when the conditions of possibility change. If, following Butler (1997b), we understand the subject as a site of power's reiteration, what are the effects when power as discursive form shifts unexpectedly, as was the case in South Africa post-1994 or even post-1990? Many activists with whom I have spoken report feeling disoriented in the face of the 'transition to democracy', which was often unexpected.[22] Some report a puzzling sense of loss. As the difficulties of recovery described in the testimonies here suggest, the forms of subjectivity produced when dread times narrow opportunities are easily undermined. What we currently recognise as PTSD may then be both a traumatic response to earlier subjection, and a fierce disorientation to power's new instantiation of the subject in time. Here, recovery may require more than psychic integration of experience into self as conventionally understood: alongside these processes, it involves the work of the social – re-establishing relationships with others and with time.

EFFACEMENT'S EFFECTS

What I have described above are layers of effacement: of the grounds of possibility on which selfhood can be built, of the activities of women in resistance, of the power that produced subjects and the moral urgency that impelled resistance. The erasure of activism in the Commission's work has three important effects. One is to resignify apartheid as an index of particular violence in which 'violation' begets 'victims', thereby imputing a natural, passive subject and foreclosing an investigation of power and resistance. The Commission's definition of a victim suggests quiescence: 'Victims are acted upon rather than acting, suffering rather than surviving ... [W]hen dealing with gross human rights violations committed by perpetrators, the person against whom that violation is committed can only be described as a victim, regardless of whether he or she emerged a survivor' (Report 1998, Volume One: 59). Rights literature too depicts victims as passive, the locus of inflicted power. It follows that the work of 'rights' frequently performs the same erasure of power, with similar effects to those described here.

The second effect of elision is to undervalue women's activities in resistance, and the third, to limit the assessment of harm. The emphasis on that which is visibly embodied denies the forms and consequences of a political agency configured in relation to state power and cruelty's effects. The Commission's findings on women, clustered as they are around an idea of bodily violation and couched in the passive tense, do not give due weight to the challenges faced by those constituted as agents in opposition to the state, particularly in the face of cruelty. They do not admit the foreclosure of the scope of possibilities through which to generate coherent fictions of self over the long term, or acknowledge the effort required to reorient the self when accustomed forms of agency are disconcerted.

4 NARRATIVE THREADS

One of the assumptions behind the juridical reckoning of truth is of a mimetic relation between memory and event. (Das and Kleinman 2001: 14)

The event is not what happens. The event is that which can be narrated. (Feldman 1991: 14)

Everything can be narrated. But what is narrated is no longer what happened. (Daniel 1996: 208)

[I]f story is truth, then truth is never absolute ... Story provides insight but never closure. (Scheub 1998: 1)

[S]tories require interlocutors, and the right to establish authoritative versions never rests with the individuals telling the story alone. It shifts from communal institutions and collective memory to the domain of experts and beyond – to market forces and the power of the state. (Lambek and Antze 1996: xvii)

The opening epigraphs describe a movement that traces narration's disconcerting effects: gaps emerge between experience and words and between words and what they purport to represent. They instantiate a puzzling relationship between interlocutors and others. Acceptance of testimonies rests on the presumption of congruity between event and description, yet this raises problems of representation. Narration performs the bridge between event and knowledge, yet in so doing undermines the ontological certainty of the former and the epistemological confidence of the latter. Time is implicated. In this chapter, I consider these problematics by closely examining the production and reception of testimony in the context of assertions about the founding nature of voice. This chapter marks a transition between the sites of the human rights violations hearings and my research in Zwelethemba, the focus of the remainder of the book.

There has been a recent flowering of studies on testimony. Most consider structures of testimony, the complexities of its demands on language, and problems of witnessing (Coady 1992; Felman and Laub 1992; Langer 1991, 1995; Agamben 1999; Bar-On 1999), usually in relation to testimonies of survivors of Nazi concentration camps. Their emphasis on testimony's literary characteristics, while important, underplays the significance of context and the local conventions that shape how testimonies are received. Recounting harm is not simple and acknowledgement not straightforward. Few studies have yet focused on the social ramifications of testimony or on the political uses to which it is increasingly put through mechanisms such as truth commissions. Those that have (see below), usually approach the problem from a psycho-social point of view. The widely cited work of Ingrid Agger and Soren Jensen (1990) is a case in point. They consider testimony to be a powerful mechanism through which recounting experiences of harm enables psychological remedy. Describing testimony as a universal 'ritual of healing', they argue that through it, the individual reintegrates painful experience into the self (thereby becoming 'whole') and makes a public statement about harms inflicted, thereby serving both to record harm and to denounce those who inflicted it.[1] Ingrid Agger writes, '"Testimony" as a concept has a special double connotation: it contains objective, judicial, public and political aspects as well as subjective, spiritual, cathartic and private aspects. Testimony thus contains the quality of uniting within its structure the private and the political levels' (1994: 9).

Others who are engaged in trying to assist in healing after traumatic experiences draw on such models (see for examples, Herman 1992; Gurr and Quiroga 2001), and too, they have echoes in the projects generically described as 'truth commissions'.

In the South African instance, the equation of the speaking self with the healed self was anticipated to be effected through the linking of 'voice' and 'dignity'. Section 3c of the Act required that the Commission 'restore the human and civil dignity of victims by granting them an opportunity to relate their own accounts of the violations of which they are the victims'. Victims were encouraged (by means of radio and newspaper adverts, posters, word of mouth and via the networks of NGOs) to 'come forward' and relate experiences of harm. This process, often described as 'story telling', was constituted as an authentically African mode of communication. Posters featuring a portrait photograph of an elderly, black, unnamed woman alongside an invitation to people to 'Tell Your Story', made by the Centre for the Study of Violence and Reconciliation, advertised the Commission's work prior to the first hearings. Commissioners and committee members frequently spoke of the healing power of story telling. Here is Archbishop Tutu: 'Storytelling is central, not only to many religious practices in this country but also to the African tradition of which we are a part. Ellen Kuzwayo is quoted ... as saying: "Africa is a place of storytelling. We need more stories, never mind how painful the exercise may be ... Stories help us to understand, to forgive and to see things through someone else's eyes"' (1996: 7).

The Commission explicitly used 'story telling' as part of its methodological approach to ascertaining 'truth':

By telling their stories, both victims and perpetrators gave meaning to the multi-layered experiences of the South African story ... In the (South) African context, where value continues to be attached to oral tradition, the process of story telling was particularly important. Indeed, this aspect is a distinctive ... feature of the legislation governing the Commission ... [:] The Act explicitly recognised the healing potential of telling stories. [Report,Volume One: 112]

Posters that decked the walls of hearings outlined the harms that might result from an inadequate knowledge of the past. One read, 'The truth hurts: silence kills'; another, 'Revealing is healing.' By implication, it was a civic and moral duty to narrate one's experiences of violation and pain and thereby bring about both personal healing and a healing of the national body. The Commission Report is explicit about the relationship between individual and national healing: 'People came to the Commission to tell their stories in an attempt to facilitate not only their own individual healing processes, but also a healing process for the entire nation. Many of those who chose not to come to the Commission heard versions of their stories in the experiences of others. In this way, the Commission was able to reach a broader community' (Volume Five: 169).

In these formulations, the constitution of both the subject and nation in the post-apartheid era is hinged on 'voice' and its foundational link with dignity. Achille Mbembe (2000) points out that this composition is distinctive of post-slavery, post-colonial and post-apartheid discourse in Africa. In an oral presentation in August 2000, he characterised the formulation as 'I can tell my story, therefore I am' (see also Werbner 1998). Here, authenticity is thought to rest in the individual's capacity for self-expression. Voice implies authenticity: speaking is considered to be an act that fully, completely and absolutely describes the self. This is clear in the Commission's assumptions about the relationship between 'experience' and 'story': the narration of experience was assumed to be a simple act, a release of 'stories' of pain that already existed intact within those who had experienced violations. All that was apparently required was a forum through which these could be released and channelled. Yet, as I show below, testimonies and their effects are complex. Remarkably little attention has been paid to their contents, their complex modes of production or the contexts within which testimonies are shaped and received.

Testimonies were a product of dialogue between a testifier and a member of the HRVC, shaped by the interpretation of the Commission's mandate, the statements given, and the empathy and interaction between the Commission representative and the testifier. Each process of eliciting testimony was unique. Commission members had different techniques for eliciting stories of harm: some were silent in the face of pain; others probed testifiers' accounts, seeking greater detail of and explanation for the experiences they described. Statements were produced through a lengthy process of decision making, narration, distillation and crystallisation of experiences and transformed into 'data' using a positivistic methodology (Buur 1999). The cumulative effect was to reduce and decontextualise narratives to produce uniform, comparable data for statistical purposes (Buur 1999: 29; see also Wilson 2001: 33–61). Richard Wilson (1997) argues that such reification is characteristic of human rights reportage.

Giving public expression to violent experience was an ambivalent experience for some: as the report points out, 'Not all storytelling heals. Not everyone wanted to tell his or her story' (Volume Five: 352; see also Volume One: 112). Priscilla Hayner states that the Trauma Centre for Survivors of Violence in Cape Town found that between 50 and 60 per cent of testifiers suffered difficulty after testifying (2001: 144), although the nature of difficulty is not described. Despite this, the Commission Report claims that on the whole, telling one's story was beneficial, claiming, 'Many ... were able to reach towards healing by telling the painful stories of their pasts' (Volume Five: 352). The claim is illustrated with extracts drawn from the testimonies and post-hearing debriefing sessions of three testifiers, one of whom is a woman named Yvonne Khutwane. Her testimony, the focus of the present chapter, warrants close attention for a number of reasons. She was one of the few women activists to testify before the Commission and the only woman activist in Zwelethemba (the area that became a focus of my research) to testify in a public hearing of the HRVC. She was the first woman to include a description of sexual violation in her public testimony, a factor that, as I have shown, was a matter of considerable import to the Commission and gender activists. Few testimonies are cited in the Report and fewer still appear more than once.[2] Extracts from Yvonne Khutwane's testimony are cited in four places (Volume Three: 448; twice in Volume Four: 298; and Volume Five: 352–3) where they are offered mainly as illustrations of sexual violence visited upon women. The telling and reinterpreting of her experiences at the human rights violations hearing, in media reports, academic studies and in the evaluations offered by political activists resident in her home town, offer a critique of simplistic assumptions about violence and voice, testimony, truth and healing.

A HUMAN RIGHTS VIOLATIONS HEARING IN WORCESTER

The public hearing on Human Rights Violations in the Boland was held in Worcester, in the heartland of the Western Cape's wine and fruit-growing region. Between 24 and 26 June 1996, 24 residents of the towns that dot the Breede River valley – Worcester, Rawsonville, Robertson, Ashton and Montagu and their townships[3] – testified about gross violations of human rights at Songhe College, a teacher training institute. Lying between the town centre and residential areas previously decreed Coloured, the college is close to what used to be Potjiestraat and Sakkiesdorp, areas from which 'African' residents were forcibly removed in 1954 when the region was proclaimed a residential area for Coloured and White residents only.[4]

Africans were removed to Zwelethemba, 'Place of Hope', some five kilometres away from the college, across a river that residents believe was diverted to create a buffer zone between the Black and White areas of town.

The 24 testifiers represented approximately 14 per cent of the total of 177 deponents in the area. The testifiers or those about whom they spoke are named as victims in the Commission's Report. Five people spoke about killings; eight (a woman and seven men) described detention and torture and eleven described injuries. Police were identified as responsible for harm in 18 of the testimonies: they had tortured eight of the testifiers; shot and killed four men; shot and injured three men and one woman; and beaten and injured two women. Members of the Zolani vigilante group known as the *Amasolomzi* (Eyes of the Community) injured four men. Police were also implicated in two of these cases. One man reported that he had been shot by 'comrades'. A civilian killed a youth during a protest march.

Three testifiers were middle-aged women. Eight testifiers were middle-aged or elderly men. With one exception, all testifiers were Coloured or African. Approximately half of the testifiers had been young when the incidents they described to the Commission had occurred. Thirteen young men were under the age of 25 at the time of the violation they or others described. Nine testifiers were residents of Zwelethemba. Two of the nine (Maria Bahume and Yvonne Khutwane) were women. Seven (Xolile Dyabooi, Zandesile Ntsomi, Amos Dyantyi, Yvonne Khutwane, Nyembezi Makhubalo, Mzikhaya Mkhabile, and Nthando Mrubata) spoke about their own experiences of violation. Maria Bahume testified about the death of her son, Nation, in 1985 (see Chapter 5). Mbedele Dyasi spoke of the death of his son, William, also killed by the police in 1985. Seven of the Zwelethemba testifiers described the violence in the township in the mid-1980s. Two elderly men (Nyembezi Makhubalo and Mzikhaya Mkhabile) described events in 1960, when residents in Zwelethemba protested influx control laws. Both men were arrested and tortured and Mkhabile was imprisoned on Robben Island for twelve years.

Eight of the nine testimonies made by Zwelethemba residents at the hearing concerned violations committed by the police and/or Security Branch. The same policemen, Warrant Officer van Loggerenberg, Lieutenant Nieuwoudt, and Sergeant McDonald, were frequently named by testifiers as perpetrators of gross violations of human rights.[5]

All the Zwelethemba residents who testified about their own experiences of violation considered themselves to have been politically active; some as students engaged in protest and boycotts, others as members of the ANC 'underground'.[6] The hearing was unusual in that in previous hearings, the majority of testifiers did not describe themselves or the people about whom they testified as politically active. The image presented to the public was of committed activists confronting the state in its manifestations as the police force and the infamous Security Branch.

Taken together, the accounts offered by residents of Zwelethemba point to the strength of anti-apartheid resistance in the area over a long period. It was in this context that Mrs Yvonne Khutwane gave her testimony.

A WOMAN'S PAIN

Yvonne Khutwane, a middle-aged woman dressed in red and accompanied by her friend, Mirriam Moleleki, a 'community debriefer' (see Chapter 6), was sworn in at 3.10 pm on 24 June 1996 before a panel consisting of four Commissioners (Denzil Potgieter, an advocate; Wendy Orr, a doctor who had exposed torture of detainees while a district surgeon in the Eastern Cape; Alex Boraine, previously a Member of Parliament in opposition to apartheid, now a primary instigator of the idea of the Commission and its Deputy Chairperson; and Mary Burton, one-time head of the Black Sash, an organisation of women that monitored state repression) and Pumla Gobodo-Madikizela, a psychologist and the HRVC member assigned to assist Mrs Khutwane with her testimony. She was the sixth person to testify that day and the fourth to testify about events in Zwelethemba in the 1980s. Her 40-minute testimony was given in Xhosa[7] and began with a warning that her memory for dates was failing. She then began to describe a political meeting held in the Zwelethemba school hall after mourners returned from the funeral of the 'Cradock Four' – Matthew Goniwe, Fort Calata, Sparrow Mkhonto and Sicelo Mhlawuli – in Cradock in 1985 (see Chapter 2). A few minutes into her description, Ms Gobodo-Madikizela interrupted her and asked, 'Are you trying to clarify how you got involved in politics?' Yvonne Khutwane replied, 'I started in 1960 to be involved in the ANC struggle. I was still a young girl. We worked underground, and it was very difficult for us even to hold meetings. I became prominent specifically when the Municipality offices were establishing community councillors, as you see this lady next to me on my left [a reference to Mirriam Moleleki], we were the people who didn't like that.'

Ms Gobodo-Madikizela intervened again and asked her to explain the events that led to her arrest and trial between 1985 and 1986. Mrs Khutwane said that she had been interrogated in 1984 about her involvement in protest against local councillors. She was a founder member of the Zwelethemba Residents' Association (affiliated to the Western Cape Civic Association, a grouping that stood in opposition to the state's local councils.) She explained to the Commission that when she had made a statement to the police, she realised that she may inadvertently have betrayed a comrade: 'It is then that I was affected severely, to the extent that, even today, I cannot explain [how it came] about that I should seem [to] have betrayed my friend. But fortunately ... [he] won the case, he was acquitted.'

Immediately after this Yvonne Khutwane embarked on a long, detailed explanation of her arrest in 1985 after the meeting to which she had alluded when beginning her testimony. The description was punctuated by questions from Ms Gobodo-Madikizela. On one occasion, the latter asked, 'In other words you are giving a statement in which you were degraded by the police: could you please just explain that?' Mrs Khutwane described being interrogated about weapons possession and the burning of the municipal bar in Zwelethemba in June 1985.[8] She had been called to the magistrate's court by a local black policeman, who told her that she was wanted in connection with charges she had laid against a young man who had stolen a car battery from her some months previously. She had dressed smartly for her court appearance and had gone with the policeman willingly, only to find that she had been duped. Instead of going to court to give evidence in the case, she was taken to the police station for interrogation. During the interrogation, she was hit in the face and verbally abused by a white policeman 'young enough to be my son'. She fought back:

When the fight continued, you could hear that there was somebody coming along and then they were ridiculing me and then saying I am a John Tait and a Gerrie Coetzee, the boxers. At the end I could see that they were also embarrassed because some of the black detectives came in. My shirt was in tatters and then one of them said, 'Are you fighting back, you *kaffir?*' Then they kept on insulting me.

Later, she heard the 'children' with whom she had been detained screaming and crying in the cells alongside hers. In response to questions posed by Ms Gobodo-Madikizela, she explained that she had been pushed into a police van and driven to the township in leg irons and handcuffs.[9] She was taken to her house which, she said, was 'infested' with policemen searching for weapons and the makings of petrol bombs. 'When we got there ... there were still a lot of policemen around my place. You would think that a male person was arrested!', she recalled. Although no weapons were found, Yvonne Khutwane was arrested.

At this point in the narration, Ms Gobodo-Madikizela intervened, prompting, 'Excuse me mama, can you please tell me what they did to you?' Yvonne Khutwane explained that she was locked in a cell with a warning:

They [the police] said if I defy them I will be detained for years and I will never get out of prison again ... I said I didn't care; they can do whatever they liked. I was arrested and I was detained again. I was alone in the cell ... I was really in solitary confinement. I was concerned about my child because I left him whilst I was taken to those offices. So I didn't know where they have taken him.

She then explained that that night two policemen had taken her from the cell and bundled her into an armoured vehicle, a 'Hippo', that drove out of Worcester and through Rawsonville, a village some ten kilometres away. As Mrs Khutwane embarked on a careful description of the route, Ms Gobodo-Madikizela intervened, prompting her to address the incident of violation: 'What were they doing to you, as you are here?' In response to persistent

questions posed by Ms Gobodo-Madikizela, Mrs Khutwane described how
two young white uniformed men sexually molested her:

I was just alone at the back of the Hippo and they were just driving – it was pitch dark
outside. They alighted from the Hippo and then they came to take me out of the Hippo.
One of them said to me can I see what [situation] I have put myself in, and then they
asked me when did I last sleep with a man. I was so embarrassed by this question.
And I felt so humiliated. I informed them that I have nobody: I didn't have a partner.
Then they asked me with whom am I staying. I informed them that I was with my
family. The other question that they asked me is how do I feel when ... I am having
intercourse with a man. This was too much for me because they were repeating it
time and again, asking me the same question, asking what do I like with the
intercourse? Do I like the size of the penis? Or what do I enjoy most?

So the other one was just putting his hand inside me [into] the vagina, I was crying
because I was afraid. We had heard that the soldiers are very notorious for raping
people. This one continued putting his finger right [into] me, he kept on penetrating
and I was asking for forgiveness and I was asking them, 'what have I done, I am old
enough to be your mother. But why are you treating me like this?' This was very, very
embarrassing.

At the end ... I think maybe God just came inside them and the other one said, 'Let's
let her go', and then at the end they took me back to this police station and then they
locked me up in the cell again. When I got inside there, I could see that there was one
person inside the cell, I was afraid because this person was also – looked as if he is a
male also, I was not trusting anybody now, I was suspicious of anything that was
moving around.

A day later, Mrs Khutwane was interrogated by members of the Security
Branch. She accused one, Lt Nieuwoudt, of emptying the breach of his gun
of its bullets and hitting her repeatedly on the head with its butt as the other
questioned her. Mrs Khutwane's description of the interrogation was
interrupted again by Ms Gobodo-Madikizela's questions about what
information the police sought from her. Yvonne Khutwane replied, with a
hint of impatience, 'I am still saying my story.' She continued by describing
multiracial meetings held in Zwelethemba. Ms Godobo-Madikizela
intervened once more, returning to the event of sexual violation. She asked
Yvonne Khutwane to describe how she had felt about the experience of being
molested by the policeman:

I want to know and want to identify the situation that you were [in] while these people
detained you. You have given us the – the other way that they treated you during
that period and we got what you are trying to say and the way they treated you while
you were in the van ... As I was sitting ... there listening [to your testimony] I couldn't
take it, because our mothers are just the same age as yours and yet there are people
who ... couldn't respect you – dishonour you as little [young] as they were. I just had
the feeling that you could be my mother.[10] That's where the pain is. We would like
you to tell us, how were you feeling that time?

Yvonne Khutwane replied that the event had been painful and humiliating,
not least because the men involved were young enough to be her children:

'It was so painful because I couldn't stand it, because these kids were young and ... they had all the powers [that is, ought] to respect and honour me. They were just the same age as my children and what were they doing to me. I ... think maybe they thought that I was just a black person who is out of her mind ... not knowing anything.' Ms Gobodo-Madikizela responded, 'Yes, it's like that, because like the one who slapped you hard on your face he was also a youngster. So I think they dishonoured you, humiliating you, lowered your dignity as much as they can.'

A series of questions pertaining to her family life was then posed, from which it emerged that Mrs Khutwane had four adult children, had been married but was divorced and owned her own house: that is, she was a woman of independent means. The questions were posed deliberately: Ms Gobodo-Madikizela continued, 'I am just saying that you are also a mother. It's because I am imagining the way these children, these policemen ... treated you. I had a picture in mind ... [of] the way they were treating you.'

Yvonne Khutwane went on to describe the appalling conditions of the jail, the lice in her cell and the brutal interrogation sessions in which she was repeatedly partially suffocated. She had contracted meningitis in jail, and, when she complained of the cold, had been given wet blankets. She was refused medical attention until a lawyer intervened and she was hospitalised. Afterwards, she was sent back to prison and was released when a friend paid her bail. At the end of a trial in which she stood accused of inciting public violence, she was acquitted. During the trial, her house was bombed:

During the period when I was detained, I was just in confused state. I didn't know what was happening to me. I didn't even know whether I was going to be acquitted or I was going to be kept for quite a long time. One of the people informed me that while I was detained my place was burnt down while I was in prison[11] and I was informed that ... [a] petrol bomb was thrown at it. So, one of my children died because he had an epileptic attack.[12]

When she returned home after her acquittal, she was alienated by her political community. Ms Gobodo-Madikizela asked her to describe her feelings and the responses of residents in Zwelethemba and Mrs Khutwane answered, 'I thought that as I was one of the ANC members they wanted me to withdraw from the ANC not to hold meetings again because I would know what will be the treatment I will get, even now ... .'

Ms Gobodo-Madikizela re-posed the question, 'Were there people who said you betrayed others?' Mrs Khutwane replied by describing her feelings of alienation: 'I could see that even the community was ostracising me – I was being ridiculed by everybody because my house was destroyed through arson. But I have never turned my back against them. I am still an ANC member.'

Ms Gobodo-Madikizela summarised Yvonne Khutwane's requests to the Commission: 'In your statement, you mentioned that we should find out why your house was burnt down ... why you were degraded and why you were reported as an informer.' Mrs Khutwane agreed, asking that the case be investigated. Ms Gobodo-Madikizela then asked whether Mrs Khutwane knew the names of the men who had verbally abused and sexually molested her. She did not. Ms Gobodo-Madikizela asked what Mrs Khutwane would say to the young men if they were to ask for forgiveness. Yvonne Khutwane answered that she would tell them that 'they should try to have manners.' At this point, her testimony came to an end. One third of the time had been taken up with questions and answers about the event of sexual violation. The panellists did not pose questions. Dr Alex Boraine, the chairperson for the day, concluded,

You have been through a very hard time. Not only were you very badly molested and insulted, imprisoned, solitary confinement, charged, kept waiting for two years before your case was heard and found not guilty [but] then to find that your own friends and comrades suspected you of giving information and informing. You lost your house, your family has been unwell, you have suffered very, very deeply and we are very aware of the pain that you have experienced.

After thanking her, he asked her to step down from the stage and called the next witness. Yvonne Khutwane and her companion left the stage.

Three years later, during one of the interviews I conducted with her,[13] she described her feelings after testifying:

When I sat there in the seats [after testifying], the time came when I felt that I was not there. My brain was *deurmekaar* [Afrikaans – 'confused']. I returned to my seat alone. No one from the Truth Commission talked to me [that is, she was not debriefed]. We went out of the hall. The members who had spoken to the Commission had to leave first and the others last. After the hearings there were people from Zwelethemba who were going home. People congratulated me. You know, I did not know if I did right or wrong. I asked myself if I should have gone before the Truth Commission. I did not know if people would understand. I just told myself [prior to testifying] that I would tell the truth and hope. That was the end.

There were lots of people at the Truth Commission that day. Some of them said, 'we did not know what happened to you'. They said that they would not have been able to speak themselves about something like this. They congratulated me for being so strong. Others thanked me. Many said I was very strong. I did not think so. I felt I had to speak the truth I knew.

No one has mentioned it since except a woman from Ashton who came about reha-bilitation.[14] I told her that I am okay, I don't need to be rehabilitated. I am not sick, I am alright. I said, 'I am strong, I do not need trauma help, *ntoni, ntoni*' [Xhosa – 'and so on and so on']. The second time it was the priest with no hands.[15] I said, 'I am not feeling anything [bad]. I do not need intervention.'

One white woman stopped me in the street. She said, '*Ek het jou 'speech' by die Waarheids Kommissie gehoor*' [I heard your speech at the Truth Commission]. I used to work for a dentist – *inslaapwerk* [live-in domestic work] – and she [the dentist's wife] saw me in town and she said she had heard me.

I didn't know it would be like this.

You know, people came from Groote Schuur Hospital to Masikhule [a centre from which several former women activists run development initiatives – see Chapter 6] one Sunday [before the Commission hearing]. They said, 'You must not keep things inside. Speak it out. You can't sit and think always, thinking, thinking, thinking.' At the Truth Commission I said I would speak out so that the world would know that we were under such conditions, so that even the people who did these things would change and would know that we are also people and they did not have the right to do such things to us. [Interview, June 1999]

Yvonne Khutwane envisaged long-term interest in her testimony. When I gave her a copy of her testimony transcript, downloaded from the Commission's site on the Internet, and of the newspaper reports, she put them in a large brown envelope and tucked them away under a table damaged in the arson attack she described in her testimony. 'For my grandchildren, so they will know about me', she said. Her actions were unusual: a number of women activists who did not make statements to the Commission told me that they did not want to expose their humiliation to future generations.

Many of the experiences about which Yvonne Khutwane testified (including solitary confinement, torture, beating, sexual molestation and arson) fell into the ambit of the Commission's definitions of gross violations of human rights, and she was found to be a victim.[16] In 1998, the Reparation and Rehabilitation Committee of the Commission granted her an Urgent Interim Relief payment.

A DIVERSITY OF HARMS BECOMES A STORY OF SEXUAL VIOLATION

In her testimony, Mrs Khutwane described diverse experiences of harm and damage that included the severe punishment meted out to political prisoners and the torture that women experienced. Her testimony described the connivance of the medical and legal systems in her ill treatment; common complaints among the testifiers in the Boland. There is substantial evidence from public hearings of the Commission of collusion between state, police, and certain medical and legal institutions and practitioners throughout the country (Report Volume Four: 109, 154, 155–7). Mrs Khutwane told of the fragile and fraught nature of community relationships during violence: the apparent ease with which accusations of betrayal led to arson and ostracism, notwithstanding her claim to 25 years of work in the underground structures of the ANC. Her testimony linked several events into a continuous narrative of both tribulation and commitment. She described her experiences as a series of disasters that followed on from one another in rapid chronological and accumulative order and that were mediated by her self-conscious political knowledge. Carefully, she charted the intrusion of violence into her life: practices of violence that moved from her body to the community, a widening spiral of violence that once again impinged on the space of the domestic in the damage to her home. The descriptions presented her experiences as a seamless set of activities and relations in which she, as a political activist, was pitted against the state and as a consequence later came into – and appeared to have overcome – conflict within the community. Both

Yvonne Khutwane and the Commission portrayed her story as emblematic of the experience of some activists: under surveillance by the police, detained or arrested, interrogated, tortured, her kin threatened, released, faced with community suspicion.

Yet, despite the diversity of harms that Mrs Khutwane described, many of which fell into the Commission's definition of gross violations of human rights, the print media and later the representations of her testimony in the Commission's Report depicted her as the *victim of sexual violation*. As I have shown in earlier chapters, prior to Mrs Khutwane's testimony, few women had testified about their own experiences of violation and none had spoken in public hearings about experiences of sexual violation although these had been intimated in some testimonies and described in the Gender Submission (Goldblatt and Meintjes 1996).

Mrs Khutwane's testimony at the Worcester hearing was not an unmediated flow of words that described her experience but was marked and shaped by interventions and questions from Ms Gobodo-Madikizela. The latter had been present at a meeting between some Commission members and members of Cape Town's NGOs on 14 June 1996 at which Commissioner Mapule Ramashala had expressed her concern that 'the whole story' of apartheid violation would not be told if women did not testify about their own experiences of harm (see Chapter 1). Ms Gobodo-Madikizela's interventions were important in view of the fact that Mrs Khutwane did not include the story of sexual violation as she told it before the Commission in her prior written statement. The statement apparently[17] described her arrest and torture, the arson attack on her house and the accusation that she was a sell-out. It also stated that she was 'threatened' with rape. Ms Gobodo-Madikizela later told me that she did not know about the incident of sexual violation, saying that the first time she had learned of it was when it had emerged from the dialogue of the testimonial process (personal communication, 5 April 1999). In response to my questions about Mrs Khutwane's testimony she wrote:

Her testimony about the behaviour of the young military police[18] came to me as a total surprise. It would be more correct to say I *identified* more closely with her story ... But because I am a woman there has to be something more intriguing in the story than simply the fact that I was identifying closely with the story of another woman, because of the humiliation I shared with her at that point, which only another woman can understand ... I think ... that there is something between a TRC member and a witness that elicits certain responses from the witness. [emphasis in the original e-mail, 5 April 1999, cited with permission]

Particular facets of Mrs Khutwane's experience were emphasised in the public record as a result of the empathy and personal engagement described by Ms Gobodo-Madikizela. Mrs Khutwane seemed reluctant to talk of sexual violation. She sometimes evaded the questions posed, or answered them briefly. She did not offer her emotional responses until prompted. Sometimes she responded impatiently. She was not reticent in describing the other violations she had experienced. She told of being threatened, hit, beaten with the butt of a gun, strangled, suffocated, squashed. She described arson and her child's death, and her feelings of alienation from her political community. In so doing, she located the sexual violation as one harmful incident among many, but the questions posed by Ms Gobodo-Madikizela returned her on several occasions to the event of sexual harm. Indeed, as I sat in the audience at the hearing, it seemed this violation was presumed to be *the* traumatic event and the *primary* violation. The process appeared to be predicated on an assumption that that which happens to or is inflicted on the body endures as pain remembered in a different and more profound fashion than the pain of, for example, a loss of community trust and engagement.

The Commission and the audience at the hearing did not learn how Mrs Khutwane coped with her experience of detention and the harms inflicted there. They did not learn about the consequences of being ostracised by political peers or about how Yvonne Khutwane was able to cement relationships sufficiently to remain in the community that she believed considered her to be a betrayer. The testimonial interaction revealed only the details of one specific event-period in her life – an event that, as I show below, she had not intended to describe in such detail. In the following section, I trace the distillation of testimony through representation.

The press reports that followed the hearing represented Mrs Khutwane's testimony as having been about sexual violation and betrayal. The South African Press Association (SAPA) reported the story as follows:

WORCESTER June 24 1996 – Sapa
WOMAN TELLS TRUTH BODY OF SEXUAL ABUSE

A Worcester mother of four on Monday told the Truth and Reconciliation Commission how she was sexually molested and tortured by security force members following her arrest in June 1985 for her involvement in African National Congress activities. Testifying before the commission at its hearings in Worcester, Yvonne Khutwane gave graphic details of the abuses she suffered after two white soldiers removed her from her cell in the middle of the night and drove her to a remote spot in a Hippo armoured vehicle. She was in her mid-40s at the time of the attack.

"They asked me when I had last slept with a man. They asked how I felt when I had intercourse with a man. I was so humiliated. I told them I did not have a partner. One of them put his finger into my vagina. I was just crying. He kept on penetrating me. I kept on asking for forgiveness and asking why they were treating me like this. I said I was old enough to be their mother. One of them then said 'let her go'. I think God came into him."

Khutwane, a former member of the Western Cape Civic Association, said she also suffered terrible injuries when she was interrogated by Paarl-based security police. She named one of her alleged torturers as a Lt Gerhardt Nieuwoudt, who she claimed sat on her chest. "They also tried to suffocate me with a towel. I was bleeding all over my body. My condition was very bad and I was taken to hospital."

During her detention her house was petrol-bombed after rumours spread that she had become a police informer. In spite of being shunned by her community, she had remained a loyal member of the ANC, Khutwane said.

© South African Press Association, 1996
<www.truth.org.za/SAPA/9606/S960624C.htm>

The SAPA report describes Mrs Khutwane in diverse ways: as a mother of four, a middle-aged woman, a person involved in ANC activities. Her political 'involvement' in ANC 'activities' is posited as secondary to the fact of her motherhood. Her identities are described in almost the reverse order to her own presentation of self in the hearing. The story highlights the sexual violation and excludes Ms Gobodo-Madikizela's shaping interventions. The testimony is presented as an uncomplicated narrative of sexual molestation and torture and it is only in the last two sentences that the complexities of returning to her community are mentioned.

The *Worcester Standard*, the town's local weekly newspaper, mentioned Mrs Khutwane's testimony in its description of the week's hearings (*Worcester Standard*, 28 June 1996). Under the caption '*WVK hoor talle verhale*' ('TRC hears diverse stories'), Mrs Khutwane's testimony is summarised in one paragraph. Despite the variety of harms and violations Mrs Khutwane described, her testimony is reduced to a narrative of sexual violence and political betrayal: '*Volgens Yvonne Khutwane, wat sedert 1962 'n ANC lid is, is sy in Julie 1985 seksueel gemolesteer deur 'n polisieman. Haar huis is deur inwoners van Zweletemba afgebrand omdat hulle geglo het dat sy 'n polisie-informant was.*' (Yvonne Khutwane, an ANC member since 1962 [*sic*], was sexually molested in July 1985 by a policeman. Her house was burnt down by residents of Zwelethemba because they believed that she was a police informer.)

Her testimony was also reported in the Cape Town daily newspaper, the *Cape Times*, on Tuesday 25 June 1996 (p. 3). The article, written by journalist Roger Friedman, differed in important respects from Yvonne Khutwane's testimony. Friedman did not interview her after the hearing. (My comments on the difference are italicised alongside the report.) The story read:

ANC veteran tells of sexual abuse

Soldiers the same age as her own children sexually assaulted African National Congress veteran Mrs Yvonne Khotwane [*sic*].

Khotwane told the Truth and Reconciliation Commission yesterday her involvement in the struggle went back to before 1960 – 'I was still a young girl' – but it was in 1985 that she was made to suffer the greatest indignity of her life. (*She did not make this claim.*)

Accused of giving local youths petrol to make petrol bombs (*the accusation followed interrogation and a house search*) – she was prominent in the Zwelethemba township community's action against the community council system – Khotwane was arrested in June 1985 and held in Worcester.

Tortured, beaten and threatened continually after her arrest, Khotwane did not dream things could get worse. *(She did not make this claim.)* Then they did. *(Again, she did not state this in her public testimony. The statement implies that the incident of sexual molestation was worse than any other experience.)*

One night, two young soldiers loaded her into a car and drove about. Then they broached the subject of sex.

'They were asking me horrible things about intercourse. They wanted to know what I liked about intercourse, whether it was the size of the penis.'

One touched her.

'The other one was putting his hand inside me, on to my vagina. I was frightened because we had all heard how notorious the security forces were about raping people. He kept on penetrating me, and I was asking for forgiveness ... I was old enough to be his mother, I was very frightened.'

'They were very young children. They were just the same age as my own children. I think maybe they just thought I was a black person ...'

When she cried, they threatened to shoot her. *(Mrs Khutwane did not state that she cried or that the men threatened to shoot her.)*

Then they took her back to the police station. The threats and torture resumed.

After three months in detention, Khotwane was charged with public violence. The case dragged on for two years before she was acquitted. But her suffering was not over.

Some members of the Zwelethemba community thought she had cracked under the torture and passed information to the police.

Her house was burnt down.

'But I have never turned my back on them. I am still an ANC member.'

All of the newspaper articles focused on the event of sexual violation as *the primary event of harm.* Those that covered the story in some detail used extracts from Mrs Khutwane's testimony to describe the sexual violation but not any of the other instances she described. Two of the reports conclude with her assertion of political loyalty, a point to which I return. In all the media representations, Yvonne Khutwane's story was presented as complete: none of the reports showed how the testimony had been constructed, drawn from her through persistent questions and repetition. Rather, the event of sexual molestation was presented as though she had intended to speak of it all along and had done so without prompting. Her testimony is represented in a manner that suggests that it pre-existed the Commission's intervention, as if there was a coherent narrative, 'a testimony', intact in form, awaiting an opportunity to be spoken in public.

The print media was not the only representation of Yvonne Khutwane's testimony that focused mainly on sexual violation. Summaries of or direct quotes drawn from her public testimony are included in four places in the Commission's 1998 Report. All but one describe the event of sexual violation. In Volume Three (p. 448), quotations relating to sexual violation are quoted verbatim in a discussion of torture practices in the rural areas of the Western Cape. The interventions by Ms Gobodo-Madikizela have been erased from the narrative. In Volume Four (p. 298), Mrs Khutwane's description of the humiliation of being asked questions of a sexual nature by young men is included in a discussion of humiliations suffered by women. Note that at no point is there a discussion of the possible humiliation of being asked questions about sexual violation by a young woman in public before an audience and in the knowledge that hearings were broadcast live on TV and radio and reported in the print media. A short description of the fight in which she was described as a 'Gerry Coetzee' is also included in the chapter of the report that deals with women (Volume Four: 298). In Volume Five (pp. 352–3), in a section dealing with reconciliation and restoring the civil and human dignity of victims, extracts describing sexual violation are quoted in a discussion of the possibilities of healing offered through testimony. The chapter's unnamed author states that Mrs Khutwane did not include the incident of sexual molestation in her statement concerning gross violations of human rights and states that the public hearing was the first time that Yvonne Khutwane had spoken about her experience of sexual violation: 'Quite often, witnesses revealed far more in oral testimony than they had in their written statements. This is illustrated by the testimony of a middle-aged woman, Ms Yvonne Khutwane, at the Worcester hearing' (ibid.).

The discussion continues by quoting her description of sexual humiliation and molestation. None of Ms Gobodo-Madikizela's interventions are included; the testimony is presented as unmediated. The author of the volume then states, 'In her written statement, Ms Khutwane had made no mention of this sexual assault. In her debriefing session,[19] she said that this was the first time she had spoken of it and that she felt tremendously relieved' (ibid.).

According to the Report, Yvonne Khutwane did not intend to testify about sexual violation. This was confirmed in our later discussions. Her written request to the Commission, included as part of the written statement and summarised in the hearing by Ms Gobodo-Madikizela, was that the Commission investigate why and how the house was burnt, why she was 'degraded' and who described her as an informer. These facets of violence were displaced in the ways in which her experience of sexual violence became the focal point of the panellist's interventions, and later, the media reports and the Commission's use of her testimony in its Report. Initially an event that she did not intend to describe in public (if her written submission to the Commission is read as a statement of intent), the event of sexual molestation was interpreted in ways that gradually repositioned Mrs Khutwane as a victim of sexual abuse, and was depicted in both the print media and the Commission's Report as the defining feature of her testimony.

This reframing is not particular to Yvonne Khutwane's testimony or even to South Africa, but has wider resonance. Rajeswari Sunder Rajan shows how literary representations of rape or sexual violence assume that women's lives end at the traumatic event. Women are depicted both as isolated in the moment of violation and as unable to move beyond the experience of violence. Rajan comments that the effect is to turn the woman into a symbol, 'a cypher', and to detract attention from the woman's concerns (1993:72).

The structuring of Mrs Khutwane's testimony by the panellist and the subsequent media reports resemble the pattern Rajan describes.

The testimony has since been taken up elsewhere, and its framing in terms of sexual harm retained. In *Between Vengeance and Forgiveness*, Martha Minow's study of the alternatives that face countries in confronting and dealing with genocide and mass violence, Yvonne Khutwane's testimony is summarised in the context of a discussion on the limitations of truth commissions in attending to women's voices. Minow writes, 'One woman volunteered testimony about a sexual violation committed by police that she found extremely humiliating; she had not mentioned the incident in her written statement' (1998: 84).[20]

In Chapter 3, I argued that the Commission elided political activism in its focus on 'the victim'. Yvonne Khutwane's testimony offers a particular instance, demonstrating how the status of 'victim' was produced through the Commission's work. The discussion above demonstrates the elicitation, condensation and crystallisation of testimonies in circulation. Different forms of violence are obscured, violence is reified to that which is inflicted on the body, and is further concretised in relation to sexual harm. Mrs Khutwane's political activities were ignored by Commissioners and overwritten in press reports. They were, however, the site of contestation among her political peers in Zwelethemba. There, her testimony was subject to different interpretations.

LOCAL INTERPRETATIONS

Much of the research that informs a growing literature on testimonial interventions has been conducted with people living in exile from their home communities. However, where testimonies are made may matter. Having gained what Liisa Malkki describes as 'voice' – 'the ability to establish narrative authority over one's circumstances and future, and, also, the ability to claim an audience' (1997: 242) – in one context (the public hearing), Yvonne Khutwane's testimony became a social fact, open to discussion and disputation. Some of her truth claims, made and accepted in one context, were contested in others. In Zwelethemba, her truth claims were re-evaluated in the light of events that were not necessarily central to the concerns of the Commission but that nevertheless carried both explanatory potential and moral weight in local contexts.

Not everyone responded in the same way to her testimony, news of which was spread through radio and television coverage and by word of mouth of those who had been present at the hearing. In Zwelethemba, people seemed to have paid less attention to the claims of sexual violation. A few believed her to have fabricated the claims. Part of the reason for their response may lie in the fact that her testimony intruded on patterns of silence that are conventional about matters of sexuality and sexual violation: where sexual violence is considered to have shamed the survivor, speaking of it draws attention to the shame (Henderson 1999). That Yvonne Khutwane testified about such violation is indicative of her bravery; the disbelief of some in her community suggests the fragility of social acceptance of testimonies that go against the grain of established convention. In such contents, public utterances may rebound or have unanticipated effects.

In Zwelethemba, Mrs Khutwane's testimony was scrutinised in the light of recent and past political events in the township. The press reports and Commission Report did not pay much attention to the arson attack on her home. Yet Yvonne Khutwane considered it sufficiently important that in both her written and oral statements she asked the Commission to investigate. The remainder of this chapter examines the arson attack and the events that followed it. Drawing from interviews with Yvonne Khutwane and other activists in Zwelethemba, I focus on local interpretations of the incident and on competing claims for legitimacy by those articulating different kinds of moral and emotional discourses in the context of confrontation with the state and its aftermath. In order to examine these, I begin by tracing her experiences in prison and during the trial in 1985. Unless otherwise indicated, the material presented in the remainder of this chapter is drawn from my field research in Zwelethemba and not from the Commission hearing.

Illness, Bail and the Arson Attack

When Yvonne Khutwane was incarcerated as an awaiting trial prisoner in 1985, she was not allowed visitors for the first few weeks. She protested the prison food, describing her hunger strike feistily: 'No one told me about this hunger-strike story. No! I thought, "Not a damn! I will not eat this!"' As described in her Commission testimony, she fell ill with meningitis. She complained about her illness to the prison warder, who, she said, gave her a single Disprin (an aspirin-based painkiller) and watched her drink it, saying that if she were not watched she might use the Disprin to make 'Mandrax' (a recreational street drug. Here 'Mandrax' refers to 'home made' drugs made from crushed Disprin and tobacco). She was later taken to a doctor who asked her to tell him whether she was sick and what the problem was. 'He wanted *me* to tell *him*! I couldn't even speak![21] The saliva was dripping down my face.' He gave her tablets that, she said, made her feel worse. She was sent back to the cells. Held in a cell close to but separate from the young male scholars and activists who had been arrested with her, she was accustomed to sending them messages of support:

I was the only woman. I was Accused Number One. I was in the cell alone. The boys were next door. They used to speak. They told me they did not feel like they were in jail because at least they were together. I was alone and they were ashamed because I was arrested with them. I did not want to make them weak. At night they would sing, not loudly, just quietly. In the boys' quarters they were *toyi toyiing*: 'We know Mandela is our father.' One day, they [the police] threw teargas into the boys' cell to stop them singing. Where can you go in a cell? Where can you move?

When the youths did not hear from her for a few days, they learned that she was ill and asked their lawyer, Vali Moosa, to make enquiries. Yvonne Khutwane said, 'You know, if that lawyer hadn't arrived, I would be dead now.' She did not have a lawyer to intervene on her behalf. Moosa insisted that she be taken to a doctor. Dizzy, vomiting and unable to stand alone, she was bundled into a police van, its floor covered in sheep dung in which she rolled as the van sped to the hospital. She was unconscious by the time she arrived.

Three days later she awoke, initially thinking that she was at home:

I was so glad. I opened my eyes. The first thing I saw was a big white policeman. I looked at him. He did not speak. He just looked at me. I asked, 'How am I here?' He said, 'I don't know.' I asked for tablets. He said, 'I am not a doctor.' I asked for water. He brought water. I asked him to help me sit. He helped me sit.[22] I was saying in my heart, 'God is there.' I was longing for my mother and my children. I was wondering, 'Where are my children now?'

After two days she was allowed to receive visits from her mother and friends from Zwelethemba. The police, who had guarded her in two shifts, 24 hours a day, were no longer present at her bedside. After four days in hospital, the magistrate and court interpreter came to visit. She recalled that having checked that she could speak and understand Afrikaans, the magistrate said, '*As hulle jou 'discharge', moet jy huis toe gaan en op hierdie datum moet jy op die hof verskyn*' ('When they discharge you, you must go home, and on this date you must report to the court'). Yvonne Khutwane wryly commented, 'As you can imagine, I was not happy about that. The day I was discharged I knew they would arrest me again.' Discharged the following day, weak and scarcely able to stand, she was sent to the dispensary to collect her tablets. There, two Coloured policemen asked if she was Yvonne Khutwane. When she concurred, they told her they were taking her to court. She argued, saying that the magistrate had said she was to go home, but they took her, protesting, back to the court: 'Outside the court, there were people *toyi-toyiing, toyi-toyiing*. They were jumping high and the police had dogs and they were *toyi-toyiing, toyi-toyiing*. Yo! What a goings-on!' She was led into the docks in court. The courtroom was full of people from Zwelethemba: 'People in Zwelethemba wanted to see me. They had heard I was ill and they wanted to see if I was still alive. They wanted to see me. They couldn't believe it was me, I was so sick.'

The magistrate postponed the case for three months and she was sent to the communal cells to await trial. The jail warders seemed surprised to see her and asked her what she was doing there given that she was ill but had been discharged from hospital. She did not report her reply.

She spent two weeks in the communal cells during which time many people visited her. Permitted to visit only one at a time, they were told by warders to speak Afrikaans, 'not *Bantutaal*' [Afrikaans – 'Bantu language'; a pejorative reference to African languages, in this instance, Xhosa] so that the warders could understand the conversations. Conditions in the prison were horrific: the cell was cold and lice-infested; the food almost inedible. Women prisoners were treated very badly. As an example of the conditions in the cells and the callousness of the warders, Yvonne Khutwane described an occasion when a young woman who had been arrested for sheep theft gave birth unassisted in the cell. She had told Mrs Khutwane that her stomach hurt: 'Then her waters broke: she was giving birth! There was blood everywhere and out came a child. [But] the child was dead already.' The guards would not help. Eventually two men were called in to take the woman to hospital. Yvonne Khutwane demanded to see the prison authorities and complained about the way the women were treated in the prison. 'Yo, I was cheeky in those days!', she recalled.

Then one day, she was called to the cell door: 'The worst sound of all in jail is the sound of those bunches of keys', she remembered. She was told to collect her coat and leave: she had been released from prison on R500 bail. It had been paid by a friend and not the UDF as she had anticipated: 'They [UDF representatives] told me they had no money for my bail', she said. 'When I was told I could go, I thought they were joking, but they weren't', she recalled. She was surprised that she had been granted bail: her first application had been turned down: 'The first time, my comrades had to make an appeal for me in Cape Town for bail. They [the court] said I could not be bailed because I was misleading the children in Zwelethemba.' None of the young men with whom she was arrested were granted bail.

In terms of the bail conditions, Mrs Khutwane was to report to the police station in Zwelethemba every day. She refused to do so, saying she was too ill to walk from her house to the station. The police said she should report weekly. She agreed to do so if she was well enough, but did not. She was not allowed to attend meetings or gatherings although she frequently slipped out of the house at night.

A few weeks after her release, she met a colleague, who warned her that she was suspected of being an informer: 'I was still on bail. [She] told me that she had heard rumours that I was a sell-out. I thought it was a joke.' A few days later, the house was attacked in the incident she described to the Commission. Mrs Khutwane, her mother and two of her three children were watching television in the sitting room. Her daughter was asleep in the bedroom. Her son saw lights outside and lifted the curtains to look. He called to his grandmother but she disregarded him:

They threw bombs in the windows. They burnt the curtains and the mat. My baby girl was sleeping in bed. They threw bombs in the other window. Luckily she was not facing the window.

My neighbours were afraid to help me in case the youth [that is, youth activists] were watching and they would also be burnt. My child was bleeding from the glass [of the window that had shattered when the bomb was thrown through it]. I was throwing water on the flames [in the other room]. Then my mother called me to see the child. We rushed to hospital. I was worried about my family at home and I phoned to make sure they were okay.

The arson attack did not cause death or serious damage, although it could easily have done so.[23] A few days after the attack, Yvonne Khutwane approached members of the youth organisations in the township to ask for a meeting to discuss the attack. A preliminary meeting was held, but she was not allowed to be present. She was told that she was accused of breaking the consumer boycott that she had been instrumental in implementing and enforcing. For the duration of the boycott people were not permitted to purchase goods from shops owned by whites. Yet a few days after the decision to boycott was implemented, Mrs Khutwane was rumoured to have a new bedroom suite in her home. A worker at the company from which the suite was bought confirmed the purchase. Yvonne Khutwane countered this interpretation, saying that she had purchased the suite prior to the boycott and had simply taken possession of it during the boycott. She was told that she stood accused of breaking the rent boycott implemented some months earlier (she denied the claim) and of having betrayed a comrade to the police during interrogation.

Yvonne Khutwane approached the Zwelethemba branch of the United Women's Congress (UWCO) to take action on her behalf. At a meeting called to address the situation she asked how she came to be called a 'sell-out' given that she was on trial for her political activities and had not been granted immunity as a state witness. In our interviews, she recalled that the meeting had been tense and had been called to a close without resolution.

When she testified before the Commission, Mrs Khutwane described the cause of the attack as her inadvertent betrayal. In interviews with me, she described tensions in Zwelethemba as running high at the time of her release from prison on bail. At that time, Zwelethemba was wracked with violence. Police guarded the only entrance to Zwelethemba; policemen patrolled the township on foot and in open vans; there was a curfew in place from 6 pm to 6 am. By late 1985, most of the adult leadership of the underground and resistance organisations was jailed, detained or in exile. Leadership in resistance activities had been taken over by young people. Boycotts and protests were the order of the day. Between August and November 1985, eight people had been killed in confrontations with the police. The police appeared to have a well-developed network of informers in Zwelethemba and 'the Movement' was under considerable threat.

In later interviews, Mrs Khutwane attributed the arson to the complexities of personal and political matters in Zwelethemba in the tense circumstances that prevailed in the 1980s. She believed that the rumours that she was a sell-out had their basis in personal and not political relations:

'Someone was jealous of me and told the comrades I am a sell-out and they must not trust me.' At the time of the attack, she had been having an affair with the wealthy ex-'boyfriend' of 'a powerful woman comrade'. It was he who had paid Yvonne Khutwane's bail of R 500. Yvonne Khutwane believed that the jilted woman had spread a rumour of political betrayal and that

Her children were jealous when they saw me riding about with their mother's ex-boyfriend. They influenced the youth. It was only an old people's affair that was the reason my home was burnt. People said to me, 'Why did you take her boyfriend?' I said, 'No, he left her.' They said, 'This is why you were burnt.' She accused me of taking her boyfriend. I said, 'No, he told me he was not involved with you.' She was cross with me. Maybe she spoke to the children and made their anger even bigger.

Yvonne Khutwane's interpretation traces the power relations between women in a small town: here, the personal and political are linked in ways that liberal theory, with its distinction between public and private, cannot easily accommodate.

Other explanations I have been offered have not clarified the reasons for the attack. For example, one young man who had been a leader in underground structures at the time attributed the attack to *imigwenya*,[24] undisciplined followers, some of whom may have been double agents for the police. His interpretation further complicates the narratives of blame that accompanied the explanations for the arson attack.

Notwithstanding the attack on her home and her failed efforts to understand the reasons that lay behind it, Yvonne Khutwane remained in Zwelethemba. She stood trial with 18 young men on charges of public violence in connection with the burning of the municipal bar. The state witness who was to testify that Yvonne Khutwane had provided the youths with petrol for bombs and with arms did not appear before the court. Yvonne Khutwane pleaded '*Andinatyala, dankie, makhosi!*' ('not guilty, thank you sir!'), and was acquitted in 1987. Several of the young men with whom she had stood trial went immediately into exile. Two joined MK and were killed in 1989 in the Angolan war where MK cadres fought alongside the MPLA against incursions by the SADF into Angola. Yvonne Khutwane recalled that local community leaders suggested that she should also leave the country but she refused: 'I said, "I am old and my mother is old and I have small children. Who will look after them if I go?"' She remained in Zwelethemba and continued mobilising support for the campaign to render the townships ungovernable, a national campaign that, together with mass protest, stay-aways, boycotts, strike action, sabotage, attacks by armed wings of liberation movements, and international measures, was eventually successful in forcing the Apartheid State into negotiations with the liberation movements.

After the ANC was unbanned in 1990, she returned with vigour to political campaigning. She believes that her work in recruiting membership for the ANC was respected and she was reincorporated into the political fold: 'I volunteered ... I was running around like a mad dog! Every morning, I closed my shop to go and teach people [about politics]. On the street corners, on the farms, I taught the people. I went to Swellendam, Ceres, the farms, all around. I have a driver's licence. I can drive. I asked a friend to loan me a *kombi* and I collected all the old people to learn to vote.'

Yvonne Khutwane intended to run as a ward candidate in the municipal elections of 1995: 'Then it was the time of the local elections. I took the forms and gave them to youths to go door-to-door. I began with the first house in Ward 10. House to house, house to house, house to house, house to house, house to house ... When I was finished, I came to the next street. When I was finished that one, I came to the next street. *Njal' njalo*' (Xhosa – 'And so on and so on').

She had been confident of winning the candidacy race. The ward is historically the centre of resistance activities in Zwelethemba; she was well known, had been instrumental in organising popular resistance to the Apartheid State and had canvassed extensively for the ANC in the period preceding the 1994 elections. Yet she lost the candidacy to a young man, also an ANC member but acknowledged as having limited 'struggle credentials'. Mrs Khutwane linked the candidacy defeat explicitly to the arson attack (and implicitly with the accusation of betrayal) on her home ten years previously and to the memory residents in the township still hold of it. In interviews, she ascribed her loss in the candidacy race to her opponent's ability to manipulate the social imagination of the community:

[He] called the youth and said I must not be councillor. I saw no parents at the meeting, only children. When I asked at the meeting, the children started to *toyi-toyi* and do funny [strange] things. He hyped them up. When I heard the children singing again like that, ooooh! I decided to go home. They chose him. He wasn't a single day in the struggle! He hyped them up. 'Yvonne, you are no good. Your house was burnt. We will not elect you as councillor', they said.

Yvonne Khutwane is not the only person to link the failure in the election with the memory that people held of the attack on her house. A number of people stated that the attack provided material evidence of betrayal in the past and imputed a consequent untrustworthiness in the present. A negative value was retrospectively inferred from a remembered event. The arson attack became a marker of value that carried weight. It was partly to counter such negative evaluations that Yvonne Khutwane had made the public assertion of loyalty and commitment, 'I am still a member of the ANC', at the end of her Commission testimony, seven months after her defeat in the ward candidacy race.

The failure to win enough support to stand as a candidate in the local election did not rest solely on the memory of arson, however closely Yvonne Khutwane and others tied the two events. Youth activists described changes in leadership ideas that made her political claims, which rested on her past activism, seem outdated. One man from Zwelethemba stated their views succinctly: 'Power does not only reside in your "resistance C.V."', adding, 'the discourse of remembrance is not very reliable in politics.' Yvonne Khutwane accepted the defeat and remains a member of the ANC. She did not run for candidacy in the 2000 local government elections.

Some of the personal tensions generated over the arson incident were short-lived. Although resolved at the political level, however, personal tensions between Yvonne Khutwane and some of the women endured for almost a decade, despite the fact that the women live close to one another and are members of the same political organisations. Indeed, it was only at a meeting of the ANC Women's League in March 1999, three months prior to the second general elections in South Africa, that Mrs Khutwane formally made peace with the woman she held responsible for the attack on her home. Their 'reconciliation' served an expressly didactic purpose: it was designed to set an example to the young people of Zwelethemba prior to the elections. Yvonne Khutwane explained, 'We were saying there should be no divisions between us [or else] the youth can say that the ANC is no good because its members fight each other.' She continued, 'Before, [we] were not sitting together. We were not at one fire together. Now [we] are sleeping with one blanket.'

This was not the only instance of what Mrs Khutwane describes as 'reconciliation'. She described her pleasure when, walking in the street one day after testifying, she was recognised by a woman who had been the prison wardress. The woman, now retired and running a bicycle shop, asked her forgiveness and invited her to visit. Mrs Khutwane said that when she visited, the woman introduced her to her husband, saying, 'This is the woman who I treated so badly. She has forgiven me.'

Not all the tensions have been resolved. She remains unhappy that the youths who had sexually violated her were not found and brought to her to ask forgiveness. She works in a forum to facilitate interaction between the police and community members. Alongside her works the policeman who had beaten her with the butt of his gun during the interrogation in 1985. He has never shown signs of recognising her or of remorse. 'I hate that man', she said.

MODELS, INTERPRETATION AND SOCIAL HEALING

The diverse interpretations of Yvonne Khutwane's testimony and the events she described offered by key participants do not lie simply in competing memories or inadequacies of recall but in different models that inform the reception of utterances and have their own historical roots. In the first, Yvonne Khutwane's Commission testimony, the model holds the violation of *bodily integrity* as the primary locus of harm. A close focus on the body allows the testimony to stand as an embodiment of similar damage done to others, a mnemonic device for representing and recalling harm and damage. In the second, Mrs Khutwane describes the betrayal of *relationships*. The third, narratives of struggle into which her testimony was slotted in Zwelethemba and against which it was measured and found partly wanting, draws from notions of the *collectivity* of political struggle in which the collective, the community in resistance, is itself envisaged as under siege. Read in conjunction with one another, the models indicate that retrospective examination of events is complex. They hint at the conflicting conventions by which utterances are assessed and weighed and suggest that the reception of testimonies as truth and the acknowledgement of testifiers as truthful do not follow automatically from testimonial interventions.

The reworking and re-evaluation of testimonies in different contexts and over time matters in relation to claims that speaking 'truth' gives rise to 'healing'. Once spoken, claims do not rest but are reworked and revised in accord with various conventions. Rather than understanding the reconfiguration of testimony as aberration, a deviation from an original, authentic spoken word, it can be understood as part of the work of forming the everyday in violence's aftermath. In that case, this chapter may be read as outlining a methodological approach to understanding social reconstitution. Tracing the continuities and discontinuities of testimony and its reception over time illuminates the extent to which local discourses reflect and refract larger processes, and vice versa (for example, Yvonne Khutwane's framing of her encounters as 'reconciliation'). Such a method may shed light on the ways in which new norms are articulated and previous experiences acknowledged or silenced. I am suggesting here that spoken words and silences sculpt one another and may take on a kind of tangibility, a traceable life of their own. In future, scholars will be better able to map the carving of utterances from the conditions of possibility and to trace their effects over time. Anthropology, with its commitment to long-term research of an intimate kind, is well-suited to the work.

Veena Das and Arthur Kleinman comment that part of what they call the remaking of the world 'is also a matter of being able to recontextualise the narratives of devastation and generate new contexts through which everyday life may become possible'. They add a caution, 'communities formed in suffering do not always succeed in this' and 'life can drain out of the words that signify healing and overcoming of tragedy' (2000: 6). The material presented here is suggestive of the contingency of interpretation and the unevenness of reception. Different responses to truth claims suggest that some forms of violence may be acknowledged while others are denied. Perhaps it is asking too much to expect accustomed frames of reference to shift quickly to accommodate new knowledge, but where the immediate reaction is to refuse acknowledgement, individuals may feel isolated and vulnerable.

The material presented here raises questions about the wider efficacy of coupling voice and self. Forcing the self to see the self as though from the outside may feel damaging, and, as I described in the Introduction, in a context in which voice and dignity are explicitly linked, individuals' lack of control over their testimonies may be experienced as alienation and appropriation. The effects of testimonial interventions may be uneven over time: the relief they offer may be short-lived, partial, or may only have its desired effect much later. In addition to the sense of power that surfaces in coming to voice, testimonial efficacy may be cut through with denial and loss.

The literature generated from testimonies tends to totalise: to assume that the subject is the same as the testifier and that the testimony describes the self completely. 'Self' and 'utterance' are frequently presumed to be coterminous, but stories, testimonies and telling are fragments, parts of people's narration of their lives. They are particular instances, synopses of experience, told at given times for specific audiences and located in distinct spatial and temporal contexts. In tracing the telling of a single set of events over a period of more than three years, in a time of great change, it becomes clear that the memory of violence is neither isolated nor singular. Its recall is an act of imagination that incorporates the self and others in relationships that change over time. This suggests that scholars should seek signs of recuperation not solely in the integrated psyche but also in the extent to which there is acknowledgement of individual harm within communities of affect. This does not presume that, once woven into acceptance, narratives are rendered inert. Events may return them to social life, reactivating and redirecting their force. In the model I suggest, coherence over time may be less important than tracing the shifts of interpretation, the processes of social reworking, the grounds of acceptance on which narratives come to rest, and the light these shed on understanding and remaking in the face of suffering.

5 CONSIDERATIONS OF HARM

What is political activism, anyway? I've been asking myself.
It's something both prepared for and spontaneous – like making poetry.
When we do and think and feel certain things privately and in secret, even when thousands of people are doing, thinking and whispering these things privately and in secret, there is still no general, collective understanding from which to move ... But these thoughts and feelings, suppressed and stored-up and whispered, have an incendiary component. You cannot tell where or how they will connect, spreading underground from rootlet to rootlet till every grass blade is afire from every other. This is that 'spontaneity' which party 'leaders', secret governments, and closed systems dread. Poetry, in its own way, is a carrier of the sparks, because it too comes out of silence, seeking connection with unseen others. (Rich. 1995: 57, emphasis in original)

Thus far, I have considered the forms of witness women bore before the Commission, the experiences about which they testified, and the ways in which testimony was elicited and reconsidered in multiple contexts. I turn now to a consideration of the Commission's work in recording and measuring harm. I do so in relation to young women. This chapter draws on the methodological challenge described in Pamela Reynolds' quest to document both 'accounts of culture from the point of view of youth' and 'intimations of their voices' (1995b: 193) by reflecting on the lives of young women in Zwelethemba who grew to adulthood in the 1980s. The Commission's regional findings and the findings of research with ex-detainees, exiles and political prisoners in Zwelethemba provide a backdrop against which both young women's experiences and their exposure to violence may be read, and the Commission's methods of eliciting experiences of harm assessed.

THE COMMISSION'S FINDINGS ON VIOLENCE IN THE WESTERN CAPE

The Cape Town office of the Commission received 1,780 statements that represent 8.4 per cent of the total number of statements received by the Commission. The statements reported on 4,267 violations, of which 3,122 constituted gross violations of human rights and 1,145 were 'associated violations' (violations that did not fit the categories as established in the Act and elaborated in the Commission's work. See Volume Three: 3, note 1. It is not clear what these were: no reference is made to 'associated violations' in the section of the Report dealing with definitions or in the Act). The statements identified 2,350 victims; on average 1.3 victims were identified in each statement and each victim suffered 1.8 violations (Volume Three: 3). In other words, a large number of those who testified in the Western Cape, as elsewhere,[1] described more than one event of violation and identified more than one victim in each instance. Most deponents in the Cape were young men. More than one-third of statements concerned violations committed in 1985 and young men between the ages of 13 and 24 were the primary victims (Volume Three: 393).

For the period 1983–89, 53 per cent of violations reported in the Cape concerned severe ill treatment; 16 per cent concerned torture; 14 per cent concerned killings and 12 per cent described associated violations. Three per cent of statements concerned attempted killing and 1 per cent of statements concerned abduction (Volume Three: 393). Age and gender analyses of the data by year and by sub-region are not provided in the Report. It is therefore not possible to describe local variations or particularities in patterns of violation, reporting or consequences.

Seventy-seven residents of Zwelethemba made statements to the Commission. Twenty-six women (representing approximately one-third of Zwelethemba deponents) made statements. As far as I have been able to ascertain,[2] nine of the women made statements concerning their own experiences of violation.

In addition to numeric data about violence, the Report provides a narrative description of events in each region. Describing events in the Cape in the 1980s, the period on which my research in Zwelethemba focused, it states:

The political revolt unfolding in the rest of the country reached the western Cape in 1985. The first six months of 1985 saw extensive unrest in the rural areas of the southern Cape, Karoo, Boland and the northern Cape ...

With some notable exceptions, the high levels of open street confrontation seen in 1985–86 generally subsided during 1986. The countrywide state of emergency imposed in June 1986 [*sic*] led to large-scale detentions in both rural and urban areas ...

The period 1983–89 generated the highest peak of violations in this region, in both the urban and rural areas. [Volume Three: 419]

In a section dealing with rural violence (Volume Three: 428–30), the Report describes violence in Zwelethemba in 1985:

During 1985, protest meetings were often broken up violently by security forces and street protests became more militant. Many towns saw at least one or two deaths of youth activists during 1985, which served to propel the townships into wider protest and attacks on those seen as collaborators...

Worcester

In Worcester [Zwelethemba], the spark was provided by the killing of Mr Nkosana Nation Bahume, after which a cycle of deaths and injuries took place until the end of the year.

On 16th August 1985, student activist Nkosana Nation Bahume (CT00547),[3] aged twenty-one, was shot dead by the security forces. On 30th August, the local magistrate issued restriction orders on the funeral of Bahume, who was to be buried the following day.[4] At the funeral, police fired on mourners, killing Mr Mbulelo [Nondatsu] Kenneth Mazula (CT00528), aged twenty. An eyewitness testified that 'police dragged his body to the vehicle and took him to the mortuary'. People were assaulted, shot and detained by security forces in the uproar.

Mbulelo Mazula was buried on 8 September without incident. However, on 21 September 1985 Mr Andile Feni (CT08402) and two others were shot and injured by a policeman in Zwelethemba after a crowd had thrown a petrol bomb at a police officer's house after a mass meeting that had resolved to chase all police from the area following the killings.

On 1 October 1985, Mr Thomas Kolo (CT08400), aged 18, was shot dead by security forces. He was buried on 11 October and the funeral was restricted by the magistrate. The following day, security forces shot Mr Zandesile Ntsomi (CT00320). Ntsomi's leg was amputated and he was discharged from hospital back into police custody the following day ...

On 13 October, Douglas Ndzima (CT00821) was shot twice by police in Zwelethemba. That day Ms Martha Nomathamsanqa Mooi's house (CT03026) in Zwelethemba was petrol-bombed by UDF members. Mr Mpazamo Bethwell Mbani (Yiko) (CT03026), her brother-in-law, was shot dead and his body set alight.

On 2 November 1985, Mr Cecil Roos Tamsanqa van Staden (CT00132) was shot by police and died two days later. The following day, Mr William Dyasi (CT00823) was shot dead by police in Zwelethemba. An inquest was held and Constable Michael Phillip Luff was found responsible for the murder but he was not prosecuted. At the intervention of the Commission the case was reopened, following which Luff applied to the Commission for amnesty (AM3814/96).[5]

On 9 November, at the night vigil of one of the victims, Mr Buzile Fadana (CT00131) was shot dead after the police arrived and an 'armed encounter' resulted. His death marked an end to this cycle of killings and injuries that year.

By November 1985, an extreme environment [*sic*] of repression existed in Zwelethemba, which was declared out of bounds to all except residents. Roadblocks were set up and residents were only allowed to go to their homes on producing identity documents. There were twenty-four hour foot patrols, and searchlights swept the streets at night. Residents reported a heavy presence of Zulu speaking policemen.[6] Funerals of unrest victims were restricted to only fifty people and the family of the deceased. In one instance, forty young people were detained whilst participating in a funeral vigil.

The Report adds: 'The Commission finds that the killing by police of Mr Nkosana Nation Bahume on 16 August 1985 triggered a sequence of violence in which numerous residents of Worcester were killed or injured by police and a number of persons or buildings were attacked in retaliation. The draconian response of the authorities, including curfews, roadblocks and sweeping detentions, only aggravated the situation.'

The Report's description of Zwelethemba offers a litany of death, interspersed with accounts of injury and torture. Police killed six young men, one man was burnt to death, five men were injured by police fire and several people were assaulted, shot and detained. One woman's house was burnt. There is no mention of the attack on Yvonne Khutwane's house (see Chapter 4). The police and legal authorities imposed curfews, roadblocks, detentions, restrictions and surveillance mechanisms.

The Report says little about the conditions of resistance or the contexts of violence in Zwelethemba. It stipulates that violence was triggered by the death of Nkosana Bahume. In fact, Bahume's death occurred after fierce protest in Zwelethemba against the Black Local Authorities ('councillors', as they are locally known) began in 1983 and reached its zenith in 1985. Bahume's death followed in the wake of at least two school boycotts; one in recognition of the deaths of the 'Craddock Four' (see Chapter 2) and the other in support of children and youths in detention. There had been a heavy police presence in Zwelethemba since 1981 and a large number of young people had been detained or arrested on political charges between 1980 and Bahume's death. According to research notes compiled by members of the Commission and issued to the media during the Worcester Hearing, 52 people had been detained and charged with public violence on 10 August 1985, a week before Bahume's death. Twenty-five of them were under 18 years old.

Other research findings suggest that violence was more widespread than the Commission Report implies. In 1995, the Cape Town-based Trauma Centre for Victims of Violence and Torture conducted a study (Skinner 1998) and found that there were 71 ex-detainees and 18 ex-political prisoners in Zwelethemba. Most had been between the ages of 18 and 30 years at the time of trauma. Twenty per cent (n=14) of the ex-detainees were women. It should be noted that the study reports only those who experienced detention periods of longer than 48 hours. My work indicates that a large number of women were detained for shorter periods. For example, young activists with whom I worked identified 25 women who, as students, had been detained in 1985 alone. None was over the age of 22 at the time of detention. Few were held for periods longer than 180 days and most were held for periods ranging between 24 and 72 hours. It cannot be assumed that the treatment of the latter was any less brutal or the effects on family and community less destructive than if they had been held for longer periods. Five of the young women with whom I worked closely were detained but were not included in the Trauma Centre's research.

There is scant mention of women, particularly the young, in either the Commission Report or the Trauma Centre's findings. The omission matters. The Commission Report makes the point that protest activities were both gender- and age-specific, and that young women were more likely to be exposed to state violence than were older women:

> In the 1980s, for example, when much of the activity was undertaken by scholars and students, these young women did not have the same social constraints against engaging in the struggle that might have been felt by slightly older women or those with more family responsibilities. In terms of the public/private distinction, women scholars and students were more firmly located in the public sphere, the sphere in which political action is most explicit, and where it was most likely to provoke state retaliation. (Volume Four: 292).

The remainder of this chapter draws from my research with ten women who had engaged in resistance activities that ranged from school boycotts and protests to attempts to join MK in exile, to consider young women's exposure to violence and responses to harm as they grew to adulthood in Zwelethemba.

AN INSTANCE OF DETENTION

Noluntu Zawukana, her friend Xoliswa Tywana, and Ntsoake Phelane, Xoliswa's cousin, were detained in three separate incidents on the same day in mid-July 1985, a time of considerable tension in Zwelethemba. Students at Vusisizwe Secondary School were engaged in a school boycott; earlier that year, angry residents had razed the local rent office, post office and the offices of the Advisory Board, and youths had destroyed the municipal beerhall. Police patrolled around the clock and a six-to-six curfew was in place. Residents of Zwelethemba had created a range of institutions to manage civic life. Local branches of the Civic Association, United Women's Organisation (UWO) and Congress of South African Students (COSAS[7]) had been formed and with the Zwelethemba Youth Organisation (ZWEYO) were affiliated to the United Democratic Front. Street and area committees administered matters of local governance.

On the day of her detention, Noluntu was one of a group of young people who were boycotting school. The police patrolled the township in Casspirs (armoured vehicles). They chased children and youths, beating them with whips and forcing them to attend school. As a Casspir approached the group of young protesters, of which Noluntu was a part, the young people scattered. Fleeing, they vaulted fences into yards. Five of the youths ran to Noluntu's grandmother's house in Hlalele Road. The old woman assessed the situation rapidly. She bundled the youths indoors and locked the doors from outside, telling them to keep quiet. Then she left the house, hoping that the police would think that no one was home.

Unfortunately, the police had seen them run inside. They kicked down the door and began looking for the youngsters.

Noluntu, who, at the time, was 17 years old, had hidden behind a door in her grandmother's bedroom. The four young men had slipped under the beds in her grandmother's room and the room next door. They heard the sounds of the police breaking the door and searching the small house. A policeman entered the room with another close behind him. Opposite him there was a wardrobe. Its door was open and, horrified, Noluntu realised that its mirror reflected her image to the police. They grabbed her and flushed out the others.

All five of the young people were captured.[8] Two were youth activists who had long been sought by the police. A third was a student on holiday from Durban and was not known to the police. Noluntu and one other were students at Vusisizwe High School in Zwelethemba. Neither had a position in the leadership structures of local anti-apartheid organisations. All five young people were pushed into the Casspir. There, Noluntu recognised other students and scholars, including Ntsoake Phelane (aged 17) and Ntsoake's cousin, Xoliswa Tyawana, who was 15 years old.

They were taken to the Worcester police station cells and detained. They were not told under which law they were detained nor were they permitted to make any phone calls. The five were not the only young people to have been captured that day: police had detained students boycotting school and young people on buses and the police station was full of people.

Noluntu was held in the cells with others for two nights. On the afternoon of the third day, she was taken from the cells and driven to a vacant piece of land in the mountainous area near Worcester, she thinks, near an area known as De Wet. There she was tortured with electric shocks. The policemen told her that she could scream all she liked because she would not be heard. Even now, 14 years later, Noluntu finds it difficult to describe the torture she endured. The words to express harm do not come easily in either Xhosa or English.

In July 1996, Noluntu made a statement to the Commission. In October 1998, she was found to be a victim of gross violations of human rights and her name is recorded in the Commission's Report.

Xoliswa was detained when the police set up a barrier at the only entrance to Zwelethemba and searched the bus on which she was returning from shopping in the town of Worcester nearby. The police held all the young people on the bus for questioning in connection with razing of the Zwelethemba post office a month previously. She and others were taken to the police station where they encountered others detained in the township, Noluntu among them. At the police station Xoliswa was told to write her name down. The police recognised her surname: they had long been seeking her 'cousin-brother' (father's brother's son), Christopher Tyawana, a UDF leader involved in organising youth resistance in the area. They asked Xoliswa about her relationship to Christopher. She replied that he was her cousin-brother. They began to interrogate her, first questioning her and then beating her with fists and a whip.

The police took Xoliswa with Noluntu to be interrogated. In her statement to the Commission, Noluntu described the torture that Xoliswa endured. As a result, the Commission found that Xoliswa was also a victim of gross violations of human rights.

Xoliswa was detained a second time shortly afterwards for questioning concerning Christopher's whereabouts. Again she was tortured. She did not tell the police that Christopher, like other activists, was no longer sleeping at his home but was hiding in the graveyard and elsewhere at night. She was detained for 90 days. She shared a cell with 20 other women and was not allowed to see a lawyer or any member of her family. At the end of the three-month period of detention, she was released. No charges were laid against her. She was not detained again, in part, she believes, because in 1986 Christopher Tyawana was captured and detained under Section 29 of the Internal Security Act after a collaboration between the members of the Security Branch and the Allied Bank in Worcester (Commission Report 1998, Volume Three: 439).[9]

Xoliswa is troubled by memory and hearing losses as a result of the beatings that were inflicted on her during both periods of detention.

Ntsoake, Xoliswa's cousin, was detained on the same day as Noluntu. Like Noluntu, she had been part of the group of students who had scattered at the sight of a Casspir approaching. She and others ran into the house next door to where Noluntu sought refuge. There, too, the owner of the property locked them inside, vainly hoping to thwart the police:

The policemen [broke] the property's windows and doors and beat us with *sjambokke* and led us to the vans. We were all arrested and sent to the detective offices in town. We ... [had] our photos taken and we were divided and kept in different cells. There was a list of names of comrades who were well known and during this time we were privately investigated [interrogated] to give relevant information about what is happening in school and the location and who are the perpetrators ...

We were sent to the magistrate's court and kept there for three days under unfavourable conditions ... I was with Noluntu and Xoliswa Tyawana, experiencing this terrible torture. Refreshments were unstrained black coffee, without sugar, and brown bread. As we were living there we carried on singing freedom songs, praying. There was also a time during singing when we were sprayed with teargas to keep us quiet. Comrades were taken individually to go for investigation and tortured privately. I was in the third group to be tortured and investigated by the authorities.

Like the others with whom she was detained, Ntsoake was questioned about student activities in Zwelethemba. The policemen had a list of names of student and youth activists and they interrogated detainees about people on the list, demanding the details of their activities. After seven days in detention Ntsoake was taken from the cells. Together with a group of men she was put into a van and driven out of Worcester:

The van that was carrying us was covered with black plastic [so that we could not] see where we were and how [we got] there. When we arrived there, we were individually carried out for torture and the ones who are left behind will just hear the screaming and crying as if you are near, because of the echoing sound which was heard.

Only men comrades were tortured on this day but it was late and when it was nearly my turn they stopped and sent us back to prison. We were free then to go home ... Their aim was to torture us to death but luckily [we] were saved and escaped death because the officials had a quarrel among themselves. [The men] were sent back to the cells and kept.

Ntsoake was not detained again, but the memory of detention and the scars she bears from the beating she received remain with her: 'My entire body was scarred with *sjambok* marks that won't fade away for the rest of my life ... In 1987 I went back for schooling with emotional and physical hatred and scars. I [later] passed my Matric.'

The Commission considered detention without trial and beating to be forms of severe ill treatment that qualified as gross violations of human rights, but, although like Xoliswa in that her name was included on Noluntu's statement, Ntsoake was not found to be a victim. She did not volunteer a statement to the Commission.

Each of the three women's experiences bears similarities to the experiences of young people elsewhere in the country at the time. The power of state officials, the extent of violence and damage, the ways in which police harmed youths in lieu of those for whom they sought and the nature of resistance are important components in how young women describe the recent past.

Powers of the State

The Commission found that:

Detention was a major weapon in the former state's armoury of terror and repression. At times, during the years of greatest conflict, children under the age of eighteen years of age represented between 26 per cent and 45 per cent of all those in detention. All the available figures indicate that the largest number of children and youth was detained between 1985 and 1989, during the two states of emergency. Of 80,000 detentions, 48,000 were detainees under the age of twenty-five. [Volume Four: 261]

The Report states,

Very early on, the former state became aware of the pivotal role of children and youth, identifying them as a serious threat and treating them accordingly ... Children and youth faced the full force of state oppression as they took on their role as the 'foot soldiers of the struggle' – as what were called the 'young lions'. Youth challenged the state by organising and mobilising their schools and communities against illegitimate state structures. [Volume Four: 252]

Although Noluntu, Xoliswa and Ntsoake were involved in protest activities, they were not leaders in local politics or in youth organisations. They were detained for different periods of time and for different reasons and were severely treated. None of the three women recalls having been told under which Act they were detained. They were fortunate to be held in Worcester as detainees were not automatically held in their home towns, and frequently were shifted from prison to prison, or were held in prisons at a distance from their homes or the places where they were captured (see Reynolds 1995a; and Skinner 1998: 177). For example, on one occasion Nokwanda Tani was held in terms of Section 50 of the Internal Security Act, which allowed for 'preventive detention' of 14 days. A person 'deemed to be threatening to public safety' could be detained by a low-ranking police officer. Nokwanda was detained after she was 'picked up' during a random police check on buses in August 1985. The bus stopped at the roadblock at the entrance to Zwelethemba, three policemen boarded it, the occupants taunted them and the policemen retaliated by randomly detaining people. Nokwanda was selected and was sent to Pollsmoor Prison in Cape Town, 120 kilometres away. There she was held in a communal cell with a number of other women from the Boland. She says that she was held for four months, although the law provided only for detention of 14 days. She was released without being charged. Her mother had been unable to trace her until she was released.

The holding of detainees at a distance from their homes caused considerable distress for families who had first to trace the detainees, then to secure visiting privileges and then to muster the resources to travel for visits. Detention was emotionally draining for families of detainees. Nokwanda's sister, Mandisa, remembered Nokwanda's second imprisonment as being the hardest for her and the family to bear: 'We had to take her food and when I first went into the cell I saw my sister, to whom I was very close, cowering like a child in the corner. I cried and cried and could not be comforted.'

Nokwanda had been detained in May 1986 after youths set fire to a delivery van in Zwelethemba as part of the ongoing protests and consumer boycotts. She was the only female detained and was held for a week in solitary confinement. She was charged with public violence and was released on bail of R200, paid by her family. The charges against her were eventually dropped.

The experiences of the young women in Zwelethemba indicate the arbitrariness with which detention powers were exercised. Ntsoake's friend, Noluthando Qaba, remembers that the police were often brutal in their efforts to force young protesters back to school:

When I was in Standard One or Two [in 1981: she was aged eleven], the police were beating our sisters and brothers. We ran from class. We were afraid of the police. I cried. In Standard Three, still the police were coming, and in Standard Four. If we were not going to school at that time, they would come door to door and beat us to go to school. We ran in our nighties and without shoes to go to school. At school they harassed us ... In 1985 at Vusisizwe, [when] I was in Standard Six or Seven [and aged fifteen] ... we marched [that is, protested] for our education. They threw teargas. They took us in a van to the police station. I was young then. The police released us.

In addition to the uncertainty and fear of detention, many in Zwelethemba considered contact with prison cells to be defiling. Detention was believed to expose young people to (symbolic) pollution and on their release, some young people, including Nokwanda, were ritually cleansed (*ukuhlanjwa*) in an attempt to remove the effects of contact with evil and to protect against a repetition of detention. Not all families subscribed to the ritual but even those who did not felt defiled by their contact with prison.

Violence

Physical violence, suffering and cruelty

All detainees reported having been harshly interrogated and cruelly treated. They were hit and beaten and whipped. Noluntu was tortured with electric shocks. Ntsoake reported that police threw teargas into the confined space of a cell to stop the youths from singing to keep their spirits high.

The women's accounts include descriptions of other kinds of suffering. All detainees spoke about bad conditions in cells and the inadequacy of the food. Xoliswa was not allowed to see her family or a lawyer for 180 days. When they were detained, none of the women knew for how long they would be held nor where. Ntsoake heard the screams of others being tortured and anticipated that similar violence would be inflicted on her. She described the sense of fear and insecurity of detention and when being confronted with a list of names not knowing what the police knew about those listed and therefore what would be safe to reveal.

The treatment to which the police subjected the young seems to have been deliberately calculated to terrify. An example, described by Nokwanda, relates to the death of Mbulelo Mazula, killed at Nkosana Bahume's funeral. The Commission Report (1998, Volume Three: 428) records only that Mazula's body was dragged to a police vehicle and taken to the mortuary. Nokwanda, aged 21 at the time, and two others were hiding from the police in an outside toilet at the time of the attack. The police saw them. Nokwanda recalled the incident:

They saw us and told us to take the body into the van. Can you imagine that? Three women to carry a dead person into the van. There was a roadblock at the entrance [to Zwelethemba]. They took us [captured us] at Tusha Street with the dead person. They kept us for three hours in the van with the dead body. We had already seen that he was dead ...

We were taken to the mortuary and the body was put there.

'Your man is dead, so now you may go', they said.

Violence and space

Noluntu and Ntsoake described how the police kicked in doors, and displaced and damaged furniture in their search for the children. Others in Zwelethemba said that policemen entered homes and small shops and took food from shelves and cupboards. Properties, including churches, still have bullet holes in walls. Walking through Zwelethemba, Noluthando described sites of violence and fear: a tree where a youth hid from the police, a church whose minister was detained after he hid fleeing youths in the vestry, the vacant patch of ground where Nondatsu was killed, the toilet where Nokwanda hid from the police.

The Commission Report states that throughout the country the police and security forces operated within 'a culture of impunity' (Volume Five: 160). Several testifiers at public hearings described how policemen entered their homes at will and by force if they so wished. The damage to property indicates that even domestic space could not be considered safe, and neither privacy nor safety could be secured. Many householders in Zwelethemba left the doors to their houses ajar day and night to enable young people and children fleeing from the police to escape or take shelter. Yet homes were too dangerous as places in which to hold young people who were involved in anti-apartheid protest or who had been injured. Young people and elders met under cover of darkness to hold meetings and plan protests. Many youths stopped sleeping at home regularly. Their absence from home generated an extraordinary mobilisation of resources and ingenuity on the part of those who cared for them as women took it in turns to cook and deliver food to 'safe-houses', the siting of which changed frequently. Women had to avoid being seen delivering extra food to those who were hiding their children lest they inadvertently gave away the hiding places. If injured, people were afraid to go to home in case police found them there. They feared seeking medical attention in hospitals because personnel reported injuries to the police. For this reason, Nokuzola Mtamo spent three days in June 1985 hiding in a church in Zwelethemba. Her knee had been badly injured when attempting to jump over a fence to escape police who were chasing protesting youths during a march after a memorial service for those who died in the Soweto Uprisings of 16 June 1976. Afraid to seek medical attention, she treated her damaged knee with salve. It healed badly. In 1994, when she sought to become a member of the South African National Defence Force (SANDF), she was found medically unfit.

Violence and the structure of time

Violence not only permeated physical spaces but worked its way into the structures of time. Vuyelwa Xusa's accounts of her political commitments and family history show the effects of violence on time and the quotidian world. She traced the emergence of a political consciousness to her childhood:

I was involved because I was suffering. *Ek ken nie my ma se gesig nie. Die ouma wat my groot geraak het was my ma se ma. Ek het gesukkel om skool toe te gaan. My ouma was oud, sy kry pension.* [I do not know my mother's face. My mother's mother brought me up. I battled to go to school because my grandmother was old, a pensioner.] (In 1973 her pension was worth R45 a month).

In 1978, she met and fell in love with a man who was a student at the University of Cape Town and involved in the underground movement. In that year, she became pregnant with his child. She recalled:

It was difficult to be pregnant. That guy *was te besig met die storie van* 'umzabalazo' [was too busy with the story of 'the struggle']. The police were searching for him so he could not live here, and so I *sukkeled* [battled]. When he left Worcester, the child was one-and-a-half years old. We were still together when he left. I never received any support for the child and I was a school child myself.

Her partner went into exile in 1981 and returned to South Africa in 1992. After he left, the police harassed Vuyelwa but when they realised he had gone they left her alone.

Vuyelwa was never detained nor did she suffer what the Commission identified as gross violations of human rights. That does not mean that she did not encounter violence or that danger was distant. Members of her extended family were no strangers to political engagement and police harassment. Vuyelwa was brought up to consider members of her grandfather's clan as her immediate kin. One relative, Miriam Colidiza, was detained during the pass law protests of 1960 and spent several months in prison before being released. While in prison, she contracted tuberculosis. She had an operation on her lung but the damage to her lungs continued to cause her considerable distress until she died in early 1999. In our conversations, she attributed the root cause of her chronic lung ailments to the tuberculosis she contracted in prison. Members of her family believe that her condition was aggravated by the dampness of the walls of her home, which was attributed to the use of cheap cement blocks 'that soak up the water', and a high water table in the area. They claim that the water table is the remainder of a small seasonal river that was diverted in the early 1950s in order to separate Zwelethemba from Worcester. Their explanations for her death rest heavily on a history of state aggression: detention, forced removal to Zwelethemba, a resculpted landscape, and inadequate housing are all features of their explanation.

During the 1980s States of Emergency, police killed two of Vuyelwa's relatives. On 2 November 1985, police shot Thamsanqa van Staden. He died two days later. Earlier that year, on 8 September, Thamsanqa's cousin (*kwinana*: mother's sister's son) Brasilo Jacobs was shot and injured when he tried to assist a friend, Mbulelo Mazula, whom the police had shot in the street. A friend of Brasilo's, Ntando Mrubata, described what followed: 'The police threw a tearbomb into the toilet when Brasilo ran to hide from the police … He ran out. The police were there; they shot him right there [that is, at point-blank range]. They dragged him round the front of the house. His mother was standing at the window. She saw it. They lifted him and threw him like a sack of wool into the van. They took him to hospital.'

When Brasilo was released from hospital, he went to live in hiding in Cape Town. He was killed there. His mother, Nombuyiselo, believes that police shot him in error. They had long sought his brother, Booysie, who had escaped into exile earlier in 1985. She said that after Brasilo was killed the policeman who was responsible for his death boasted to her that he had killed Booysie. She did not lay charges against him. Young activists in Zwelethemba suggest that he died in a confrontation between taxi-owners during the 'taxi wars' in Cape Town.[10] Nombuyiselo made a statement to the Commission and Brasilo is identified as a victim in the Commission's Report.

It was not only Brasilo's death that was violent. Vuyelwa's uncle, Sibango Jacobs, told the story of his birth:

Brasilo was born the day of a terrible raid in Zwelethemba. On 28th March 1960, a week after the Sharpeville and Langa protests, we [the residents of Zwelethemba] engaged in a pass protest of our own.[11] Young people went door-to-door collecting [each adult's] *dompas* [the pass that recorded people's rights to live and work in urban areas]. We burnt the passes in Freedom Square in Zwelethemba, then we marched towards Worcester to protest. When we got to the entrance to Zwelethemba, police barred the way. They wanted the leaders to come forward to negotiate. At first the people said that they were all leaders, to protect their leaders. Then, negotiations began and lasted for half an hour. Then someone shot. Everyone scattered back to the township, then we realised we were not safe at home and so we ran to the graveyard, where we jumped into open graves. Open graves! Six foot deep! And we lay there without moving for four or five hours before we dared to show our heads and creep out and go back home.

Nothing moved in the township after all that shooting: not a dog or a bird. When I got home I saw that my sister had a son, Brasilo. Our sister got a baby that day, a boy, the one who was shot, Brasilo. Now he's a dead somebody.

Support and Bodily Substitution

All of the women with whom I worked identified school peers as having been most instrumental in their politicisation, but those women whose activism was the most sustained and enduring are also those whose kin are recognised as having been important in political struggle. This is not accidental. Youths brought up in homes where political activity was an accepted part of the domestic world were more likely to be supported in their stances by parents than those unfamiliar with political activity. Kin groups also mobilised because the police frequently detained siblings and parents instead of those for whom they sought. Even where individuals were not engaged in acts of resistance or protest, they were not exempt. State violence reverberated through social networks, affecting everyone's lives. Many cases were reported to the Commission of young people abused in lieu of their siblings or parents. Extreme pressures were brought to bear on young people who were detained in place of their kin. Sometimes siblings of activists were detained and tortured. The police set out to persuade young people and children to act as informants, betraying the activities and whereabouts of their siblings. The damage wrought to family relationships in such instances is enormous and may be hard to repair.

All former detainees report having been questioned about the activities of others. Sometimes the questions were about youth activities in Zwelethemba and at other times detainees were questioned about named youth leaders. Sometimes young people were hurt during interrogation. Another of Ntsoake's cousins, Zanele Kolo, was detained and tortured by police who sought information about her family's political activities, particularly those of Thomas Kolo, a youth activist. In 1985, police killed Thomas as he returned from the funeral of a young man, Mawethu Mzima, in Zwelethemba.[12]

In addition to the direct impact on individuals and their immediate families, violence affected the extended kinship networks that provided both social and material support. It may be that the brutal treatment inflicted by police was deliberately intended to damage social relations beyond repair as seems to have been the case elsewhere. Marcelo Suarez-Orosco, describing Argentina's 'Dirty War', argues that the state made its power known through a 'grammar of terror' inscribed into communities through harms inflicted on the bodies of its members (1992). He suggests (1987: 238) that the state's objective was to reorganise society, a reorganisation effected through sundering the family in highly visible ways: through torture, dis-appearance and other forms of a 'theatrics of power' (1987: 244; see also Perera 1995; Taussig 1984, 1992; Taylor 1997).

The Commission Report states that, 'indiscriminate victimisation was intended to serve as a warning of the dangers of dissent' (Volume Five: 160). Yet, if social reorganisation of the scale envisaged in Argentina was the aim in South Africa, violence did not always have the intended effect. In some instances, violence consolidated political commitments, confirming the apartheid system as an evil one and one against which struggle was just.

THE NATURE OF RESISTANCE

In the mid-1980s, young people's lives were marked by intrusions of violence and by structures of oppression and poverty. Often, the latter formed the basis from which young people developed their ideas about politics and justice. Ntombomzi Siwangaza framed her emergent political consciousness thus:

It was not very nice to be grown in Zwelethemba through poverty. We had no choice, we had to accept. It is like being in prison. I have not been in prison. I accepted blackness. Poverty pulled us.

During the early years we had to accept poverty. We went to school with no shoes. Sometimes we had no jersey if it was washed. My mother used to smear Vaseline [petroleum jelly] on us to warm us. Sometimes I wore my mother's jersey, even if it was too big.

I accepted it until I was grown and then I felt that enough is enough, despite our parents' fears.

A too-large jersey, a body covered in petroleum jelly, the pull of impoverish-ment: everyday features were powerful material influences on young people's recognition of injustice. The mundane aspects of enforced inequality and its disastrous consequences propelled a fiery vision of resistance. Ntombomzi described the pull to protest in the mid-1980s: 'In the day, nothing. At night, freedom songs. If you heard them, you could not stay at home, despite your parents. There was a burning thing inside you that sent you there. We used to sing in a place different to where the comrades would attack so as to distract attention from them.'

Performances, such as the *toyi-toyi* created a sense of unity and cohesion and were an important dimension of protest activities. *Toyi-toyi* and liberation songs gave people a sense of purpose and power, a sense of the collective and of future possibility.[13] According to Nana Khohlokoane (1998), an anthropologist and youth activist from Zwelethemba, they were a powerful means of mobilising support in Zwelethemba and elsewhere, and, Ntombomzi points out, the performances were a deliberate strategy to distract attention from the site of attacks.

Resistance took many forms. Rent boycotts, protests against apartheid education, class boycotts are all mentioned in women's accounts, as are instances of arson, stone-throwing and of people leaving South Africa to join banned political parties and armed movements. For the most part, young women were involved in student protest. Few young women were involved in banned or underground organisations or in military organisations.[14] Young men resisted incorporating women into cells, believing them to be incapable of holding secrets: 'Women were seen as potential informers' recalled one.

There were exceptions. Nowi Khomba and Nomeite Mfengu played central roles in local anti-apartheid organisations. Both were actively sought by the police for their roles in organising youth resistance in the Boland. Their chronicles of the 1980s in Zwelethemba provide insights into youths exposure to danger and the shape and complexity of political commitment that brought them into confrontation with the state.

In 1983, at the age of 18, Nomeite joined and became secretary of UWO, after having been recruited by her father's brother's wife.[15] Nomeite joined COSAS in 1985 and held the portfolio of Organiser. She was also an 'ordinary member' of ZWEYO, WOYCO (Worcester Youth Congress) and the Civic Association, and was engaged in recruiting young people to join UDF-affiliated organisations. The police knew of her activities and sought her throughout the 1980s. To some extent it was chance that enabled her to evade arrest.

Her decision to join UWO was not lightly taken. Young women's positions as students, youths and mothers offered them a range of organisational affili-ations. At the age of 16, Nomeite had borne Bandile, the first of her three children. She and Bandile lived at home with Nomeite's mother, three sisters and extended family. Nomeite was the youngest member of UWO. Her decision to join the organisation had put her into conflict with members of the youth organisations in Zwelethemba who believed she should join their structures, and with the parents of young people involved in protest who were angry that she encouraged youths to engage in resistance against the state with its attendant dangers.

Often young women faced difficult choices between the demands of political life and the traditional requirements of family life. Nomeite confronted conflicting demands when, in 1986, at the age of 21, she decided to leave Zwelethemba and go into exile. She left her two sons, Bandile, aged five, and Zuko, aged three, in her mother's care.

Once installed in a safe house in Cape Town, Nomeite changed her mind about leaving the country. In her 'struggle diary', recorded for my research, she recalled her decision:

I started to think about my two children [and] I changed my mind about leaving the country. I decided to hide at Cape Town. When I was in Cape Town I was hiding in New Crossroads ... I stayed there for six months without contact from my family and my children and I was so worried because I left my young ones and they knew nothing about where I was ... One time I tried to phone ... home because I wanted to know about the situation, because of homesickness. They said to me, 'You must not come back now because even last night the police were at home, searching the whole house looking for you'...

Sometimes I used to cry when I was thinking of my sons. When I phoned them they also cried and asked where I am and when I am coming back to be with them again ... I was [their] mother and father.

Nomeite faced stark choices: between being involved in struggle activities or not; joining the UWO or the youth organisation; going to exile or remaining at home; leaving the country or remaining with her family. She eventually returned to Zwelethemba in 1987. There she continued working alongside Nowi Khomba in organising youth structures in Zwelethemba. Nomeite is now in her mid-thirties. She is unemployed, unmarried, the mother of three children, and a member of the ANC Women's League. She did not experience 'gross violations of human rights' and did not make a statement to the Commission.

Nomeite's close friend, Nowi, is widely acknowledged as having been the most politically active of the young women in Zwelethemba. As a teenager, Nowi became involved in political organisations in part because of the activities of her family members. Her oldest sister, Nomonde, was a founder member of ZWEYO, and a member of its executive committee, as was her brother, Amos, who became a respected youth leader. The activities of the three siblings in organising youth protest in the 1980s soon focused the attention of the police on them, their home and family. Like many other young people at the time, they ceased sleeping at home in an attempt to protect their kin from the constant surveillance and interventions by policemen. Nevertheless, the police tormented the Khomba family.

A friend of Nowi's commented, 'Amos and Nomonde were double-trouble for the Khomba family and it was triple-trouble, for that matter, when Nowi joined!' They became a quartet when Mrs Khomba joined the Zwelethemba branch of UWO (United Women's Congress). Anxious about her children's activities, she used her involvement in the organisation to provide support for them and to agitate for political change. She remained an active member of UWO and its later incarnation as UWCO. After the ANC was unbanned in 1990, she helped to establish the local branch of the Women's League, of which she became the vice-chairperson. Nowi's father supported protest activities but did not join any of the anti-apartheid organisations active in Zwelethemba.

Nowi's notes on her past activities recall:

In 1985 when I was doing Standard 9[16] in Vusisizwe Secondary School, two classmates from Oudtshoorn encouraged the whole class to join COSAS ... At this time my older brother Amos [had] already passed Standard 10 and couldn't further his studies because of the financial situation. He was working at 'Slagpal', the place that was selling meat. My sister, Nomonde, was doing Standard 7, also at Vusisizwe. She also joined the Congress [COSAS]. My class was most active.

In May 1985, COSAS held a conference in Durban. Nowi was one of the students elected to represent the Zwelethemba branch of COSAS. On their return from Durban, the students negotiated with the principal of the school for permission to meet on the school premises to discuss political matters. The principal permitted them to meet twice a week for two hours. Nowi's political activities and those of her family continued:

Amos was busy recruiting those who were not scholars to join the Zwelethemba Youth Organisation, ZWEYO. Nomonde joined ZWEYO and informed the students to join ZWEYO after school. Luckily this was very successful.

Nomeite [Mfengu] and Maqoma [Dyabooi[17]] were elected to attend the umbrella committee on Wednesdays, where UDF, UWCO, the civic association, ZWEYO and COSAS members met. This committee reported back to the organisations. When ZWEYO decided to form the street committees, ZWEYO wrote a letter to COSAS asking the whole committee to attend their meetings. It was easy to form street committees because we were all from different streets.

In 1985, five of the nine portfolio-holding members of the executive committee of COSAS were women, Nowi among them.

In June 1985, news of the deaths of Matthew Goniwe, Fort Calata, Sparrow Mkhonto and Sicelo Mhlawuli, 'the Cradock Four', reached Zwelethemba. Residents collected money and arranged transport to take mourners to Cradock for the funeral. Sixty thousand people came from all over South Africa to attend the funeral (Report, Volume Three: 23). Nowi was among the mourners. On their return, police were waiting at a roadblock at the entrance to Zwelethemba and dispersed the chanting mourners.

That night, a meeting was called in the civic hall. Students addressed the meeting, announcing that a consumer boycott was to be instituted nationally and requesting community support in their ongoing protests against apartheid education. The following day, COSAS students met separately. Nowi remembered:

On Monday, those who went to Cradock gave a report back to the other COSAS members about the consumer boycott. The students decided to take the zinc doors [in protest against inadequate educational facilities] to the police station. And we went to the beer hall and asked our parents not to support the beer hall. Our main reason was that it did not support the community. We also went to the *shebeens*[18] and asked them not to sell beer for a certain time and said that some of our parents spend most of their money on beer while the children have no school uniforms. Most of the *shebeens* supported the boycott.

Some people were detained [after the beerhall and school protests. Noluntu, Ntsoake and Xoliswa were among these]. The police shot Nondatsu [Nation Bahume, who, at the time of his death was president of the Student's Representative Council at Vusisizwe Secondary School] and we continued the struggle.

In August 1985, COSAS was banned. The students intensified the work of ZWEYO and held nightly meetings to educate themselves in political matters and to develop strategies of resistance. Nowi was detained on 28 November 1985. She was released on 23 February 1986, having spent three months in prison in solitary confinement in terms of Section 29 of the Internal Security Act.

Nowi's accounts veer away from the personal. She did not describe the circumstances that led to this, the first of three detentions. It was only through careful probing that the details emerged. She was detained in November 1985 after she was caught with eight others, six from Zwelethemba, while trying to cross the border ('skip') into Lesotho and exile:

I had a friend in Cape Town and they organised for me to skip. I asked, 'What about my parents?' They said, 'No problem!' Other women I worked with from Paarl had already gone into exile. The guys said that I was in the executive [of ZWEYO] and was successful so it would be easy to skip ... I asked, 'How will I get money to go?' They told me not to worry; it was already organised. So, I was persuaded.

Seven of the nine people in the group were from Zwelethemba. Nowi knew the eighth. The remaining man was unknown to the other members of the group.

In her terse style, Nowi summarised the process that led to her detention in 1985. She described the assurances she had required before she would leave: that there was sufficient money to fund their escape and that someone would inform her parents so that they would not worry. She meticulously outlined the steps that had to be taken to leave the country and get safely to exile: introductions to people who could be trusted, meetings, safe houses, forged identity documents. She detailed the careful planning of a route to exile, the speed with which the underground communication network adjusted to changes in plans and showed the reliance of activists on the hospitality and discretion of kin.

The group was to travel to Matatiele. From there they were to be taken across the border into Lesotho:

So, we left on Sunday with the Blue Line bus. They organised everything, even all kinds of food. We got to Matatiele. We did not see the people who were supposed to meet us there. Luckily, [one man] had family there. He wanted to find the family and he did. So we took the bus to Maluti, to his family. There was no problem with them: they put us up. [Two of the men] were sent to collect the bags because we were too conspicuous in that Sotho place.[19] Some of us did not speak seSotho. We did not look like the people there and we dressed differently. They wore long dresses and big *doeks* [headcloths] and the men wore old clothes.

Alarmed that the next stage of their journey was not going according to plan, the group arranged that one among their number should call their contact in Cape Town and alert him to their changed plans. The man in Cape Town told them not to worry and that transport would arrive to collect them from the new venue.

The next day the transport came to fetch us. It was Tuesday. A *bakkie* [light delivery van] came to deliver us to Lesotho. We came to Maluti Station ... You know, on that first day at Maluti, one of us disappeared.[20] Just left. We did not notice at the time. We were caught at Matatiele. There is a police station not far from there. They drove us there. The women were put into a cell. We were two. The men were put into a different cell.

Two members of the group managed to hide from the police and were not detained. They returned to Zwelethemba where they alerted their comrades to the detention of the others. The six who were captured were held in the police cells near Matatiele. The cells were close enough for the detainees to speak to one another when the guards were not present. One man struck up a friendship with one of the policemen who smuggled notes between the cells to the detainees. The young people were held for four days and interrogated singly. Not having had time to prepare a plausible story, each told his or her version. Some of the stories contradicted one another.

After four days of interrogation, the six were reunited. Nowi was handcuffed between two of the men and bundled into one police car. The others were cuffed and pushed into the second car. They were driven to East London where they spent two days in solitary confinement. They were not permitted to communicate with one another. They were then moved to Le Grange Prison in Port Elizabeth and taken from there to Cape Town's infamous police station at Caledon Square. The women and men were held in separate cells for two days while police interrogated their family members. On 28 November 1985, a week after they had been captured, they were formally detained under Section 29 of the Internal Security Act.

Nowi and the other woman were sent to Robertson prison, some 20 kilometres from Zwelethemba, where they were separated from one another and held in solitary confinement. Nowi was interrogated repeatedly by a black policeman who, at the time, she said, was living in the cells because his home in Robertson had been burnt down by community members who accused him of collaboration with the state.

Nowi and her comrades were not charged. They were released from detention on the same day and taken to Worcester police station where they met one another for the first time in three months. They were taken to their homes in Zwelethemba. Nowi was accompanied by the woman with whom she had been detained: neither trusted the Security Branch and the woman was afraid to return to Cape Town alone. Later, Nowi's parents contacted her family and she was collected from Zwelethemba.

Nowi remains reticent about describing the detention. In her written notes and during our interviews and informal discussions, she glossed over her treatment and the interrogation sessions she endured. She did not describe her experiences of solitary confinement or its effects on her, a point to which I return later in this chapter.

After her release in February 1986, Nowi intensified her activities in organising resistance to the state: 'When I was released I became more and more involved in the struggle. We launched WOYCO (Worcester Youth Congress) because we were [working] with the Coloured comrades ... After launching WOYCO we organised the Paarl youth and we formed BOYCO, the Boland Youth Congress. After launching BOYCO ... I was detained again for being the committee member of BOYCO.'

She was detained for the second time at five o'clock in the morning of 7 September 1986 and taken from her home to Worcester police station where she joined three men who had also been detained in the predawn swoop. The four, and a Coloured woman detained later the same morning, were taken to a large house near a dam outside Worcester, on the road that runs south-east towards Swellendam:

They took us from the Worcester police station. It was seven o'clock. It was very cold that morning. They put us in the van, all of us. They took us to that place, far from Worcester. They gave us food – they weren't so strict that you couldn't talk. We talked about how they found us. We ate together.

At about ten in the morning, Security Branch men came to us and separated us. The women were taken first and separated. They asked about organisations in Zwelethemba and why we were involved. They said we should tell the truth. They asked about the committee members of WOYCO, especially Nomeite. They never found [that is, caught] her. I said that I knew her and that she was a committee member.

There was no point in denying that Nowi knew Nomeite – the police already knew her name and her activities. Nevertheless, they bade Nowi tell the truth:

They said that if I did not tell the truth they would throw me in the dam. They took me there and showed me. I did not know where the others were. There was a woman with them, a white policewoman. She told me to tell the truth and then she was left with me and interrogated me. Then two men came. She grabbed me and tried to throw me into the dam. The men stopped her. I did not want to talk. I was crying.[21] I ran along the edge of the dam. The policeman stood in front of me and threw sand in my eyes. I could not see. He beat me with a *sjambok*. I cried because I could not do anything. I stood. I tried to look and they threw sand again. My eyes were swollen. [Her sight was permanently damaged.]

They took me to a single room and gave me lunch. It was past three o'clock. They apologised to me and took me to Eben Donges hospital. They said I shouldn't tell the others. The doctor gave me something for my eyes.

Then I was taken to Worcester prison. The next day they came. They took me to that place again. I did not know where the others I was detained with were. I was kept there for the day. I was given hotel food. I was interrogated for the whole day. I was also beaten. At about three o'clock, they took me to De Doorns [prison]. I was kept there. I was sick there – stomach problems. A doctor was brought there. He gave me pills but I did not drink them – I did not trust them.[22] Mirriam [Moleleki] organised a lawyer. I don't remember his name. He was a white man. He came once and I did not see him again. I was in De Doorns for the whole time, for three months. They held me in solitary, under Section 29 again.

In Nowi's account, place and time figure powerfully. She has etched into memory the places of detention and pain in the Boland: an isolated house, a dam, a hospital, a prison cell. Members of the Security Branch used a variety of places near Worcester to hold, interrogate and torture detainees. Nowi was held and tortured on a farm;[23] Noluntu was tortured in the mountainous area in Worcester's north-western environs; and young men reported having been tortured alongside the Breede River that runs south of the town.

On her release from detention, Nowi returned home and attended school. She wrote her Standard Nine examinations at the end of the year and passed the year. In 1987 she entered Standard Ten. In that year, many of the youth activists were attending school elsewhere as parents who could afford to send their children elsewhere to better schools to study did so. Nowi recalls that their absence had a marked effect on protest in Zwelethemba, which, in the absence of older scholars, decreased.

Nowi's success at school was not repeated:

I failed Standard 10 in 1987 and then in 1988 I was not learning. I joined the Civic [Association in 1987] and [a comrade] organised me to join the Unemployed Workers' Movement. I was elected as a branch secretary since the main office was in Cape Town. He was the Boland Organiser. Every month we attended a meeting in Cape Town. The structure grew very quickly and we had about 300 members in only one month.

Her account does not describe the difficulties involved in recruiting members and in holding meetings in the near-blackout conditions that prevailed in the community at the time. She continued, 'Unfortunately, I was detained in August and kept for two months.' She spent a week in the Worcester prison and then was transferred to a prison in the small town of De Doorns, some 50 kilometres away. Once again, she was held in solitary confinement under Section 29 of the Internal Security Act. She was not allowed any books and her mother was allowed to visit only once a month for two hours. Her brother, Amos, was detained at the same time although in a different prison. Nowi's family was kept busy trying to ensure the well-being of the two detainees.

Nowi did not address the period of detention at all in the written notes she kept for my research but continued:

When I came back I became active in the Women's League.[24] In 1989 we worked underground and in 1990 all the organisations were unbanned. When Comrade President [Mandela] came from prison we again involved ourselves in the struggle. The chairperson of the Women's League was Sis' Neli Mroxisa and my mother was the vice-chairperson. I was the secretary. We did a door-to-door campaign and recruited mothers to join the Women's League.

In 1991, I was elected to be a delegate in the first conference after Madiba [Mandela] was released. When we launched the ANC Women's League in Zwelethemba, I was also the committee member. I am still an ANC member [and will be] until the day I die. Long live the ANC, long live!

In her characteristic style, Nowi glossed over her fear and the harshness of the treatment she endured. The account emphasises her organisational affiliations. In 1990, at the age of 27, she was a student in the Standard Ten class at Vusisizwe Secondary School in Zwelethemba and matriculated at the end of that year. She was a member of the executive committee of COSAS until it was banned (1985); a committee member of UWCO (1986–90); an executive member of ZWEYO (1985–87); a member of WOYCO and later BOYCO (1987–90). She was a member of the civic organisation (1985–90) and branch secretary of the Unemployed Workers' Movement (1987). After 1990, she was secretary of the Women's League and an active member of the ANC.

After considerable prompting by her peers, Nowi made a statement to the Commission late in its process. The account she gave the Commission was spare. It described only one of the periods of detention and stated that her eyesight was damaged. She is not currently recorded as a victim and the status of her statement is unclear.

PROBLEMS OF METHOD

It is difficult to place the experiences of the women with whom I worked within the narrative that frames the Commission's findings on rural violence cited earlier. They do not fit easily into the 'crystallised narratives' (Das 1995: 43) on which the Commission based its findings. Young women in particular were less likely to appear in the chronology of violence or in the data collected by the Commission. The chapter on women in the Commission's 1998 Report does not provide data on the ages of deponents at the time of violation. Chapter 3 of the Report (pp. 5–6) indicates that the majority of women who were victims of killing and torture fell between the ages of 13 and 36 whereas older women tended to report experiences that were classified as 'severe ill-treatment'.

Nowi was not alone in her unwillingness to make a statement to the Commission. Despite having instituted a special focus on youth and holding four Special Event Hearings on Children: in Durban (14 May 1997), Cape Town (22 May 1997) Johannesburg (12 June 1997), and East London (18 June 1997), the Commission admits that it did not apprehend the full range of young people's experiences. The Report states,

> Given the Commission's focus on gross human rights violations, those who gave evidence at the hearings on children and youth spoke mainly of the suffering of young people. Few chose to speak of, or to report on, the heroic role of young people in the struggle against Apartheid. Many saw themselves not as victims, but as soldiers or freedom fighters and, for this reason, chose not to appear before the Commission at all. [Volume Four: 249]

In part, the Commission's failure is methodological: a problem of sample and of time-scale. In the Commission's work, individuals identified themselves as victims. A self-selecting sample contains its own biases. The Report warns, 'Many South Africans who experienced human rights violations did not come to the Commission and are therefore not represented ... Significant, too, was the fact that many women and girls chose not to testify about violations they themselves had experienced' (Volume Four: 259).

It takes time and sustained interaction to establish the relationships that form the basis of a careful accounting of violence and pain. Pressures of time and the constraints of the Commission's research methodology meant that these were often absent from its work. The Commission anticipated that those wishing to make statements would do so through its Regional Offices or through designated statement-takers (see Chapter 6). For the purpose of public hearings, the Commission's Western Cape Regional Office (based in Cape Town) divided its geographical area into six sub-regions, one of which was the Boland. A team of Commission members was allocated to each sub-region. The team included members of the Human Rights Violations Committee and the Reparation and Rehabilitation Committee, two statement-takers, a briefer, a researcher, a logistics officer and a driver. Later an investigator was added to the team. In each sub-region, the team worked in a ten-week cycle that consisted of pre-hearing (information dissemination and statement taking), hearing, and post-hearing (follow-up and referral) phases (Volume One: 433–4). Approximately two weeks of the cycle was spent in collecting statements. Only 26 women from Zwelethemba made statements to the Commission. Some did not make statements because at that time the Commission did not recognise certain experiences as falling within the definition of gross violations of human rights.[25] Those who did not make statements but whose experiences would have qualified as gross violations of human rights offered a variety of reasons for their decisions. Some were concerned that Commissioners, who were not well-known political activists,[26] would not understand them while others distrusted the local organisations through which the Commission established itself in Zwelethemba. Some felt their pain to be limited in comparison with that suffered by others. For some, the experiences of torture and loss are not widely known and they feared being labelled.

Young women's stories of harm are not lightly given. Tracing their experiences is complicated by the shifting positions that women take up in society. Few who were instrumental in resistance organisations remain in Zwelethemba. A number have married and in accordance with traditional practices of patrilocality have moved to their husband's parents' homes or have established nuclear families elsewhere. Others have followed career opportunities outside Zwelethemba. Still others, born elsewhere and sent to Zwelethemba to be educated, have subsequently returned to their natal homes. Convention and opportunity displace young people from the sites of their earlier political activities. Their absence makes it difficult to create an enduring record of activities in a place and to investigate the precise extent, nature and consequences of exposure to harm and efforts to rebuild social worlds. In their absence, a rendering of the past in Zwelethemba takes account mainly of harm inflicted on men.

Eliciting experiences of harm and resistance in Zwelethemba required methodological innovation and establishing relationships of trust. Women who had been integral in protest organisations were suspicious and initially participated reluctantly in my research. Indeed, when I began working in Zwelethemba at the end of 1996, several women refused to participate in the study. One woman wrote a letter giving her reasons: 'I don't think it is wise to give confidential information to someone you do not know. What [will that person] do with the information? Perhaps there are things that will lead to arrest, maybe in the near future. So I'm afraid to give any information about my political experiences, due to what is happening in the TRC.' She did not elaborate on her misgivings regarding either the Commission or the use to which information would be put. She wished to remain anonymous: I did not include her in the focus group and I did not interview her.

Nowi Khomba, too, initially refused to participate, saying that she did not see the point in being interviewed about her experiences. In comments and a letter, she gave seven reasons for not participating: (1) She felt that researchers who conducted research seldom reported on their work to their research subjects, but (2) they made money by publishing the findings. (3) She had not been interviewed, nor (4) been offered psychological support or counselling by the Trauma Centre for Victims of Violence which had conducted research on political violence in Zwelethemba in 1995. (5) She had heard about the Commission but had not been invited to make a statement, and (6) she believed that the money being spent on the Commission and on research would be better used in 'building the new South Africa'. (7) She felt that those who had contributed to the demise of the

Apartheid State through their political activities at 'grassroots level' had not been given adequate recognition in the new political dispensation. In short, she recognised that there is often little benefit to research subjects who participate in research, and made it clear.

Once she had agreed to participate in the research, the outline of Nowi's political activities described above took patient work, drawing on many techniques,[27] to piece together from fragments that emerged over the research period. Notwithstanding our mutual efforts, the description of her political activities that Nowi offered was spare, lacking detail and emotional content. Her qualities – courage, a willingness to risk, care for her family and comrades, a lively sense of justice and a strong commitment to ideals – and her frailties, and the difficulties she faces in everyday life were not all evident in her telling and were difficult to elicit. She did not easily admit the harm she suffered; she found it difficult even to talk of her partial blindness. She refused psychological assistance or other forms of support.

It may be that the lack of emotional content in her description of the past is indicative of healing, a mastery of pain. It may be a refusal to admit pain. It may be a front, a mask carefully established to hold the memory and consequences of harm at a distance from herself and her family. It is difficult to know: intrusion may undermine her achievements or damage her efforts at recuperation. She holds herself with dignity, and is widely respected and recognised as a powerful figure. Members of her family and her community know no more than is presented here.

In the aftermath of apartheid, some kinds of knowledge are held to the self. It takes time and the establishment of trusting relationships to elicit people's experiences of violence, especially where the forms and extent of violence suffered are not widely known. The Commission's tasks had to be completed within a specified time period and its methodology was such that its representatives were able to spend very little time collecting statements in an area. The result has been a sample that the Commission admits is biased by gender and age. Its findings, based on that sample, do not reflect the extent of young women's suffering or the enormity of the damage wrought by apartheid.

GAUGING HARM

Considerations of harm offer prognoses for the future. They identify the extent of damage and may enable remedial action.

The Commission's Report (Volume Five: 125–6) states that:

The consequences of repression and resistance include the physical toll taken by torture and other forms of severe ill treatment. The psychological effects are multiple and are amplified by the other stresses of living in a deprived society. Hence, lingering physical, psychological, economic and social effects are felt in all corners of South African society. The implications of this extend beyond the individual – to the family, the community and the nation ... Human rights violations can also trigger a cascade of psychological, physical and interpersonal problems for victims that, in their turn, influence the functioning of the surrounding social system.

Drawing from a sample of two thousand statements weighted by region, the Commission concluded that exposure to violence produced a wide range of problems (see discussion in Chapter 3). Its findings on the consequences of gross violations of human rights are generalised and heavily reliant on research conducted elsewhere and reported in the psychological literature on trauma. The Report does not describe the impairment of social functioning save to state that there is an association between domestic violence and 'social strain' (Volume Five: 156). It identifies families and communities as damaged, perhaps irreparably so. It does not differentiate between adults and children. Its findings in respect of youth are limited: it found that youths who were armed and trained in the mid-1980s to resist apartheid were dehumanised, desensitized and criminalised and that they have not been reintegrated into and made valued members of society (Volume Five: 256). It suggests that this has 'created the potential for [them to commit] further gross violations of human rights' (Volume Five: 256) but does not say why this should be so. These findings hold mainly for men and the Report makes no findings about the consequences of gross violations of human rights for young women.

The findings of the Trauma Centre study (Skinner 1998: 184–7) are more specific in relation to Zwelethemba. The study sample was drawn from those who had been detained for periods of longer than 48 hours, although, as Noluntu's experiences indicate, one cannot presume that those held for shorter periods were less badly treated than those whose detentions were longer. Indeed, on learning that the most aggressive periods of interrogation usually occurred within the first three days of detention, the Commission 'eventually agreed that detention without trial itself constituted severe ill-treatment, leaving the specific period open and assessing the individual cases on their particular circumstances' (Burton 2000: 18). The Trauma Centre study identified medical and psychological problems among its sample of 45 respondents. The data are not compared to a control group. When responses to questions were expressed as percentages, the following features emerge:

- 22 per cent of respondents reported headaches, 'physical weakness' and 'other body pain'.
- 51 per cent reported feeling 'sad or down' and 40 per cent indicated that they cried easily. One-third of respondents reported being unable to 'feel emotions'; 55 per cent felt anxious when they thought about the trauma and 33 per cent reported feelings of anxiety, fear or worry.
- 55 per cent of respondents said that they tried to stay busy so that they did not think about the trauma but 28 per cent of respondents reported that they could not stop thinking about the trauma.

- 58 per cent of respondents identified themselves as angry and 55 per cent reported hating 'those involved in the old system'; 42 per cent felt that they had become less trusting.
- 13 per cent reported drinking or taking drugs, although the majority of these reported that they 'seldom' did so.

The study notes high levels of unemployment and limited health and social services in the area (1998: 170–1) but does not attempt to correlate these factors with the reported symptoms. Instead it assumes that the symptoms are expressive of previous experiences of violence and violation and concludes (1998: 186) that respondents' profiles indicate PTSD (post-traumatic stress disorder).[28]

Neither the Commission Report nor the Trauma Centre study draws conclusions about young women nor about the effects of violence in constraining the social possibilities that define the scope of young people's futures.

Consider the diversity of responses to violence of young women with whom I worked in Zwelethemba. Some stood firm in the face of danger while others withdrew. Some prioritised familial needs while others braved both convention and their own fear in order to act on their vision for a different world. Some were exposed to danger as a consequence of their political beliefs while others were caught in the emotion of the moment or were drawn into protest through the activities of kin, friends and peers. Some families supported the activities of their children; some forbade young women from participating in political activities; some were ambivalent, afraid or withheld support. Members of a few families sought to influence young people by becoming involved in political organisations. Others became involved in order to protect their children. Of those young women who were engaged in protest activities and who remain in Zwelethemba, some remember their roles in opposition, even where these might be judged limited, with pride. For some, an exposure to violence has harmed trusting relationships. Others have worked at restoring social bonds.

Now consider the young women in relation to five markers of social success. The markers – achievement in education, employment, motherhood and marriage, independence, and self-care – are drawn from local social and cultural registers that together describe a broad range of socially sanctioned possibilities for women:

- *Education:* All of the women returned to school after 1990. Nine completed the Standard Ten school leaving examinations. Four have further qualifications: Xoliswa Tyawana recently completed her Bachelor of Arts degree; Noluntu Zawukana has completed a secretarial course and will soon complete a computing course; Vuyelwa Xuza has received 'Girl Friday' training; Ntsoaki Phelane will soon qualify as a teacher. Nowi Khomba and Gertrude Siwangaza attended college in Worcester. The last two fought hard to be awarded scholarships and subsidies by the local municipality but when the money ran out, they could not complete their education.

- *Employment:* Only three of the women were fully employed at the time of research: Noluntu on a three-year contract as a clerk on a government project; Vuyelwa as a labourer on the same project and Noluthando as a part-time assistant at a domestic violence crisis centre.
- *Motherhood and marriage:* All of the women have children. In four instances the children born of one mother have different fathers. None of the women is married and 'damage payments' to their families for pregnancies were paid in only a few instances.[29] Some of the women receive maintenance assistance from the children's fathers but most do not. In only one instance is there a lasting relationship between a woman and her child's father.
- *Independence:* Only one of the women and her children lives independently of parents or kin. After the death of her parents, Noluntu and her daughter continued to live in their house. Vuyelwa shares a house with three other people but a relative in Zwelethemba cares for her three youngest children and her oldest daughter lives with the child's father in Johannesburg. The other women continue to live with their parents or kin.
- *Self-care:* Some of the women care for themselves well. Others are ill but do not always stick to treatment regimes. Some drink heavily and some have relationships that are frowned on by family and friends.

In short, the women have tried to further their education but are not employed; they have entered motherhood in ways that are not socially sanctioned; they receive little support from the fathers of their children; they remain dependent. They report feeling helpless, angry and despairing in the face of change that does not recognise skills learned in conditions of protest. The women have worked to develop new skills but their efforts have not always been either successful or rewarded. Despite their efforts, they are not well equipped to enter a neoliberal economy and their capacities to innovate have been reduced in the face of social and personal hardship. The gap between the registers of the ideal and reality continues to expand.

It is difficult to interpret the social facts described in the bulleted section above. They may indicate individual trauma, such that people are unable to form lasting relationships or to be independent. They may be markers of apartheid's destruction of social conventions and possibilities, or reconfigurations of the possibilities at hand that may become socially sanctioned in time. It is equally difficult to predict from the data what might become of the women. They may admit to harm and seek assistance; they may be able to rework their social arrangements into forms that more closely approximate social ideals, or their current configurations of family life may become more widely acceptable. Their relationships may solidify and men may take responsibility for their children and partners. The women may have the capacity to invest in their children's futures, to find employment and to forge independent lives.

What is clear in the present is that there has been a foreclosure of the grounds of possibility, a narrowing in the range of options and a distancing of the horizons of success for young women. It is felt particularly by those who engaged in protest against the Apartheid State, who feel that their stake in the future has been curtailed. For example, during a workshop in July 1998, some of the women expressed their frustration:

Nokwanda: For that matter, you get people asking some questions, like, 'You said Nowi was active in 1980, 1985, but why today she is sitting there not having any jobs?' [Or people say] 'You said Nokwanda was very active but now she's sitting there, having nothing, just sitting with a baby she must feed.'
Ntombomzi: And then you get some questions from other people who were not active. And they will ask you, 'What has the struggle done for you?'
Nokwanda: (interjects) [They ask] 'What is the pay-back?'

The activities that young women in Zwelethemba describe – their participation in youth protests, school and consumer-boycotts, street committees – and the threads that wove together protagonists in networks of commitment, comradeship, protest, endurance, and (though it is seldom mentioned) fear, overflow the edges of the compartmentalised categories for understanding violence that the Commission provided.

It is difficult to identify the full extent and nature of violence and its effects on young people. In any attempt to recognise impairment and coping, it is important to take into account both what is considered to constitute violence and the ways it is recorded. Too close a focus on particular facets of violence may obscure other dimensions of harm. An emphasis on victims may displace from the historical record the agency of those who mobilised in the face of repression or who confronted additional dangers as a consequence of their political ardour. Considerations of harm that reframe resistance as suffering may undervalue people's experiences and their commitments, expectations and skills. They may conceal the variety of responses to violence and disguise the full range of consequences and strategies to cope.

It matters that the experiences of the young have not been documented. In the first instance, the data provided by the Commission and other studies do not enable an understanding of the extent to which young women were exposed to danger or of the nature of efforts at or obstacles to recovery. In the second, as yet the record contains few stories of experiences that lie outside of conventional narratives of heroism and suffering that are usually masculine (Reynolds 1995b). Reynolds suggests that it is important to incorporate alternative stories into a repertoire so that new scripts for living can be held, enacted and offered for the future. In their absence, any understanding of violence and its effects is narrowed, women's experiences may be undervalued or unrecognised, and the possibility of expanding or legitimating the range of repertoires upon which people can draw in reconfiguring their lives may be missed.

6   IN PURSUIT OF THE ORDINARY

To recover is not the same as to uncover or to discover. Recovery ... is more akin to regaining one's balance, albeit in a new place and time; it is a coming to terms with contemporary forces that buffet without allowing these forces to overwhelm. Recoveries often do entail radical rearrangement of meanings and forms, but they do not necessarily presume radical ruptures, nor do they deny all continuity, all memory – whether real or imagined – and all familiarity. (Daniel, 1996: 73).

On 17 June 1996, shortly before the Commission's public hearings in Worcester, four short autobiographies by Mirriam Moleleki, Neliswa Mroxisa, Nothemba Ngcwecwe and Nongeteni Mfengu, key figures in the formation of 'struggle organisations' in Zwelethemba and the Boland in the 1980s, were published.[1] The books trace the development of the women's political consciousness and activities and describe the contexts of women's mobilisation: poverty, the harsh conditions of farm labourers and domestic workers, trade union activities, youth activism, and growing state violence.

The autobiographies were Mirriam Moleleki's idea. She wished to create a record for her children of the activities that she and others had undertaken: 'There was no chance for us to explain to our children what was happening. If you are an activist, you move time and again out of the house, you go to meetings, you go everywhere and you've no chance even to sit down with your children and explain' (Moleleki 1997: 1). She wished also to provide an example to farm labourers, particularly women: 'I feel that books must go to the women, to give the women a chance ... to show that we cannot stand only in the kitchen. We can march out ... and do something else. I am a strong woman: I can do things in my own way. You can do something: you must trust yourself as a woman' (p. 2).

The books offered a perspective on women that was different from the images of 'secondary witnesses' that had emerged from the Commission's early hearings. At the time the books were published, the Commission's language had deeply permeated the public imagination and book reviews made explicit connections between the Commission's work and the books. Barry Streek, a political writer for the Cape Town daily newspaper *Cape Times*, described the autobiographies as 'powerful testimonies to the role played by women, particularly in rural areas' and quoted the women as saying that they hoped the books would help rural women 'break their silence' (*Cape Times*, 17 June 1996: 2).

The women know one another well. In the mid-1980s, Mirriam, Neliswa and Nothemba worked with two others from Worcester and with the assistance of the Black Sash, ran an Advice Office in Worcester.[2] Together with Nongeteni Mfengu, they worked closely in UWO, the UDF, the Civic Association and later the ANC and ANC Women's League. Three of the women were detained: Nothemba Ngcwecwe was held several times for periods of less than 48 hours; Mirriam Moleleki and Neliswa Mroxisa were detained three times each, sometimes in solitary confinement. Their children were involved in student protests and were also detained.

At the forefront of protest and support structures in the Boland in the 1980s, Mirriam Moleleki is well known in the Western Cape's circle of anti-apartheid activists and non-governmental organisations (NGOs). As head of the Masikhule Rural Development Centre, a community-based organisation (CBO), she was approached by the Commission to facilitate their work in the Boland. She has an extensive knowledge of the violations committed in Zwelethemba and surrounding areas. Masikhule became the main conduit for collecting statements concerning gross violations of human rights and for distributing information about the Commission and its tasks.

Masikhule was not unique in this regard. The Commission drew on CBOs and NGOs throughout the country to establish networks of communication between local residents and the Commission and to improve the collection of statements concerning gross violations of human rights. Initially, the Commission drew on NGOs and CBOs to disseminate information, assist with logistical planning for hearings and provide support for those who had given statements (Volume One: 407). According to Nomfundo Walaza (2000: 251–2), Director of the Trauma Centre for Survivors of Violence and Torture in Cape Town, however, NGOs received little support from the Commission in the work of sustaining deponents and testifiers. They drew largely on their own resources and received no funding from the Commission.

The Commission later trained local residents to take statements, a process that was formalised through the 'designated statement taker programme'. The tasks of 'designated statement takers' were to identify victims, fill in protocols, liaise with the Commission and provide referral services. The programme was useful in generating statements from victims in rural areas (Volume One: 141) and in providing corroboration of the events described by deponents. The Commission Report states, 'The local recruitment of statement takers meant, too, that victims could tell their stories in their mother tongue, often to people they knew, thereby enhancing the quality and reliability of the testimony and reassuring victims who felt apprehensive. Some, however, chose not to share intimate details with neighbours and others from their own communities' (Volume One: 140).

The Report is contradictory about the success of the programme. The Western Cape Office reported that:

It was ... regrettable that the official designated statement taker programme did not get off the ground earlier in the region, especially in the rural areas. In 1996, a total of sixty-two community statement takers were trained in four of the eleven sub-regions in anticipation of the launch of this programme [Zwelethemba was in one of the four sub-regions]; but funding only became available in April 1997, too late to be of significant use. [Volume One: 398]

Despite the delays in funding, Masikhule Centre had early been involved in the Commission's work. Through Mirriam's office, the Commission trained three designated statement takers – Mirriam's daughter, Mimi; Gloria Makoetlana, and Nobantu Bushwana. In addition to assisting deponents fill in statement protocols, the women identified those who had suffered gross violations of human rights in the period under review and encouraged them to make statements to the Commission. In fact, Mirriam did most of the work: she is well known in Zwelethemba, and many people saw her role as a continuation of her previous activities in the Advice Office. In some ways, this was detrimental to the collection of statements in the area, as Mirriam's relationships with many political activists have been strained by the fact that she is employed and they are not, and that money is often channelled into Zwelethemba through the Masikhule Centre, and they feel themselves to be on the margins of development possibilities in the region.

Mirriam was well placed to identify victims and corroborate their stories of violation. Born in De Doorns in 1944, she had come to Zwelethemba in 1963 when she was abducted from home by the father of her child, her husband-to-be. She began working at the Langeberg factory in Worcester in 1964, shortly after her marriage. As soon as blacks were allowed to join trade unions, she joined the Food and Allied Workers Union (FAWU) and within a few years was a shop steward. In 1976, the Langeberg factory closed. Alongside seasonal employment on the grape farms of the region, it had been the main source of employment for many Africans in the area, and single women and widows were particularly badly affected by its closure as it was difficult for them to obtain work elsewhere. In 1976, Mirriam and others represented residents of Zwelethemba at a meeting in Parliament in Cape Town. The residents were demanding an end to the Coloured Labour Preference Policy that curtailed the access of Africans to employment throughout the area of the Western Cape demarcated by the 'Eiselin Line'.[3]

When they returned to Zwelethemba a school boycott was under way and police were deployed throughout the township. Mirriam attended the mass meeting called by the youths to explain to the parents the reasons for the boycott: the use of Afrikaans as a medium of instruction, inadequate educational facilities, untrained teachers and no secondary school. Her son, Tumelo, aged 14, addressed the assembled meeting, asking for the support of parents in the struggle against 'Bantu education'. Mirriam then addressed the crowd, encouraging residents to support the scholars.

During student protests in Zwelethemba that year, several children were detained, including Tumelo. Although she was involved in community-based politics, Mirriam did not know much about her son's activities. He ceased sleeping at home, and spent many nights at school in political meetings. Sometimes he returned home late at night, sometimes not at all. In 1980, shortly after a service in memory of the students who had been killed in the Soweto uprising of 16 June 1976, she confronted him, offering her support for his political activities. Three days later, he was arrested. He was held in solitary confinement for two weeks in mid-winter and was badly beaten. It was the first of four periods of detention.[4]

Mirriam travelled to Cape Town to seek assistance from Oscar Mphetha, the head of FAWU in the Western Cape and a member of the ANC underground. He told her to seek legal advice from Dullah Omar, a young lawyer. The two men assisted her to obtain money for bail from a network of sympathisers. Tumelo was charged with public violence and released on bail. After a six-month trial it became clear that the state had insufficient evidence to convict him and the charges were dropped. As a consequence of his arrest and her efforts to secure his bail and legal representation, Mirriam's network of acquaintances became wider and her exposure to political activists deepened.

Shortly thereafter, the Zwelethemba Residents' Association (ZRA) was reactivated in opposition to the local community council.[5] Mirriam was elected to serve on the executive committee of the Association.

Later that year, Mirriam and her husband sent Tumelo to relatives in Qwa Qwa, a Bantustan approximately one thousand kilometres away, to continue his education. As I show below, it was an action that was to have considerable repercussion on her efforts to mobilise women's support in the struggle against apartheid.

Mirriam remembers her son's arrest as having been instrumental in determining the shape of her political involvement: 'I was not always so political, you know. But after my son's arrest I was starting to be very involved. I became a politician. But I was not the kind of politician the Apartheid government was calling a "political radical". I was a very disciplined politician. I was the person who fights in a very quiet way' (Moleleki 1996: 32).

Her reputation and experiences give lie to her words. She had been detained in 1977, held in solitary confinement and questioned for 48 hours: 'They detained me because of my work with the old people. I remember the day very well. The old people were standing in queues for their pensions and the police hit one of the old women. I took the thing he hit the lady with and I started to hit him.'

Mirriam was questioned about her political activities and those of the ZRA. During her detention, Mirriam promised the police that she would desist from political activities, but after her release, returned to her political activities. She used her contacts with protest organisations and NGOs to assist those in need in Zwelethemba and to coordinate protest activities.

She became a member of the anti-apartheid organisations, while at the same time her husband worked for the municipal police. Ironically, his job as a municipal policeman whose task it was to enforce the pass laws provided her with a source of information about the activities of the police. When he was able to warn her of an impending pass-law raid, she spread the word to those who did not have passes. He carried messages from those arrested or detained whom Mirriam then visited and for whom she tried to arrange bail.

By 1985, she was a member of the Civic Association, a founder member of the UWO in Worcester, a member of the Regional Executive Committee of the UDF, and head of the Worcester Advice Office. Closely linked with the ANC's underground movement, she had received limited organisational and weapons training. In the 1980s, some of those wishing to leave and go into exile came to her and she organised safe passages for them. Some remember her as their 'mother in the struggle'.

After the launching of the UDF in the Boland in 1984, she became increasingly involved in recruiting people for its component organisations. Her methods were innovative. Sometimes she would dress in her church uniform and request permission from farmers to preach to farm workers. She had grown up in the farming region and knew how to use the language of *baasskap* to good effect.[6] Having received permission to minister to the workers, she would gather them together, remove her uniform and, clad in the civilian clothes hidden beneath the uniform, would preach fiery messages about the political state of South Africa. Her methods succeeded in swelling the ranks of UDF-affiliated organisations.

In August 1985, she was detained again. She was captured early one Sunday morning during a night vigil at the home of Nkosana Bahume, who had been shot by the police on 16 August 1985 (see chronology in Chapter 5). Bahume was related to her husband, Zacharias; his father's brother's grandson:

I remember that night. The mother of that boy was distraught. The parents were angry that the child was killed and angry with the organisations that put children into that situation. We as community leaders had to speak and show that it was the System [apartheid] that killed the children, not the [anti-apartheid] organisations.

There were many women sleeping there. At two in the morning there was a bad [that is, rude] knock. It was the police. The Security Branch. After they arrived, they looked around at the people. They were looking for me. One person said, 'She's not here'. One of the black Security Branch policemen said, 'She is here'. They found me. I was so shocked. I didn't expect that.

They picked me up and took me home. My children were there. Thabi was three years old. They searched. They were looking for pamphlets and papers. Thabi was crying for me. The police threatened him. My daughter was pregnant. In my room there were many pamphlets. She went in there and she took off her clothes and they could not enter. That is how things were saved: because there was a naked woman in the room!

The police tried to push Mirriam into a van. She refused to enter it, saying, 'I am not a criminal.' She demanded that they send a car for her and when she got into it she said, 'I will sit like *'n respekbaar persoon* [Afrikaans: 'a respectable person'], a Parliamentarian. I am Mandela's Parliamentarian.' Accompanied by a policewoman whom residents believed to be a karate expert, she was taken first to Worcester police station, then transferred to Bonnievale prison, some 70 kilometres away. The blankets in the cell in which she was held were covered in lice. The brown bread that was her dinner was stale. She refused to eat. She collapsed. A doctor said she was not well enough to be held in prison. Instead of being taken to hospital, she was transferred to Robertson prison and then to Paarl women's prison where she spent the duration of her three-month detention period.

During the first 30 days of her detention neither her family nor comrades knew her whereabouts. A Black Sash member, Di Bishop (now Oliver), eventually tracked her down and obtained legal support for her. Detained in terms of Section 29 of the Internal Security Act No. 74 of 1982 that had been implemented on 2 July 1985, Mirriam was held in solitary confinement. She was not allowed visitors. She was interrogated regularly by members of the Security Branch. Once, four policemen whom she identified in interviews as Heunis, van Loggerenberg, Nieuwoudt and McDonald went to her home and assaulted her children and her husband. They then returned to the prison and told Mirriam what they had done: 'They would tell me in prison, "Today we beat your children very badly." And when I came out, my son told me, "Mama, the police came to beat us." And he showed me the marks from the *sjambok*. I was in jail: they hit the children. Can I forgive them? No' (Moleleki, 1996: 37).[7]

After her release from prison in October 1985, she went into hiding for six months. She disguised herself in the traditional clothes of a married woman – head-scarf, shawl and apron knotted over her dress – and moved frequently throughout the Western Cape. She spent time in Mossel Bay, Outshoorn, Cape Town and Zwelethemba. In the first part of 1986, she gave evidence for the defence in the Delmas Trial, in which 22 UDF leaders were charged with treason. A leader of UWO, the Civic Association and the UDF, Mirriam was called by the defence to describe their activities in peaceful protest.

In June 1987, she attended a meeting held in Cape Town at which the underground leadership discussed how best to re-establish political structures destroyed in the police crack-down during the States of Emergency. She believes that someone revealed her name and whereabouts to the police, as she was captured on her way back to Zwelethemba. Once again, she was held under Section 29 of the Internal Security Act and served a three-month period of detention in solitary confinement. In the interim, in the face of police harassment, a funding crisis and accusations of misman-agement, the Advice Office closed.

On Mirriam's release from prison, she returned to Zwelethemba and helped to establish the Masikhule Rural Development Centre. Funded through the offices of the Catholic Welfare Bureau, it operated from the premises of the local Roman Catholic church. Masikhule drew on the talents of some of the women who had worked in the Advice Office and in UWO and the Civic Organisation. It concentrated on community development through facilitating education bursaries, offering literacy classes to adults and providing leadership training to women. It was a nodal point for groups meeting to discuss land reform. The centre also boasted a crèche and, until 1998, housed a rape crisis and domestic abuse counselling facility headed by Thandiwe Silere, who had been involved in political activities in the 1980s and became president of the local branch of the ANC post-1994.

In 1989, Mirriam was detained for the fourth time and held in Pollsmoor prison in Cape Town. She does not know why she was detained: she was neither questioned nor charged. She was held in a communal cell with women who had been detained from all over the Western Cape and spent five months in detention before being released.

Mirriam's community and political activities did not end there. Between 1996 and 1999, she was a member of the Community Policing Forum, an organisation established after the first democratic elections to liaise between the police and the Zwelethemba community. She was a member of the ANC Women's League and various committees. She protested vigorously against abuse of women even before her daughter, Cecilia, a pre-school teacher, was raped and murdered in 1996. Mirriam raised funds and built a crèche in Zwelethemba in her memory in 1998.

Although she had been detained four times, held twice for three months at a time in solitary confinement, and her home had been subject to police surveillance and searches, her children threatened and beaten, and her life threatened, and although she was in regular contact with the Commission, Mirriam did not make a statement about gross violations of human rights.[8] She stated that others had suffered more than she and that, as she was employed, she had no need of reparation. Instead, she took on a nurturing role in relation to the community. In addition to acting as liaison person, she was a community briefer for the Commission's public hearing held in Worcester between 24 and 26 July 1996. In this capacity, she accompanied testifiers, sitting beside them on the stage as they spoke to the panel of Commissioners and members of the HRVC and comforting them if they cried. She provided support for testifiers and deponents even after the hearings ended, when she continued to liaise between the Commission and Zwelethemba residents. Her efforts in that regard were not always successful as people held her responsible for the Commission's failures to communicate information. Mirriam also facilitated referrals to the Cape Town-based Trauma Centre and created links with a programme called the 'Healing of the Memories' that provided support for testifiers.

In many ways, her efforts have been directed at social recuperation: through attempts to secure better working conditions and proper local governance, through support for young people's protest and the activities of anti-apartheid organisations, through assistance to the poor and harshly treated, through the establishment of community development projects. They are activities aimed at assuring the future of variously defined communities. They have not always been successful: as I explained above, many activists hold her at a distance and she has been accused of nepotism. Yet her efforts in reshaping social relations have wider resonance with the ideals and experiences of women of her generation and political persuasions in Zwelethemba. I suggest that they have to do with labours in the remaking of everyday life.

REMAKING THE EVERYDAY

In considering the everyday and its reconstitution, I draw from Njabulo Ndebele's (1984) keynote address to the conference *New Writing in Africa* held at the Commonwealth Institute in London. In his paper 'The rediscovery of the ordinary: some new writings in South Africa', he compared what he called 'literature of the spectacular' with what he characterised as 'the rediscovery of the ordinary'. The literature of the spectacular (often known as 'protest literature') is characterised by 'a highly dramatic, highly demonstrative form of ... representation' (1994: 41) that uses a simplistic causality to generate a shock response. It consists of 'stories revealing the spectacular ugliness of the South African situation in all its forms' (p. 44). Ndebele views the spectacular critically:

The spectacular documents; it indicts implicitly; it is demonstrative, preferring exteriority to interiority; it keeps the larger issues of society in our minds, obliterating the details; it provokes identification through recognition and feeling rather than through observation and analytical thought; it calls for emotion rather than conviction; it establishes a vast sense of presence without offering intimate knowledge; it confirms without necessarily offering a challenge. It is the literature of the powerless identifying the key factor responsible for their powerlessness. Nothing beyond this can be expected of it. [p. 49]

He is more approving of the shift in the late 1970s and early 1980s towards a literary concern with 'the ordinary'. The opposite of the spectacular, 'the ordinary is sobering rationality; it is the forcing of attention on necessary detail' (p. 53). A focus on the ordinary engages with the complexities of people's efforts to constitute themselves and their relationships in the contexts of apartheid. Ndebele holds the rediscovery of the ordinary to be core to both the individual and society. He claims that it produces a growth in individual consciousness (p. 53) and provides an impetus to social regeneration through recognition of apartheid's infliction of ugliness on people's lives and of their efforts to manage the distorted possibilities it permitted (p. 57). Ndebele points out that:

... [w]e must contend with the fact that even under the most oppressive of conditions, people are always trying and struggling to maintain a semblance of normal social order. They will attempt to apply tradition and custom to manage their day-to-day family problems: they will resort to socially acquired behaviour patterns to eke out a means of subsistence. They apply systems of values that they know. Often those values will undergo changes under certain pressing conditions. The transformation of those values constitutes the essential drama in the lives of ordinary people. [p. 55]

Ndebele makes no claims about the efficacy of efforts to sustain and reconstitute the ordinary. Rather, his argument suggests that by examining both people's efforts and their assessments of these, scholars may come closer to an understanding of harm, recognising that efforts at social reconstitution are not always successful.

Of course, as feminists have long pointed out, achieving the ordinary may not be intrinsically liberating. Susan Griffin cautions: 'Ordinary. What an astonishing array of images hide behind this word. The ordinary is of course never ordinary. I think of it now as a kind of a mask, ... a mask that falls like a dead weight over the human face, making flesh a stationary object ...' (1992: 120). Implicit in her comment is a warning that attempts to re-establish the ordinary draw from cultural repertoires that are not neutral and may have detrimental effects. Nevertheless, in actual contexts of extreme repression and violence (as opposed to their literary representation), such as those that prevailed in the mid-1980s – the repeated States of Emergency, the extremes and increasing scale of state repression and violence and the challenges of resistance – the ordinary must have taken on elusive qualities. Perhaps here 'recreation' of the ordinary might be more apt than Ndebele's 'rediscovery' – a dreaming of and acting on new possibilities to achieve an 'ideal everyday'. In an ideal everyday, facets of life scarcely imaginable under apartheid – the possibilities of living coherent lives unhindered by pass laws and exploitative work conditions, for example, or the cessation of violence, or the non-disruption of efforts to secure valued goals – might be achievable, might even come to be taken for granted. In short, 'the recreation of the ordinary' draws attention to efforts toward a *desirable* ordinariness, rather than simply the *possible* ordinary or the *permissible* ordinary available to those enduring apartheid.

Among the events remembered with pride in Zwelethemba is the 'Peace March' held on 18 August 1985. A State of Emergency had been declared in 36 magisterial districts in South Africa on 21 July 1985. Worcester was not one of them, but the police presence in Zwelethemba was marked. Police patrolled the township on foot and in motor vehicles, sometimes in plain clothes. Informants recall that a surveillance tower was erected in the middle of the township and was manned 24 hours a day by armed policemen. A police tent was erected at the sole entrance to and exit from Zwelethemba. Police conducted random searches of buses entering the township and sometimes detained people arbitrarily. Youths boycotted school. The police response was brutal: they chased children, whipping them back to school and locking them inside the school property. At night, the youth organisations and members of banned organisations ('the underground') met to strategise and hold political discussions. They were constantly harassed. Many people were detained and their treatment was cruel.

Determined to put an end to police surveillance and violence in the township, Neliswa Mroxiswa addressed the members of UWO after a vigil for Nation Bahume who had been killed by the police on 16 August 1985. She remembers that she addressed them boldly:

Moeders, wat kan ons maak as hulle ons lokasie so deurmekaar is. Ons slaap nie meer nie, want bly die doef-doef-doef deur die yard in. Moet net die deur oopmaak dan hardloop die kinders in, dis onder die bed in, en reg rondom die huis, in die toilets en ek weet nie wat om te doen.

Moeders, julle weet julle kan teen by die dinge staan. Die kinders gaan seerkry. What kan ons eintlik maak? Ek is die voorsitter van die Women's League, wat kan ons maak? ...

Is julle bang? Laat ons vir hulle kan loop 'face', laat hulle kan uitgaan ...

Moeders, ons gaan vir hulle sê ons baklei nie, en hulle gaan sien ons is moeders. Ons baklei nie, ons doen niks met onse hande nie, ons kom praat net die dinge. [Mroxisa 1997: 41]

(Mothers, what can we do about the turmoil they've caused in our location? We don't sleep any more because of the 'doef-doef-doef' [the sound of bullets or explosions] in the yard. We open the door and the children run inside, hide under the bed and run through the house, into the toilets, and I don't know what to do.

Mothers, you know you can stand against these things. The children will be hurt. What can we actually do? I am the Chairperson of the Women's League [UWO]: what can we do? ...

Are you afraid? Let's make them [the police] turn around and leave ...

Mothers, we'll go and tell them we are not fighting, and they are going to see that we are mothers. We are not fighting, we are doing nothing with our hands [that is, we are not armed], we come only to discuss things.)

The women were afraid. They had just cause: police brutality was clearly in evidence. Yet they agreed to march to the tent-base at the entrance of the township. They set to work: spreading word of the proposed march, planning the route, briefing the proposed speakers and making placards. Some people tried to stop them. Men, including church ministers, warned that they would be killed or that the march would bring further reprisals on the residents. The women were not deterred. Neliswa remembers telling one minister who tried to prevent the march:

As ek moet dood, sal ek net vandag dood. Maar ons gaan nou nie meer dit toelaat laat die boere uit die dorp hier kom bly tussen ons nie, en ons slaap nie. Ons kinders hardloop op en af die hele nag. [Mroxisa 1997: 42]

(If I have to die, I'll die today. But we are no longer going to allow the whites[9] from the town to come and stay here and disrupt our sleep. Our children run up and down the whole night.)

On 18 August, the day of the march and two days after Bahume's death, afraid but determined, the marchers lined up in rows of five and strode to the entrance of Zwelethemba. Gradually, they were joined by the most radical members of the youth organisations and by men. Neliswa estimated that half the township joined the march, but research notes supplied by the Commission to the media during the Worcester hearing state that there were 300 protesters.

As they approached the police station, Neliswa told the marchers to stop singing: *'Julle moet doodstil staan ... net doodstil loop. En julle kan sien as ons voor die polisie kom, gaan julle almal op julle kniëe val, and julle roer niks nie.'* ('You must stand dead still ... walk dead quietly. And when you see that we are in front of the police station, you must fall to your knees and do not stir up anything.')

Led by the women, the procession came to a halt before a row of policemen who stood with their weapons at the ready. The women were afraid. No one wanted to address the police. Nongeteni Mfengu, a recent recruit to UWO and heavily pregnant, stepped hesitantly forward and began to speak. Neliswa took over. She explained that the marchers did not come to cause trouble but to talk. She addressed the head of the police, Mr Swarts, and negotiated an agreement: if the township was quiet then the police presence would be reduced.

As she relayed the settlement conditions to her comrades, they shouted, *'Viva!'* in approval. Suspicious, the policeman asked Neliswa what they were saying. *'Nee, hulle se maar net, Dankie! Dankie!'* ('No, they are just saying, Thank you! Thank you!') He seemed satisfied with the answer. The marchers chanted *'Qabane! Qabane!'* ('Comrade! Comrade!'). Again the policeman asked what they were saying. Neliswa replied that they were saying, *'Die baas is groot!'* ('The boss is great!')

The marchers returned home and spread the word of the agreement. The policeman, Swarts, asked to see Neliswa and Harris Sibeko (a member of the 'Committee of Seven', elected from the members of the Zwelethemba Residents' Association to negotiate with the local authorities) in private the following day. Fearing a trick, Lizo Kapa, also one of the members of the Committee of Seven, told Neliswa to let Sibeko go alone to discuss whatever events might arise during the night. Sibeko met with Swarts who told him that the police had been undisturbed that night and that should they pass another night in peace, they would begin to withdraw from the township. Another night passed quietly. Neliswa recalled that the following day, a Wednesday, when she returned home from her work at the Advice Office, her husband met her at the door. Laughing, he lifted her into the air and told her that the police had left: *'Nee man jong, julle vrouens is mos sterk. Julle het so gepraat, die groot tent is uitmekaar uit, daar's nie meer 'n tent nie!'* (He exclaimed: 'You women are so strong. You spoke: the big tent has been taken away; there's no longer a tent there!') (Mroxisa 1997: 45). A sole van remained to patrol the township.

Neliswa's recall is selective. The march was not as successful in reducing the police presence and consequent violence as she remembers it. On 25 August 1985, a week after the Peace March, a delegation of Black Sash members held talks with the police to try to defuse conflict in Zwelethemba, and Mirriam Moleleki was arrested between the time of the march and Bahume's funeral on 30 August. Whatever the reduction in the police presence, it did not last long. On 30 August, Nation Bahume was buried and, as described in Chapter 5, by November 1985, there existed an environment of extreme repression in Zwelethemba.

Notwithstanding the selectivity of Neliswa's account, the work by those that planned the march and participated in it points to their faith in a vision of normality that prevailing conditions seemed to make entirely impossible. Seeking to regenerate a community in which time and space were not defined by the presence and actions of policemen, the women knew that they ran a considerable risk in marching. They tried to defuse the risk by walking quietly and in formation, rather than *toyi-toyiing*; by supplication and negotiation; and by presenting themselves as mothers, typified, perhaps, by the bravery of a pregnant woman in addressing the police. Their gamble seemed to have paid off, confirmed in the meeting between Harris Sibeko and Swarts, and later in the police withdrawal from the township. The peace was short-lived.

Some women, like Neliswa and Nongeteni, can easily be described as heroines. Risking their lives, they stood firm in the face of danger. The actions of others are less amenable to conventional scripts of heroism. Theirs is an elusive activism. It is easy to overlook their contributions but their presence as mothers was essential to the aim of the march: to present a group of women who were concerned about their children and community and thereby win a reprieve from violence.

MOTHERING AND WOMEN'S MOBILISATION

The Peace March was undertaken in the first instance by women who had mobilised in terms of their identities as mothers of children under threat. Yet the forms of women's mobilisation and the patterns of their support for scholars and youth protesters were not universally accepted among women. Here, Neliswa Mroxisa and Vuyisile Malangeni (a young man who had worked closely with Neliswa in resistance organisations), describe to me women's mobilisation, the Peace March and the consequent changes in women's relationships with one another:

Vuyisile: There were boycotts that began in the 1980s and women were brought into the struggle because their children were being victimised by the system. UWO began in Cape Town – we got organised from there.

Neliswa: ... We had no public meetings, only house meetings. You would meet women and explain, recruit them in the street and in your area and explain to them why they should join. That was in the early '80s. The main problem was the question of the school boycott. The children were harassed and arrested and this took up a lot of women. The organisation [UWO] got a lot of members.

That was the 1980s. Women were afraid to join the organisations but the organisations captured women ...

During 1983 there were UWO campaigns like the rent issue ... when the rents went up. And then there was this thing with the unmarried women: they were not allowed to keep their houses and they were just thrown out, evicted by the councillors.

Vuyisile: ... Old women did everything. There was the 'One Million Signature campaign' of the UDF [a campaign to petition Parliament with signatures of those opposed to apartheid]. The women were the main people [involved]. After the UDF was launched, the women embarked on the questions of the bus boycott because the fares went up. The [company] was forced to lower its prices.

Neliswa: In March 1983, the Advice Office was formed. I worked there ... [Its] committee ... involved [representatives of] all the organisations. Women spearheaded it. It was for legal issues, especially at work, at home. We gave advice and then the person who came [seeking advice] would join UWCO or the Civic or the Youth [organisations]. After we helped, they would join ... Then in 1985 there was the big march.

Vuyisile: ... The women with the Youth Congress organised the march ...

Neliswa: No! The *women* organised the march and the youth joined to make it big.

Fiona Ross: You see! Already these youths are changing history! ...

Neliswa: Some of the women hid themselves but they left children to be involved in the struggle. They did not want to go to jail, so they denied they were involved, but they were part of the struggle.

The conversation describes patterns of recruitment into local organisations in the 1980s. Those who sought assistance from the Advice Office often became members of UDF-affiliated structures; women were recruited by word of mouth to join UWO (later UWCO); people joined organisations after the successful resolution of disputes such as increases in rent and bus fares. Neliswa observes that women were afraid to join organisations. Their fear was justified – after all, the punishment endured by activists was well known and police brutality was an everyday feature of life in Zwelethemba. At other times, the fear derived from having seen the hurt experienced by an older generation that had confronted the State Security Forces. For example, Nothemba Ngcwecwe, who recruited women from Robertson to the Boland branch of UWO and who later worked with Neliswa and Mirriam Moleleki in the Advice Office, was initially afraid to join UWO. Her mother had been active in the ANC's political activities in Worcester in the late 1950s and early in 1960. She had taken part in the pass protest in Zwelethemba on 28 March 1960 and had been imprisoned. In prison she was left to lie on a cold cement floor, given limited food of low quality and severely beaten; while there she had fallen ill with an untreated lung infection that continued to trouble her after her release. Despite her experiences in detention, she had continued her political activities, but her health did not recover. Nothemba attributes her mother's death in 1965, when Nothemba was 22, to the weakness that resulted from her lung infection.

Nothemba remembers that, 'I didn't like the United Women's Organisation because I thought it was something that would take women to jail' (Ngcwecwe 1997: 8). She was concerned about the effects of activism: her mother's experiences and the severe injuries sustained by her sister's child who was struck on the head when the police shot rubber bullets during the student protests of June 1976, made her wary. Nothemba remembers explaining why she was refusing to join UWO early in 1984 to her friend Mirriam Moleleki: 'I don't want to join you because if I join you maybe I will land up how my mother landed up. No, not me. My mother suffered [because of] the organisation. Not me! I am not going to follow her steps. Now I am motherless because of this ANC business!' (Ngcwecwe 1997: 9).

In 1985, Nothemba eventually did join. Neliswa came to Robertson to collect recruitment forms for UWO that she had asked Nothemba to distribute among farm labourers and residents in the small town. Nothemba handed over the forms and Neliswa told her, 'We can't take the forms unless they have the organiser's signature.' Nothemba replied that she would not sign. Neliswa reminded her that, 'Your husband works at the police station' (he was a cleaner at the Robertson charge office) and intimated that if she did not sign, people might suspect a trap: that she was planning to ask her husband to give the list to the police. Neliswa's warning contained a hint of threat. Nothemba joined the organisation and was elected to the portfolio of Organiser. She soon overcame her wariness and became deeply involved in organised resistance in the Boland.

As a direct consequence of ever more harsh state oppression and violence during the period after 1980, the ranks of organisations such as UWO swelled. Women's conventional roles as protectors of the domestic realm were reframed by those who sought to articulate a different vision of family, community and nation from the one possible under apartheid. However, women's relations with one another were neither simple nor homogenous. The activities of members of UWO generated conflict between men and women and among women themselves. Some of the tensions were expressed through the idiom of culturally appropriate mothering practices: women activists were accused of being inadequate mothers and betraying cultural ideals of motherhood both by engaging in protest and by supporting activities that placed young people in danger from the police. Young activists frequently recall their parents' concern about their activities and about the parenting qualities of those who were perceived as leading the youth in revolution against the state and in rebellion against traditional sources of authority in the home.

Nothemba Ngcwecwe described some responses to women's organisations and activities: 'Some women were angry. Some women had children who were involved but the women were not. They said we were misleading the children by encouraging them.' Mirriam Moleleki elaborated on the difficulties:

Women played a nice role, because we used the churches and the schools, you know, to pass messages when the organisations were banned. It was the only way to pass messages because the laws were so restrictive. The only way to get a message to children was in school, where they could discuss it.

But people hated some of us. They said we were misleading the children. Some women said that we were not allowing their children to be educated. Someone wrote a pamphlet [and circulated it in the high school] in Zwelethemba. It said, 'Do not listen to Mirriam Moleleki. She has sent her children to school in Qwa-Qwa and now wants to use you against the government.'

Mirriam's son, Tumelo was, at that time, attending secondary school in Qwa Qwa. Until 1980, there was no secondary school in Zwelethemba. Students wishing to continue with their education attended schools elsewhere in the country. Although Vusisizwe Secondary School was built in 1980, some parents who could afford to send their children to better schools did so. Parents' concerns about the loss of education incurred by children engaged in political activities indicate the importance of parental strategies to secure an uncertain future. The vision for which young people and those who supported them fought did not neatly articulate with the ideas of those who invested scarce resources in their children's education in the hopes that children might be better off than they were. To see their investment put at risk must have been hard. In response, they confronted women activists suggesting that they had deviated from valued cultural and social norms. Mirriam remembered: 'You know, they said we were acting against our culture in teaching those children politics. They said we were wrong. They told me I was betraying my culture. They used culture against us.'

Women's mobilisation in support of institutions such as the family are often read by feminist writers and scholars as conservative and as a defence of patriarchal systems of power (see Gaitskill and Unterhalter 1989; and discussion in Charman, de Swardt and Simons, 1991). The argument owes much to Cherryl Walker's *Women and Resistance in South Africa*, an historical study of women's organisations and the changing patterns of women's protest between 1910 and 1962, that was banned when it was first published in 1982. Walker argues that the mobilisation of women as mothers was inherently conservative because it did not challenge male authority or patriarchal power. In a later edition of the book, she noted 'feminist moments' (1991: xxiv) when women's demands ran counter to male domination. In 1995, Walker further modified her position. She suggested that:

The labels 'conservative' or 'progressive' are not particularly useful for understanding women's behaviour. They are normative ... and they discount both the process (the way in which identities may shift and change in relation to concrete historical developments) and women's own part in constructing their identities as mothers – identities [that] ... extend beyond relationships with men. [1995: 436–7]

Women insisted on the political nature of their roles as mothers and custodians of family life. As Judy Kimble and Elaine Unterhalter (1982) point out, women who opposed apartheid did so specifically through their under-standing of the damage caused by apartheid to family life: 'Whereas women in the West have identified the family as a site of women's oppression, women in South Africa point to the destruction of "normal family life" as one of the most grievous crimes of Apartheid' (1982: 13). The damage to family life is confirmed in the Commission's Report:

Apartheid generated a crisis in South African family life. Group Areas legislation and forced removals have both been linked to disruptions in healthy family functioning, and the migrant labour system also deprived people of family life ... In trying to deal with these problems, extended family networks came into play.

The pressure on families was relentless. [Volume Five: 142]

Hylton White has suggested that women mobilised around what he calls 'organic domesticity' (1994: 34). His study of women kin of male political prisoners held on Robben Island traces ways in which appeals to an organic notion of family had the effect of transforming kin relations into a legitimate site of confrontation with the state. In this, his argument has continuities with a growing body of literature on women's mobilisation elsewhere which explores the transformation of motherhood to make political and social demands.[10] White argues that politics 'has to do with the local worlds of morality that occupy – and are occupied by – the daily concerns of social agents' (p. 48). His argument is strongly reminiscent of Ndebele's claim that it is in the ordinariness of life that the potential for social change must lie. White's argument interrogates the too simple distinction between public and private space. He suggests that women's recourse to kinship moralities reflects their attempts 'to circumscribe the domestic arena so as to limit and reverse the damage to its relative interruption' (p. 47). In other words, formulations of kinship and of motherhood provide idioms through which an alternative image of the world *and* recuperative efforts to achieve it can be articulated.

Although motherhood was important in mobilising women, it would be misleading to suggest that political consciousness was derived solely from children's protest activities. Some of those mobilised under the rubric of 'mothering' drew from a powerful political critique generated as a consequence of appalling working conditions on farms and in factories and the establishment of and forced removals to Zwelethemba in 1954. Alongside the political education offered in resistance organisations, people drew from the examples set by predecessors, from a long history of political activities, and from their own political enthusiasms and experience. For example, although she frequently traces her political activities to her son's detention, Mirriam Moleleki had been involved in trade union activity and in the

Zwelethemba Residents' Association before his detention. Nothemba Ngcwecwe traces the roots of her political knowledge to her mother's political activities. Nongenti Mfengu, an early recruit to UWO who worked closely with Mirriam, Neliswa and Nothemba, remembers the harsh conditions of work as a child labourer on the grape farms of the region and in the packing yards of Langeberg canning factory as providing a stringent introductory political consciousness. Yvonne Khutwane was involved in pass law protests in 1960. As a young woman and an ANC member, she had gone from door to door with comrades collecting the mandatory *dompas* from each adult resident and burning the passes in Freedom Square. Like many other women, Yvonne Khutwane described her political consciousness as having its roots in personal experience and in the maintenance of everyday life:

You see, here in South Africa, we live with politics. If you say the bread is stale, that's already politics! We are not all the same. You get people who can sit and shiver with worry about a problem. You get people who don't shiver, who will stand up and say, 'Maybe I can change things.' At Vusisizwe [school] the children were boycotting. I saw children jumping over high fences. They were being chased by the police. How can you then sit and say, 'I won't do politics'? What is going on? I go there, and here come the soldiers. They were hitting children with batons. I went to them and asked why they were beating girls. He did not worry about me [that is, he didn't pay any attention] so I held his *sjambok*. Then someone threw teargas. There was smoke. I was coughing. The girl had a chance to run. The man was respectful: he did not *sjambok* me. He said, 'Go home! Your children are naughty!' Mrs Bentele brought me a wet cloth for my face to stop the burning.

Is this not politics?

One day in the cold I was standing outside in the yard of my mother's house. Two white policemen called me from a Casspir: '*Vroumens!*' [Woman!]. I said, 'I have a name.' '*Kaffirmeid*! [Kaffir girl] Why are you standing there?' 'I'm in my own mother's yard.' I stood. One came down from the Casspir. 'Can't you hear me?' he said. I said, 'Where am I standing? In my mother's yard.'

Is this not politics?

All the whites made us get into politics in South Africa. Themselves!

I was a smart [clever] teenager. One day they [representatives of the Bantu Affairs Administration Board] told us to come and collect the *dompas*. It was so hot, so hot, so hot. All of us were in a long queue [waiting to collect passes]. It was a *dompas*, in a bag to wear over your shoulder. We realised we were trapped by it.

Is that not politics?

Wat hulle vir ons gedoen het, dit maak ons politiek. [What they did to us made us political.] We had to be political. You could be endorsed out after two years.[11] I was red-stamped, '*uit Worcester uit*' [out of Worcester]. I was told to go to Mdantsane [in the Eastern Cape]. They chased me like an animal. I had to rush out of the window. Like an animal! I did not register and so I was endorsed out. It was not the ANC that made me 'mad' like this! My mother said I should go to her brother in Jamestown near Aliwal North. I refused to go. She had lawyers. They were *skelms* [rascals]. They said they could do nothing, 'It's the law.' My mother wasted her money. I grabbed my two children and went to BAAB [the Bantu Affairs Administration Board]. I said, in Afrikaans, 'Here I am with my two children. Call your police van and take me and

the children to jail forever. I will not leave here. I'll never run.' I took the children –
one was a baby – and (I wish I had a picture of it!) I sat outside the office, waiting for
the van. Sitting, sitting. I had never been to prison. Sitting. People coming in and out.
Sitting, sitting. The child said she was thirsty. I fed her an orange. Sitting. Gunther
[the head of Bantu Affairs in the area] called Soga [the translator/clerk]. He told him
to bring the reference book and he re-stamped it. I am still here in Worcester.

Is that not politics?

If I were not strong, I would not be here. Is that not politics?

My *ouma* [Afrikaans: grandmother], my *oupa* [Afrikaans: grandfather], my pa, they
are all dead here. It is just my mother who remains. A European woman asked what
was going on and she sympathised, but she would not say it was wrong.

That is politics.

Yvonne Khutwane describes political mobilisation as a consequence of the
wrongs inflicted by apartheid. Pass laws, police violence against children,
the power of state functionaries to 'endorse out', and the failure of
sympathetic whites to denounce apartheid furthered self-reliance and
continued to invigorate political critique and activism.

Some women extended the critique and formulated a political consciousness that expressly took account of oppressive gender relations. While
working to end apartheid, such women were simultaneously involved in
activities designed to empower women in a patriarchal society. Nothemba
Ngcwecwe described how she and others recruited women to join UWO: 'We
recruited by explaining and at gatherings we would speak in public. We
would say, "If we do not fight, no one will fight for *women's rights*." We said,
"We must protect our children who have begun this action."'

In Nothemba's interpretation, 'the struggle' was both to secure children's
well-being and to fight for 'women's rights' against patriarchal structures,
including 'Xhosa culture'. Her perspective is informed by personal
experience. Even a cursory examination of her life history pinpoints
numerous moments when conventional gender scripts harmed or failed her
badly or when men were able to manipulate their interests to her detriment.

In 1949, when Nothemba was six years old, her father, a teacher,
abandoned her pregnant mother, her brother and herself in Sterkstroom,
Transkei. A few years later he abducted the three children and took them to
live with his other wife in Port Elizabeth. There, Nothemba cooked and
cleaned and cared for her stepbrother. She was not allowed to attend school.
Eventually the children engineered an escape and returned to their mother.
She died in 1965, and, because Nothemba was not married, she was evicted
from the council house that she had shared with her mother. Nothemba's
first relationship ended after she had borne two children who were sent to
live with her partner's first wife in Herschel, Transkei. She attempted to
maintain contact with them across the distance. In 1980, she met another
man and in 1982 bore the first of their three children. He divorced his wife
and Nothemba went to Robertson to live with him. He had a reputation for
brutality against women but initially treated Nothemba well. By 1985,

however, she discovered that he was a philanderer. Their relationship deteriorated as her political activities increased. She decided to leave him. When she told him, he hit her with his fist and then began to beat her with a whip. Neighbours intervened and as they were calming him, she escaped. She was forced to abandon all her possessions: at the time, adult African women were not, in law, considered to have attained majority and she was unable to secure an interdict against her partner.

Mirriam Moleleki, too, describes the demands that an oppressive patriarchal society may make on women. She bore her first child in 1962, at the age of 18. An unmarried mother, she continued living in De Doorns with her mother who had agreed to support her. Relatives of the child's father tried to persuade Mirriam to marry Zacharias Moleleki, but she refused. Then he persuaded her to visit him in Worcester. She was reluctant but went. When she arrived, she was forcibly married in a traditional ceremony. She managed to run away a few days later but the family recaptured her and she remained with them. Her husband treated her well, even foregoing customary expectations that placed an enormous weight on young married women (*oomakoti*). Mirriam remembers, 'Tradition is very important ... but sometimes it can make you a slave' (Moleleki 1997: 23). She and Zacharias remain married and have five children. She persisted in her political activities, despite his displeasure. (He eventually resigned from his job as a municipal policeman in 1989.)

Sometimes women's political involvement brought them into direct conflict with men and they faced the difficulty of balancing their personal convictions and public commitments with men's demands. Nothemba described the tactics they used to reduce conflict. The tactics ranged from appeasement and conformity to conventional gender roles to assertions of rights, and drew on women's support and the threat of reprisal against recalcitrant men:

Some men tried to stop the women from attending our meetings. They did not succeed – we were very strong. We said, 'Women have rights and they have the right to go to meetings.' We used to tell [the women], 'Cook early for men so that they won't hit you.' If someone was worried about her husband [that is, afraid of a beating] then they would be accompanied by someone from the meeting. The men knew that if he beat the woman we would face them. We said they [men] should help us at home.

Not all women made clear links between gender oppression and 'the struggle'. Some women joined in resistance activities (such as rent, bus and consumer boycotts) because they were directly affected. Others contributed to the revolutionary atmosphere that pervaded the township by attending rallies, funerals, political meetings, marches and by participating in protest and boycotts. In addition to a strong sense of personal commitment, there was considerable community pressure to engage in such actions.

There are clear patterns in women's mobilisation. Periods of peak activity in Zwelethemba occurred from the late 1950s-61; 1976–78; 1985–90 and

1990–94. These periods correspond to the broader contours of change in Zwelethemba: women were actively involved in opposing the pass laws in the late 1950s until the banning of the ANC and PAC in 1960 and the incarceration of activists who campaigned against the pass laws. They were also involved in trade union activities in that period. In the mid-1970s, women in Zwelethemba joined the Zwelethemba Residents Association and between 1976 and 1977 some supported youths involved in protest. In 1980, youths in Zwelethemba engaged in school boycotts. The Bantu Affairs Administration Board deployed constables to quell resistance. Some parents tried to force their children to attend school. The children refused. Much of the youth leadership was detained and a number of young people fled into exile. By 1985, parental support of children's activities had grown considerably, due in large measure to the roles played by female members of organisations affiliated to the UDF. Women's political mobilisation solidified with the formation of the Boland branch of UWO, which provided a clear role for women. Between 1985 and 1990, during the States of Emergency, women were involved in UWO and other organs of mass mobilisation such as trades unions. Since 1990, women in Zwelethemba have been actively involved in joining the ANC and in establishing the local branch of the ANC Women's League.

Women's political consciousness drew on an awareness of harm, a determination to maintain social relations stretched to breaking point by apartheid policies and violence, and a capacity to imagine a future in which 'ordinary' social relationships might be taken for granted. The visions of the future that different protagonists in 'the struggle' held were neither homogenous nor necessarily easily achieved over time. In generating and sustaining resistance to the state, activists had to manage diverse ideas and trajectories, different commitments and multiple forms of activism. It is not accurate to suggest a simple dichotomy between those who were active and those who were not. It seems, rather, that with the exception of a few central characters, many women's political engagement waxed and waned. This does not mean that their political will was weak, or that they were harder to mobilise than men. It points rather to the diversity of routes through which women achieved political knowledge and made decisions. For many, political engagement was not determined by a single trajectory of 'the struggle' but by complex and fluctuating sets of relationships with people and institutions including the articulation of patterns of intimate relations, childbirth and marriage with the shifting contours and temporalities of violence.

Writing of women's political activities and commitments in Northern Ireland, Begonia Aretxaga proposes that

... political agency – the capacity of people to become historical subjects deliberately intervening in the making and changing of their worlds – is the product of a movement that goes back and forth from discursive possibility to experience to change in the conditions of possibility. Political agency thus presupposes a degree of consciousness and intentionality ... but it is anchored in a cultural respository of largely unconscious discourses and images, modes of thinking and feeling. [1997: 8]

She draws from Joan Scott (1991) who, in criticising social explanations that rest on unexamined appeals to 'experience', argues convincingly that agency is not an automatic characteristic of the individual but a consequence of historical discourses that constitute subjects at particular times and in certain places. Deborah Battaglia, too, suggests that agency is not fixed, that it does not attach to an autonomous individual (the 'self'), and that it has a propensity to 'travel' (1999: 141). Drawing on post-structuralist philosophy, she argues that 'the self is a representational economy' and suggests a notion of identity in which people draw from an 'integratory capacity' to create a sense of cohesion and continuity. For her, the self is 'a chronically unstable project brought situationally – not invariably – to some form of order, shaped to some purpose, consciously or otherwise, in indeterminate social practice' (p. 116). The subject is relational, emergent, its power neither intrinsic nor sovereign. For Battaglia, agency and the intentions of an autonomous individual are not coterminous. She argues that 'to represent agency as individually or constantly situated would be a breach of ethics' (p. 141) because the representation would fail to take into account the shifting grounds of verisimilitude in which subjects act or are constrained from acting. For Scott, Aretxaga and Battaglia, agency is not an attribute of the self but a product of the intersection between the mutually constitutive processes of subject formation and particular historical moments.

Some women in Zwelethemba were politically engaged for the duration of the struggle and beyond: testament to their convictions and to the efforts of organisations that they created to wrest from changing conditions of possibility the space to reconceptualise social relations. If Battaglia's argument holds true, then the efforts of those who have managed to win to themselves the possibility of sustained action so that it becomes both an attribute of the self and is externalised into realised visions, are still more admirable. If agency is but a fleeting phenomenon, how extraordinary the effort to sustain actions that make a difference.

NARRATIVE CONVENTIONS AND A TRICKSTER SCRIPT

Philosopher Stanley Cavell has suggested that agency might be considered as a coming into one's own powers, finding a voice worthy of the self (1994:135). If so, then one might expect to find different expressions of selfhood in narrative forms other than those conventionally available in the language of rights and their violation on which the Commission's work was predicated. When women who were instrumental in organising resistance in Zwelethemba describe their activities and experiences they draw on many of the same narrative conventions as did women who testified before the Commission. However, they also put tropes to work in ways that are unlike those used by many testifiers. They speak of their roles in resistance with pride and passion. They seldom draw on the Commission's powerful tropes of 'heroes/martyrs in the struggle' or 'victims' or 'perpetrators' to describe themselves. In Commission hearings, the experience of violation was often recast as 'sacrifice'. Commissioners frequently identified their task as being to alert the populace to the loss, couched as sacrifice, of childhood and youth, life opportunities, and, in some cases, lives, for the struggle. Women testifiers were thanked for the 'sacrifice' of their dead or injured kin and testifiers were frequently told that their sacrifices (of health, well-being or the lives of those close to them) had redemptive power for the national body. Suffering and sacrifice, heavily predicated on a Christian model, were depicted as consti- tutive of the foundational order of 'the new South Africa'. Older women activists in Zwelethemba seldom used notions of sacrifice when they spoke about the past. They did not often depict themselves as victors or as violated. Willing to advise about the harms inflicted on others, few accounted for the violence that they suffered themselves. Recognising damage in others, they do not easily attribute it to self.

Drawing on narrative conventions that are similar to those I have described in Chapter 2, women activists' accounts of harm are often elliptical, allusive. Yet their expression of activism is lively and confrontational. They clearly identify the self as the locus of a powerful and enduring morality. Their sense of choice and action is carried in their use of the trickster figure, that uses wit and skill to outmanoeuvre opponents. In its use, activists' narrative strategies are markedly different from those utilised by women testifiers before the Commission. In the hearings that I attended, only one woman drew on the trickster figure to describe her experiences. Testifying on 8 August 1996 before the Women's Hearing in Cape Town, Shirley Gunn described how she had convinced policemen that she was able to produce excessive quantities of breast milk for her child detained with her. She believed that the tactic made the police fearful of her feminine characteris- tics. (Her testimony and the incident are described in Chapter 3.) It may be that women are more likely to describe themselves in terms of the trickster figure when describing their own experiences, and because most women testified about men, the trope was less striking in public hearings than it was in discussions outside of the Commission. However, while older women drew readily on the trope, young women did not make use of it before the Commission or in private conversation when describing either their political activities or the harms they had suffered. By contrast, young men made frequent use of the trickster motif in our informal discussions.

I have already described Mirriam Moleleki's delight in tricking farmers by pretending to preach religion when in fact she was preaching politics. Some of the women recruited in this manner became important figures in local resistance.[12] On one occasion when Mirriam was detained, her daughter prevented police from searching one room in the house by removing her clothes and appealing to conventions of decency. I have also described

Neliswa's quick-witted translation of her comrades' words to the policeman who demanded to know what her comrades were shouting. Realising that their chants could jeopardise the concessions she had won, she not only mistranslated their words but also altered them through a language of *baaskap* to carry overtones of submission.

Examples of the kinds of trickster tales that are told in Zwelethemba abound. Nothemba Ngcwecwe, for example, described a police search in June 1985 in the small township attached to Robertson, where she was then living. The police were searching for all known political activists in the area after the local administration offices had been razed. Nothemba was one of the people they wished to detain, as they knew she was a leader in local resistance structures. While she was ironing her dry washing, a neighbour came to warn her of the police search. It was too late for her to hide. Hurriedly wetting her husband's newly washed and ironed uniform, which showed him to be in police employ, she hung it out on the line so that it was visible from the road: 'I took out his ironed shirt and put it on the sofa with his hat and trousers. Then the police arrived [conducting a] door-to-door [search]. The police, seeing my husband's clothes said, "Oh, this is a policeman's house" and left.' Their expectation that a policeman would never allow his wife to be engaged in political subversion blinded them to her identity.

In describing the scene, Nothemba placed herself into the role of trickster, outwitting the police through use of gender stereotypes. The stereotypes concerned not only women's tasks but also assumptions of gender control within households, so that a man was presumed to hold power over his wife's activities, and would therefore disallow particular kinds of political engagement.

An incident of cross-dressing enjoyed wide currency in a repertoire of stories that placed activists as tricksters in relation to unimaginative state functionaries. I tell it below as related by a male colleague, Nana Khohlokoane:

One day, news came to those in the township that there was to be a door-to-door raid to find the men. Someone in the town heard about it and hurried back to Zwelethemba to spread the word: 'All the men in the township must hide.' People knew that the consequences of detention were dire. Yet, by the time the news arrived, the men could not leave the township. Zwelethemba has only one entrance and exit and it was guarded by police. At the end of the township there is a barren wasteland and a graveyard.[13] The area offers little space for hiding and less chance of evasion. Despite the lack of escape routes, when the police arrived and conducted a door-to-door search, they did not find any of the men for whom they were searching.

The men could not leave Zwelethemba. So they dressed in women's clothes, and the police did not find them.

Clad in married women's conventional daily wear – skirts, aprons, blouses, jerseys and head-scarves[14] – men succeeded in avoiding both state surveillance and the consequences of detention or arrest. In the story, men took refuge in the protection offered by policemen's stereotypic expectations of women. In the *denouement* of the story, local notions of tricksterism are introduced. Harm is avoided through sly knowledge and quick use of stereotypes.

Many women described the use of religious objects and practices to disguise their political activities. For example, Mrs Khomba, an early member of the United Women's Congress (UWCO) in the Boland, tells a story of her activities thus:

> I remember how we used to sit here in this room, all around the table. There was tea and ... our bibles and prayer books and then we used to talk politics and read banned books. All about what was going on with our organisations and the children. And when those policemen came [on door-to-door searches] they used to think we were having a prayer meeting and they would go away. Then, we laughed!

Her words make light of the weight of the consequences that she and others would have borne had they been discovered with the banned materials they read to one another. Her son, Amos, and daughter, Nowi, both spent long periods of time in detention (see Chapter 5) in connection with their political activities, and the police had on more than one occasion damaged the Khombas' property while searching for banned materials and weapons.

Writing of crisis and its figuration of the subject, Achille Mbembe and Janet Roitman argue that in contexts of 'extraordinary tension and nervousness', 'laughter is inseparable from the fear inspired by the immediate present'. They continue: '*to laugh* means not only to hypostasize domination, but also to mark the non-correspondence between objectified violence and the fear that one endeavours to admit and avert' (1995: 351–2, emphasis in the original).

Stories couched in the trickster motif describe the manipulation of social, cultural and racial stereotypes to provide protection from the police. The stories generally fall into three clusters of social experience: to do with the domestic sphere and women's roles within it, stereotypes of gender attributes, and the religious sphere. Conventional notions of women's obedience were ironically inverted or subverted. The stories, drawing on caricatures of con-servative *boere* that abound in South African popular culture, show how wit, skill and courage were pitted against the might of the state.

The stories are remarkable for their allocation of blame: the state and the Security Forces are held clearly and unambiguously to be accountable for oppression, repression and violence. Notwithstanding the humour with which the stories are told, the subject matter is neither superficial nor petty. Women always tell trickster stories in such a way as to elicit a smile or laughter, but tellers assume a familiarity with the dangers that faced those for whom the police sought and those taken in their place.

It may be that using a trickster motif to describe encounters is part of a strategy of symbolically transforming power through ridicule. Used in these ways, tricksterism draws attention to the raw power of the state and the wiliness of those attempting to outwit it. James C. Scott reads trickster tales as a cross-cultural form of 'veiled cultural resistance' by subordinate groups (1990: 162). Arguing that there are structural connections and similarities between the position and strategies of the trickster and 'the existential dilemma of subordinate groups', James suggests that trickster stories carry public messages about power relations (p. 163), carving 'a public, if provisional, space for the autonomous cultural expression of dissent' (p. 166; see also Scott 1985).

What is important about the use of the trickster motif by activist women in Zwelethemba is its divergence from the grammar of pain offered by the Commission. In the ways that women activists in Zwelethemba use the trope, the individual is reconfigured as a site of power. The narratives construct protagonists as politically engaged, as *bricoleurs* playing cultural stereotypes off against one another in practices of resistance. They place the individual at the centre of a challenge not only to the power of the state but also to the power embedded in conventional ways of seeing and doing, including (cross-) cultural constructions of gender-appropriate behaviour. The narratives locate action at the level of the individual and highlight creativity and innovation.

There are many different ways to express harm and violence. The repeated use of the trickster trope by older women and young men contrasts with the Commission's insistence on 'victims' and 'perpetrators', that, as I have described in earlier chapters, may reify pain and violence and have the effect of objectifying people and experience. Such objectification implies passivity on the part of those that suffered violence and harm and imputes an enduring damage. Trickster narratives open a discursive space that enables a consideration of the past different from that offered by the models of heroism and victimhood. Yet, the ironic or humorous stories told about 'the struggle' in Zwelethemba may obscure important facets of human experience in contexts of violence. If the Commission testimonies are limited in that they elide the collective then the stories couched in trickster mode neglect pain by emphasising autonomy. Perhaps these stories draw from a cultural repository to ward pain away. They may be likened to amulets of words that work in much the same way as Bruno Bettelheim (1980) describes for laughter: as a means to distance oneself from evil and the knowledge that one lives with it.

HUMILITY IN ACKNOWLEDGING HARM

Women activists in Zwelethemba are reluctant to identify the self as a site of violation. The reasons are not always explicit and people proffer diverse sets of reasons. Some women, such as Mirriam Moleleki, stated that they did not testify because they neither desired acknowledgement nor felt a need for reparation. Other women wished to testify but their experiences did not neatly fit the Commission's definitions of gross violations of human rights that were, at the time of its most concentrated period of work in Worcester (June to the end of July 1996), still narrowly defined.[15] Experiences such as detention without trial, which were later recognised to be gross violations of human rights, were not, at the time, considered to be such. Some women were loath to make statements that their children might one day read: the public expression of harm ran counter to local ideas about pain's expression. In this respect, women who were mothers faced particular difficulties. Motherhood is a status that traditionally carries great weight and some women felt it damaging both to conceptions of womanhood and to their relationships with future generations to declare the harms inflicted.

In general, activists did not make statements because they felt that the Commission's ideals ran counter to those that had provided impetus for struggle. Ideas about collective action and the greater good that had informed their mobilisation seemed subverted in the Commission's insistence on the primacy of individual experience. Women involved in community struggle in Zwelethemba are proud of their achievements. Believing that resistance to apartheid was morally sound, they acted out of a powerful commitment to a future vision of the ordinary and everyday – an ordinariness that apartheid policies and strictures undermined.

Of all the women who had been instrumental in leading anti-apartheid protest in Zwelethemba, only Yvonne Khutwane and Neliswa Mroxisa made statements. Neliswa Mroxisa was invited to testify in public, but refused, saying, 'My story carries no weight.' Her assertion is an effacement of experience characteristic among women who were involved in anti-apartheid and community organisations. In fact, Neliswa had been detained three times during the 1980s and brutally treated each time. The first time she was detained was in connection with the killing on 13 October 1985 of Mpazamo Bethwell Mbani (also known as Mistake Yiko), who was accused of being a sell-out and of protecting someone believed to be an *impimpi*. Neliswa was detained with 31 young men and they were charged with attempted murder. The charges against most of the youths were dropped, but Neliswa and seven young men, including her son, Mbuyiselo, were tried in a court case that ran for three years. Charges against them were eventually dropped.

Neliswa was detained a second time after she was released from prison on bail. She had returned to work at the Advice Office in Worcester and continued with her work for the UDF-affiliated organisation, UWO. Shortly after midnight on 12 June 1986, when the renewed State of Emergency came into effect, a loud banging at the door woke her. Still half-asleep, she opened the door and Lukas van Loggerenberg, a policeman, told her that he was there to detain her. He did not say why. She was loaded into a van with four other activists and taken to the Worcester police station. The police then took her to the Advice Office where she worked. They searched the premises for banned materials but did not find any. Despite their failure to find incriminating evidence, Neliswa was not released but taken to the women's prison in Worcester and separated from the others with whom she had been detained. She was held in solitary confinement for the night. Later, a number of women from the Boland were put into the cell with her: they had been detained while shopping. The following day, the group of women was taken to Pollsmoor prison in Cape Town and held for almost three months. In September 1986, Neliswa was released. She had not been charged.

On her return, she continued to work at the Advice Office and to recruit members to the UWO. She was detained for a third time in connection with a fierce conflict that had resulted in an arson attack on the home of a family that owned a bar in Zwelethemba. Some residents believed that the family members were vigilantes and that the police supported them. The family that was attacked sought Neliswa's son, Mbuyiselo, who was a student activist and whom people claimed had been instrumental in the attack. He had fled Zwelethemba and could not be found. Her daughter, returning from Worcester, was captured by an angry mob and badly beaten. The people involved told her that they believed her mother to have instigated the arson attack. An angry crowd cornered Neliswa in a neighbour's house. Quick-witted, Neliswa's mother called the police, hoping that if her daughter were detained she would not be killed by the mob. The police arrived and detained Neliswa, holding her for a month with a group of young people. Together they were charged with public violence in connection with the attack. The youths detained with her said she had not been present at the incident and, lacking concrete evidence against her, the charges were dropped and she was released. She was not detained again.

Neliswa continues her work in the ANC Women's League. She supports her extended family. She ends her written life story (Mroxisa 1997: 77) with these words:

Ek het koue dae in die tronk geslaap. Ek het koue aande sonder my kinders geslaap. En ek het gesê dit sal my kinders se kinders se rykdom wees, wat ek voor struggle. Nou, soos 'n ouma, ek het geloof met al die dinge uitgestaan. Ek het als gevoel en gesien. Ja, en deesedae in, ons sal darem die liggie sien. Nou, daar is nog hoop. Ek het nog altyd hoop. As ons nog 'n bietjie stywer kan staan, en ons sokkies net a bietjie stywer optrek, sal ons darem die liggie sien vorentoe ... As die moeders ...(ek praat nie van die boeties en die tatas nie), ek dink die moeders sal alles sorteer as hulle net 'n bietjie sterk kan staan op hulle twee voete ... En so ons kan nou ook 'n bietjie hard praat en onse stemmetjie word ook nou gehoor.

Ek is nog nie klaar nie. Ons moet nog baie dinge regmaak.

[I slept cold days in jail. I slept cold nights without my children. And I said that my children's children would inherit what I struggled for. Now, as a grandmother, I've set all those things aside. I've felt and seen everything. One of these days, we'll see the small light. Now there is still hope. I still have hope. If we can stand a little straighter, and pull our socks up a little higher, we'll soon see that small light ... As mothers (I am not talking about boys and fathers), I think the mothers will sort everything out if they can just stand a little stronger on their own two feet ... And so we can also speak out and our voices will be heard.

I am not yet finished. We must still rectify many things.]

Her declaration indicates an acute awareness of fracture and responsibility, of the fault-lines of society and the measures necessary to render them harmless. As she points out, the work of social recuperation continues in accord with a vision – 'a small light'.

REGARD FOR SOCIAL INSTITUTIONS

Veena Das and Arthur Kleinman propose that 'the recovery of the everyday, resuming the task of living (and not only surviving), asks for a renewed capability to address the future.' They note, 'While everyday life may be seen as the site of the ordinary, this ordinariness is itself recovered in the face of the most recalcitrant of tragedies: it is the site of many buried memories and experiences' (2001: 4).

In Zwelethemba, the women most instrumental in establishing anti-apartheid organisations have remained active in political organisations and CBOs or in implementing social programmes in accordance with a vision of recovering and directing the ordinary in the aftermath of violence. Their activities have to do with a concern for social institutions. There is a direct continuity with women's mobilisation in the past: they acted in defence of community, imagined variously and changeably as the family,[16] the neighbourhood, women, workers, 'the oppressed', Africans, blacks. In less dramatic ways, women activists continue to strive towards community recovery. For example, Mirriam Moleleki helped establish the Masikhule Centre in 1987 and a crèche in 1998. She is now trying to raise funds to build a bakery that will provide both food and employment. In 1979 and 1988, while working full time, Nothemba Ngcwecwe returned to night school. She completed her final year of education in 1993: that year she also attended a Delta Training Course at the University of the Western Cape and held down a full-time job. She has put her dream of women's empowerment into place through providing adult literacy classes and women's leadership programmes. Thandiwe Silere established a branch of *Ilitha laBantu* (a counselling and legal advice centre for abused women and children). In 1994, she became the first woman chairperson of the Boland branch of the ANC. Nongeteni Mfengu runs a crèche from her small shack. Neliswa Mroxisa and Yvonne Khutwane are members of the Women's League. Women activists are members of the Community Policing Forum and of the Community Peace Initiative. They are members of the committee to oversee land redistribution, and of the ANC and its Women's League.

The women who now describe themselves as 'community activists' all report feeling tired and discouraged by the small inroads they have made. Their efforts are not always appreciated, their methods not always considered appropriate, but their vision is one that aims both to restore the family and community and to invigorate trust in social conventions. It is easy to overlook their work or to discount it when faced with the enormity of the damage caused to social institutions by apartheid. To do so is to ignore the fact that they provide a ground – a recuperative space – from which new institutions can emerge.[17]

The process of recuperation is gradual. It involves recognising the full extent of harm, envisaging forms of healing and enacting them by holding to and building on the moments when agency is possible. A re-creation of the everyday involves granting full rein to imagination: reimagining is future-oriented. It is an ongoing act of envisaging potentials that lie outside the scope of current possibilities and of striving to achieve them. It requires broad sight and a close attention to detail.

Perhaps recovery from apartheid draws on what one might characterise as a passion for the future. Those who, in their many capacities, opposed apartheid undertook such work, actively dreaming of the possibilities for a different kind of future to that figured in state policy and practice. The pursuit of a vision of an ideal everyday required daring. The outlines of the ideal were drawn from tradition and custom, the possibilities of revolutionary change, individual experience of harm and collective outrage. It was a painstaking effort that proceeded through conviction, convention, coercion, innovation, fear; that was debated and contested. Among women, it frequently had to do with the reformulation of the conditions of the domestic that apartheid had made a public domain.[18] In the aftermath of apartheid, the work of establishing an ordinary is less clear. It may be that scripts devised through struggle against the state and within communities offer fresh possibilities (though not guarantees) in the face of uncertainty.

EPILOGUE
RETURN TO VOICE AND SILENCE

How, in whose voice, or rather, in which of many voices, ought an anthropologist to tell such stories? And what does he tell when the most poignant parts of their voices are their silences? (Daniel 1996: 121)

David Morris argues that 'Silence stands in opposition to every voice, weak or strong, ordinary or unique, prosaic or poetic. The basic opposition between voice and silence matters here because suffering, like pain ... exists in part beyond language' (1996: 27). He quotes Joyce Carol Oates who, arguing that language is 'all we have to pit against death and silence', did not guarantee that 'the opposite of silence is truth' (p. 31). In a Commission that aimed to elicit and document spoken and written commentary on human rights violations committed during the apartheid era, the relationships between words, silences, elisions, truth and meaning hold special pertinence, shedding light on the complexities of the conventions by which we seek to render and understand experience.

As models of 'transitional justice' that rest on human rights gain in popularity, it is important to note their limitations, not least of all in relation to testimony and the assumptions about 'voice' that underlie their work. Remembering and recounting harm is neither a simple nor a neutral act. The Commission's rubric of harm focused on the individual and on the sayable. Permitting the expression of pain of a particular kind, it emphasised bodily violation at the expense of a broader understanding of apartheid and its consequences. Foregrounding certain forms of violence in the public record, it rendered some kinds of pain more visible while displacing other forms of experience and its expression. Its work points to the ease with which women's experiences are homogenised and the range of expressions to give voice to experience restricted. These facets are not particular to the Commission's work: Richard Wilson (1997 and 2001) has documented similar patterns in human rights reportage. Talking about certain kinds of experience may require more than a short-lived social intervention. Testimonies do not exist intact, awaiting an opportunity for expression, but emerge from interactions shaped by the complex relationships of class, race, gender and conventions of speech that are always in flux. Subject positioning is not uniform, and the social and cultural locations from which to speak may be fraught, saturated with discomforting customs that mould patterns of speech. They may render women vulnerable. The language available to express pain may be limited, lacking or fractured. Crystallised forms may become formulaic, losing the capacity to hold the attention, while recounting harm does not guarantee that it will be received in ways testifiers might wish. Attempts to express the capacity to act may elide suffering or overestimate the power of the self. Refusal to speak in terms that do not do justice to the self may be read as silence or even as moral failure. The different origins of silence – sometimes the result of processes that discount particular kinds of experience or constrain the social spaces within which to speak, sometimes a consequence of reticence, and sometimes the result of determined efforts not to speak – may be overlooked, ignored or discounted.

The restlessness and mutability of narratives of harm described in Chapter 4 stands in ironic contrast with the effects of bureaucratic processes that fix individuals within narrow subject positions. Georgio Agamben cautions against the tacit confusion of ethical and juridical categories (1999:18). While it is true that 'victim' is a legal category, it is one that carries moral weight. Given the Commission's equation of voice with the self, it is important to consider what the experience of inhabiting a subject position that carries negative social and cultural worth may be. The category 'victim' is currently imbued with negative social and cultural value. While this is not necessarily predictive,[1] the effect has been to constrain both the ranges of expressions of suffering and the institutions to which people may have recourse in seeking its amelioration. For example, in order to make claims against the state in relation to the Commission's proposed 'Urgent Interim Relief Grant' and 'Individual Reparations Grant', a person has to be identified by the Commission as a victim, to occupy and to claim that subject position. From the data presented in Chapters 3, 5 and 6 it is evident that a large number of women who may have been eligible to make statements to the Commission did not do so. One result is that they are not recorded as victims and, in terms of the current configuration of recommendations for reparation, are not eligible for individual reparation – even where their suffering was great. That limitation has important implications. Data collected in the national census of 1996 (*Census96*) locates African women at the nexus of social fragility. They represent the most unskilled members of the potential workforce and suffer the highest rates of unemployment. The poorest households in South Africa are likely to be woman-headed and are frequently reliant on state assistance in the form of pensions and welfare grants.

Considering apartheid in terms of excess phrased as violation of certain rights – as injury – has the effect of flattening and homogenising the complex social terrain of the everyday. The focus on apartheid's spectacular dimensions undervalues, even disguises, the ordinary difficulties it caused, and the limitations it imposed on the possibilities of the everyday. When carefully considered, testimonies demonstrate the intrusion of apartheid at all levels of life, including at the level of individual identity, the composition of the personal, and the voice in which it is uttered.

My research demonstrates the complexities in capturing women's experiences of activism and harm. The book's purview, too, is partial: it considered the testimonies of some women who appeared before the Commission and the lives of women who were influential in struggle activities in a small town but whose political influence, while important, was, and remains, limited. It does not reflect systematically on the experiences of women who were instrumental in organising resistance from exile or who were members of underground cells. Some women who took on more powerful roles are suspicious and reluctant to discuss the past; in discussions, one described herself and women like her as 'ex-activist housewives'. Brave, defiant and courageous, such women have received scant acknowledgement.

Susan Griffin suggests that there is a form of courage best described as 'moving against the direction of history' (1992: 156). Perhaps this quality has displaced proper acknowledgement of the role of women activists: some kinds of courage may only be recognised with hindsight.[2] Without careful attention in the present, women's participation in multiple forms of resistance and in shaping political and social agenda, along with individual acts of caring that went against the grain of established convention, will remain unacknowledged, underexplored, and in danger of slipping from the historical record.

In his study of the possibilities of moral life in concentration camps, Tzvetan Todorov distinguishes between 'heroic' and 'ordinary' virtues. The former benefit groups by using ideals and instrumental thought to achieve goals, producing 'actions that can be defined by their purpose' (1996: 286). The latter, drawing on ideas about dignity, caring, and on an active imagination – 'the life of the mind' – benefit individuals by enabling a sustained relationship to the self and by establishing relationships between individuals. Todorov points out that 'human life is inconceivable without both kinds of activities' (ibid.), adding,

> While it is true that ordinary virtue can be found everywhere and that we must rejoice in this fact ... there can come a time in the life of a society, as in that of the individual, where ordinary virtue is not enough. In such moments of anguish and despair, a different virtue is needed. The subject must then not only take upon himself [*sic*] the action he prescribes but accept the risks such action entails both for himself and for those close to him. And not only must he direct his action toward another individual, he must be willing to do so even when the individual is a stranger to him. In short, the heroic virtues, courage and generosity, become as necessary as the ordinary ones. [1996: 295]

Virtue, especially courage, has many faces whose expressions may not be easily recognised. In the South African context, achieving a desirable ordinary can be heroic. Where there is a meshing between gender ideologies and registers of acknowledgement that are insufficiently sensitive to the subtlety and diversity of efforts to act in the face of terrible constraint, the diverse forms of women's courage are underacknowledged.

In the absence of a careful accounting of harm and a perceptive register of the measures of social success against which to weigh damage, the extent and duration of harmful consequences may be underestimated. Assumptions of damage that are abstracted from social and cultural contexts may fail to recognise the scale of harm or the different impacts it may have on young and old, men and women. As I have demonstrated in Chapters 5 and 6, the Commission's register of damage does not admit the breadth of harm inflicted on residents in a small town or the depth of violence's reach into individuals' sense of the future and past. Young women and older women have dealt differently with the violence that has shaped both the quotidian world and the register of social opportunities available. The failure to attain socially sanctioned goals weighs heavily on young women who were involved in protest activities, and women's efforts to reconstitute the social fabric may be easily undermined if not acknowledged and supported.

The caveats described above suggest the need for careful attention to the constraints on verbalising experience, and an awareness of the ways that social conventions work in constituting 'linguistic bearings' (Butler 1997a: 29) – voice, silence and subjectivity. Throughout this book, I have worked against too easy an acceptance by focusing attention on the points of inter-section between voice and silence and suggesting that both are the products of social processes that give different weight to particular forms of experience and subjectivity. The process is risky: Veena Das reminds scholars that:

It is often considered the task of historiography to break the silences that announce the zones of taboo. There is even something heroic in the image of empowering women to speak and to give voice to the voiceless ... [But] even the idea that we should recover the narratives of violence becomes problematic when we realize that such narratives cannot be told unless we see the relation between pain and language that a culture has evolved. [1996: 88]

My research demonstrates the paucity of currently existing grammars to understand and give voice to both suffering and the capacity to act. Prevailing conceptions of voice – particularly the equation of speaking subject with healed subject – and the methodologies used to elicit it, do not do justice to the range of women's experiences of harm and the diversity of efforts to cope. These findings suggest the need for a new language of social suffering, one that permits the expression of the full range of experience, admits the integrity of silence, recognises the fragmented and unfinished nature of social recovery, and does not presume closure.

There is a Xhosa phrase used by storytellers, by testifiers before the Commission and by many of the women with whom I worked:

'Ndiqibile' – 'I have finished.'

APPENDIX A: SOUTH AFRICAN SECURITY LAWS

A full list of colonial and apartheid laws is provided in the Commission's Report. Here I list Security Laws that shaped resistance. I have not included laws passed in the homelands:

- Laws passed and amended in 1950, 1951 and 1954 saw a clampdown on 'communism', which was widely defined.
- In 1953, the Public Safety Act No. 3 provided for the declaration of a State of Emergency.
- In terms of various new and amended laws passed between 1953 and 1960, the Minister of Justice, the Commissioner of Police, magistrates and commissioned officers could detain, ban, prohibit, place under house arrest and banish people, and prohibit public gatherings. Those affected had little recourse to the courts.
- Longstanding resistance to the state increased. On 21 March 1960, the Pan African Congress organised a protest march against influx control measures in Sharpeville, Johannesburg. Police opened fire and killed 67 protesters. On the same day in Langa, Cape Town, police killed three people during protests. The state responded by issuing Proclamation 91 that declared a State of Emergency that came into effect on 30 March 1960 and remained in force until 31 August of that year.
- In March 1960, the Unlawful Organisations Act No. 34 was passed, and the ANC and PAC were immediately declared illegal. In 1961, *Umkhonto We Sizwe* (MK), the ANC's armed wing, was formed, and the PAC formed the Azanian People's Liberation Army (APLA) in 1967.
- As opposition to the state grew, the power of the police was entrenched through ever more harsh laws. In 1962, the General Law Amendment Act No. 37 was passed. It defined 'sabotage' in wide terms. It was amended again in 1963 to provide that any person suspected of a political crime could be held for 90 days without access to a lawyer. On their release, many detainees were immediately redetained.
- In 1965, the Criminal Procedure Amendment Act No. 96 put in place a 180-day detention, part or all of which could be spent in solitary confinement.
- The 1967 Terrorism Act No. 83 scrapped the previous detention laws and provided for indefinite detention and interrogation of detainees.

- Existing laws created what was essentially a police state. Resistance continued. In 1976, the state issued an edict that Afrikaans should be the medium of instruction in schools. On 16 June 1976, young people engaged in mass demonstrations in Soweto. The police opened fire and many young people were killed. Elsewhere in the country, mass demonstrations, protests and strikes took place. The police responded violently and 590 people were killed that year.
- The state passed the Internal Security Amendment Act No. 79 in 1976. It provided for indefinite detention.
- Protest continued. In 1982, the Internal Security Act No. 74 was passed. Section 29 of the Act provided for indefinite detention for interrogation. Detainees were held in solitary confinement. In 1985, another State of Emergency was declared.
- In 1986, the Internal Security Act was amended again to allow policemen of the rank of lieutenant colonel to decide to hold detainees for 180 days. The State of Emergency was renewed in 1986, and annually thereafter until 1990.
- During the Emergencies, thousands of people were detained (see Appendix B).
- State officials were successively indemnified throughout the period 1950–90.

APPENDIX B: DETENTION DATA

The data presented in the tables below are drawn from a variety of sources. The tables describe the number of people detained in terms of various Acts and, where data is available, the number of women and children detained. Table B.1 describes data given in to questions posed in the House of Assembly between 1960 and 1994. The data are by no means exhaustive: the state did not report detention figures unless requested in Parliament to do so, [1] and it responded only in terms of detainees held under specific legislation. Table B.1 should therefore be read as a summary of available materials and not as an accurate rendition of the scale of detention. During the late 1960s and the 1985 and 1986–90 States of Emergency, the Ministers of Police and/or Justice frequently refused to provide data about detainees, saying that it was not in the interests of national security to do so. I have italicised the data that the state refused to divulge. Detainees were held in terms of different Sections of Acts but for ease of reference I have reported data by Act rather than by Section. Detention data were not always provided by year: often the figures given in Parliament represent shorter or longer periods. For ease of reference, I have used only the annual figures where these were available. The data reported below do not include detentions in 'homelands', which had their own legislation.

It should be noted that under apartheid laws, children of different 'population groups' were considered to attain majority at different ages. African children attained majority at 16 and whites at 18. In reporting detention data, the state made use of variable definitions of childhood, so children might be those under 14 or those under 18.

The state consistently refused to reveal the numbers of people detained in terms of the Terrorism Act, and from the mid-1980s, refused to reveal numbers detained in terms of the Internal Security Act and other 'emergency regulations'.

Very little about the detention of women can be gleaned from the data presented in Table B.1. Data was seldom disaggregated by gender. The state explicitly refused to reveal the numbers of children detained in 1977 and 1986. It is not clear whether, in reporting detention figures, the state counted detainees who were held for short periods of time.

Table B.1: State detention data, 1960–94

Year	Act	Total no. detainees	No. women	No. under 18
1960	No data	No data	No data	No data
1961	No data	No data	No data	No data
1962	No data	No data	No data	No data
1963	No data	No data	No data	No data
1964	No data	No data	No data	No data
1965	SC, UO, CPA	500	No data	No data
1966	CPA	247	No data	No data
1967	CPA	282	26	No data
1968	TA	*Refused to divulge*	No data	No data
1969	TA	*Refused to divulge*	No data	No data
1970	TA	*Refused to divulge*	No data	No data
1971	TA	*Refused to divulge*	No data	No data
1972	TA	*Refused to divulge*	No data	No data
	RA	296	38	117
1973	TA	*Refused to divulge*	No data	No data
	SC	67	No data	No data
1974	SC	12	No data	No data
	TA	1	No data	No data
1975	TA	*Refused to divulge*	No data	No data
1976	RA	*Refused to divulge*	No data	No data
	Other	Referred to Cillie Commission	No data	No data
1977	TA	*Refused to divulge*	No data	*Refused to divulge*
	ISA	369	21	No data
	'Security laws'	259	No data	259
1978	ISA	No data	No data	227
	TA	No data	No data	25
1979	'Security laws'	No data	No data	48
1980	TA	49	No data	No data
	ISA	15	No data	No data
	'Security laws'	*Refused to divulge*	No data	No data
1981	Curfew regulations	10,835	No data	No data
	'Security laws'	No data	0	No data
	ISA	78	No data	No data
1982	TA	73	No data	No data
	ISA	91	No data	No data
1983	ISA	48	No data	No data
	'Crimes against state'	364	No data	0
1984	ISA	524	No data	No data
1985	'Emergency regulations'	2,387	No data	482
	'Emergency regulations'	No data	No data	2,016
	'Unrest'	18,966	No data	7,443
1986	ISA	*Refused to divulge*	No data	*Refused to divulge*
	s.29 ISA	463	67	114
	'Emergency regulations'	*Refused to divulge*	No data	No data
1987	ISA	519	22	279
	'Emergency regulations'	1,338	No data	290

Table B.1: *continued*

Year	Act	Total no. detainees	No. women	No. under 18
1988	ISA	315	No data	234
1989	'Emergency regulations'	*Refused to divulge*	No data	No data
1990	ISA	237	No data	No data
1991	ISA	171	No data	No data
1992	ISA	No data	No data	0
1993	ISA	No data	No data	0
1994	ISA	No data	No data	0

Source: Hansard, 1960–1994. *House of Assembly Questions and Answers* (Cape Town: Government Printers).

Table B.2 describes detention figures collected by a number of extra-governmental organisations and academics. The sources of the data that they quote were government figures, the media, the South African Council of Churches, the South African Institute of Race Relations, and the Detainees Parents' Support Committee (DPSC). For the period 1960 to 1976, the South African Institute of Race Relations (SAIRR) relied mostly on data provided by the state. Its later reports drew from the analyses offered by other organisations.

Although the data in Table B.2 indicate substantially higher rates of detention than those cited in Table B.1, it still remains difficult to identify how many women were detained each year. Other sources provide information for selected periods only. Coleman (in Russell 1990: 15; see also Coleman 1998) indicates that in 1985, 14 per cent of detainees under the age of 18 were girls. The DPSC (1988) estimated that women comprised 12 per cent of detainees held by the state in 1986–87 under the State of Emergency. The Lawyers Commission for Human Rights (LCHR) estimated that some 25,000 people were held in terms of security legislation in 1985, in which case, if the DPSC estimate is accurate, some 3,000 women were held in detention.

Table B.2: Detention data, 1960–94, according to extra-governmental sources

Year	Act	Total no. detainees	No. women	No. under 18	Source
1960	PSA	11,000			IDAF 1991: 67
	State of Emergency	11,727	35		McKendrick et al.
	'Dangerous'/'statutory'				1990: 412
	Offences	18,011			SAIRR 1960: 79
1961	No data				
1962	No data				
1963	Security legislation	3,246			SAIRR 1963: 52
	(Poqo)[2]	2,618	45	102	SAIRR 1965: 61
	GLAA				
1964	GLAA	987	81	4	SAIRR 1965: 61

Table B.2: *continued*

Year	Act	Total no. detainees	No. women	No. under 18	Source
1965	GLAA	1,095	76	17	SAIRR 1965: 49
1966	SC	24			SAIRR 1966: 68
	UO	130	19		SAIRR 1968: 68
	PSA	477	10		SAIRR 1968: 68
	GLAA	1,310	49		SAIRR 1968: 68
	CPA	*State refused to divulge*			SAIRR 1968: 77
1967	TA	*State refused to divulge*			SAIRR 1968: 58
1968	TA	*State refused to divulge*			SAIRR 1969: 62
1969	TA	35			SAIRR 1969: 70
1970	TA	*State refused to divulge*			SAIRR 1970: 54
1971	No data				
1972	TA	*State refused to divulge*			SAIRR 1972: 98
1973	TA	*State refused to divulge*			SAIRR 1974: 90
1974	'Security laws'	*State refused to divulge*			SAIRR 1975: 57
1975	'Security laws'	23			SAIRR 1976: 110
1976	TA	1			SAIRR 1977: 143
	ISA	453	21		SAIRR 1977: 143
	CPA	21			SAIRR 1977: 143
1977	'Security laws'	2,430		286	SAIRR 1978: 106
1978	'Security laws'	261		64	SAIRR 1978: 107
1979	TA and GLAA	No data		48	SAIRR 1980: 264
1980	'Security laws'	768		458	SAIRR 1980: 264
	GLAA	762			SAIRR 1982: 224
	TA	222			SAIRR 1982: 224
	ISA	255			SAIRR 1982: 224
	CPA	4			SAIRR 1982: 224
1981	GLAA	579			SAIRR 1982: 224
	TA	320			SAIRR 1982: 224
	ISA	68			SAIRR 1982: 224
	CPA	7			SAIRR 1982: 224
1982	'Security laws'	210			SAIRR 1983: 548
1983	TA	*State refused to divulge*			SAIRR 1983: 548
1984	ISA	530			SAIRR 1984: 758
1985	ISA	4,794			LCHR 1986: 78
	CPA	25,000			LCHR 1986: 83
	State of Emergency	8,000		2,016	Thomas 1990 439–41
1986	State of Emergency	8,800		3,000	UNICEF 1989: 87
	State of Emergency	10,000			Straker 1992: 6
	State of Emergency	25,000			SAIRR 1986: 824
	ISA	3,989			SAIRR 1986: 822
1987	State of Emergency	No data		230	DPSC 31/1/88
	State of Emergency	No data		1,338	SAIRR 1987–88: 538
1988	State of Emergency	No data		250	Thomas 1990: 441
	State of Emergency	No data		2,000	SAIRR 1985: 442
1989	ISA	316			SAIRR 1989–90: 175
1990	ISA	86			SAIRR 1993–94: 307
1991	ISA	93			SAIRR 1993–94: 307
1992	ISA	86			
1993	No data				
1994	No data				

Table B.2: *continued*

Key:

SC = Suppression of Communism Act No. 44 of 1950, as amended
PSA = Public Safety Act No. 3 of 1953
RA = Riotous Assemblies Act No. 17 of 1956
UO = Unlawful Organisations Act No. 34 of 1960
GLAA = General Law Amendment Act No. 76 of 1962 and No. 37 of 1963
TA = Terrorism Act No. 8 of 1967
CPA = Criminal Procedures Act No. 96 of 1965
ISA = Internal Security Act No. 74 of 1982
Emergency regulations = undefined regulations under the State of Emergency
Security legislation = undefined legislation pertaining to matters of national security

GLOSSARY

ANC	African National Congress
ANC WL	African National Congress Women's League
ANC YL	African National Congress Youth League
APLA	Azanian People's Liberation Army: Armed wing of the PAC
ARM	Armed Revolutionary Movement: a break-away from Alan Paton's Liberal Party
Askaris	Members of a liberation organisation captured by the police or Defence Force and 'turned' into informers and assassins
Black Local Authorities	Local authorities established by the state. The institution was widely disliked and many councillors were accused of being informers and 'sell outs'.
Black Sash	An organisation of white women that monitored and protested state repression
BMW	Bonteheuwel Military Wing – based in Cape Town and linked with MK
BOYCO	Boland Youth Congress – aligned with UDF and formed after COSAS was banned in 1985
CBO	Community based organisation
CCB	Civil Co-operation Bureau
Civic Associations	Associations formed in opposition to Black Local Authorities
COSAS	Congress of South African Students – banned in 1985
Councillor	Official representative of the Black Local Authorities
CRADOYA	Cradock Youth Association
DET	Department of Education and Training, responsible for the provision of education to Africans
DPSC	Detainees Parents' Support Committee – aligned to UDF
FEDTRAW	Federation of Transvaal Women
HRVC	Human Rights Violation Committee
IFP	Inkatha Freedom Party (previously, Inkatha)
Impimpi	'Sell-out', informer
MK	'*Umkhonto We Sizwe*', 'Spear of the Nation' – the ANC's armed wing, formed in 1960

NGO	Non-governmental organisation
NP	National Party
PAC	Pan African Congress
PTSD	post-traumatic stress disorder
SACC	South African Council of Churches
Sjambok	(Afrikaans) whip
Street committee	Local governance structures set up by Civic Associations in the 1980s in opposition to Black Local Authorities
Toyi-toyi	Protest chant accompanied by rhythmic dance
UBJ	Union of Black Journalists
UDF	United Democratic Front – a broad-based alliance of organisations opposed to apartheid. The UDF had strong links with the ANC in exile and underground. It was launched in 1983, banned in 1988 and disbanded in 1991.
UWCO	United Women's Congress – formed by the amalgamation of UWO and the Women's Front in March 1986; affiliated to the UDF
UWO	United Women's Organisation – launched in 1981 by women who had been members of the ANC prior to its banning in 1960; affiliated to the UDF
WOYCO	Worcester Youth Congress
ZWEYO	Zwelethemba Youth Organisation

NOTES

INTRODUCTION

1. See the five volumes of the Commission's 1998 report, and: Amadiume and An-Naim (2000); Asmal, Asmal and Roberts (1996); Bell and Ntsebeza (2001); Boraine (2000); Boraine and Levy (1995); Boraine, Levy and Scheffer (1994); Botman and Petersen (1996); Bozzoli (1999); Buur (1999 and 2000); Coleman (1998); Edelstein (2001); Goldblatt (1997); Goldblatt and Meintjes (1996); Hayner (1994, 1996, 2001); Ignatieff (1996); James and van der Vywer (2000); Jeffrey (1999); Krog (1998); Mamdani (1996); Meiring (1999); Meredith and Rosenberg (2000); Olkers (1996); Orr (2000); Owens (1996); Tutu (1999); Villavicencio and Verwoerd (2000); Wilson (1996, 1997, 2001).

2. I attended twelve public hearings of the HRVC: in East London (15–18 April 1996); Cape Town (22–25 April 1996); Johannesburg (29 April–3 May 1996); Durban (May 7–10 1996); Kimberley (10–11 June 1996); Worcester (24–26 July 1996); Cape Town (5–7 August 1996); Beaufort West (12–14 August 1996); Upington (2–4 October 1996); Paarl (14–16 October 1996); Cape Town (26–28 November 1996 and 20–22 May 1997). At these hearings, 390 testifiers spoke of 416 incidents of violation. Each hearing lasted from three to five days, and approximately ten people testified each day. The twelve hearings account for 16 per cent of the total number of Victim Hearings the Commission held between 1996 and 1997 and 75 per cent of the Victim Hearings held in the Commission's Western and Northern Cape Region.

3. The Greek word for witness, *martis*, is derived from the verb meaning 'to remember' (Agamben 1999: 26). Its customary English form is 'martyr' (Agamben 1999: 17). Agamben points out that in Latin there are two words for 'witness'; *testis*, which describes a person 'in the position of a third party', and the *superstes*, someone who 'experienced an event from beginning to end', a survivor. In relation to the Commission, many of those who testified were doubly positioned, having experienced apartheid and the particular violations about which they testified.

4. In a critique of Shoshana Felman and Dori Laub's (1992) argument that testimony speaks beyond words, like song, Agamben argues that 'To explain the paradox of testimony through the deus ex machina of song is to aestheticize testimony', adding 'Neither the poem nor the song can intervene to save impossible testimony; on the contrary, it is testimony, if anything that founds the possibility of the poem' (1999: 36). Recognising the validity of his argument, I wish nevertheless to mark a distinction between testimonies of Holocaust survivors and testimonies made before the South African Commission. In the latter, poetry marks boundaries of expression and efforts to communicate where ordinary linguistic forms may not suffice. As *forms*, poetry and song were important components of struggle and memorialisation in South Africa, and as I show in Chapter 2, many testimonies use lyric forms. At two hearings that I attended, poets and youths read their poetry, including one instance where a poem formed part of a description of the horrors of detention and solitary confinement. Sometimes local choirs opened the hearings with song, often hymns. For generations, protest and memorial have been conveyed in choral form, among

which features the well-known *toyi-toyi* (protest chants accompanied by rhythmic dance). There is as yet no compilation or comprehensive analysis of such performance in relation to 'the struggle' in South Africa, although they exist in relation to liberation wars fought elsewhere: for example, Pongweni (1982) and Masiye (1977) have described and analysed songs of the liberation wars in Zimbabwe and Zambia respectively. Interestingly, while visual art forms have received much attention in relation to the Commission (most conferences that I have attended have included artists or critical considerations of visual art), the absence of close studies of music in relation to violence and suffering in South Africa and more generally is both marked and remarkable.

5. See Henri (2000); the documentary video *We Tell Our Stories the Way We Like* produced by da Cahna, Paleker and van Vuuren (1999); and Hastrup (1992). An important literature considers the ways in which writing of violence may appropriate it and give offence – for sensitive examples see Daniel (1996); Das (1995, 1997, 2000); Feldman (1991); Kleinman and Kleinman (1997).

CHAPTER 1

1. Nguni word with no precise English correspondence. It incorporates ideas of 'humanity' and 'humaneness'.

2. Although no reference is made to her work here, I am indebted to Wendy Brown's *States of Injury* (1995) which I have found helpful in enabling me to think about the effects of construing social injustice, suffering and harm as injury.

3. Others include a limited land restitution programme, revised welfare provisions, a limited affirmative action campaign, and the provision of social services in accordance with the Reconstruction and Development Programme (RDP).

4. Political prisoners were released from prison or permitted to return from exile through the provisions of the Indemnity Act No. 35 of 1990 and the Further Indemnity Act No. 151 of 1992. Government officials were indemnified through the provisions of the 1961 Indemnity Act No. 61 and Indemnity Act No. 22 of 1977. Members of the South African Defence Force (SADF) were automatically indemnified through regulations governing the SADF and through Section 16 of the Public Safety Act No. 3 of 1953. During the 1993 negotiations, liberation organisations opposed further amnesty or indemnification provisions for state officials while representatives of the state and of right-wing political organisations sought a blanket amnesty.

5. Several legal challenges were brought against the Commission, the most important of which challenged the amnesty provisions. The case was brought by the Azanian Peoples' Organisation (AZAPO), Nontsikelelo Margaret Biko, Churchill Mheli Mxenge and Chris Ribeiro against the President of the Republic of South Africa, the Government of the Republic of South Africa, the Minister of Justice, the Minister of Safety and Security and the Chairperson of the Truth and Reconciliation Commission. The plaintiffs held that the amnesty provisions violated their constitutional rights to redress. The case was heard in the Constitutional Court on 30 May 1996, five months after the Commission had been established, and a judgment given on 25 July 1996 by Justice Mohammed with concurrence from the members of the Constitutional Court. The judgment found that although the amnesty provisions limited applicants' rights to settlement through the courts, because amnesty was a provision of the Interim Constitution, rights were legitimately curtailed. While upholding the amnesty provision, he found that Parliament should offer reparations to victims and that reparation could be differential.

    The Commission countered claims of injustice by arguing that its enquiry offered 'social' or 'restorative' justice in lieu of criminal and/or civil justice. In the Commission's Report, Archbishop Tutu, Chairperson of the Commission, describes restorative justice thus: 'restorative justice ... is concerned not so much with punishment as with correcting imbalances, restoring broken relationships – with healing, harmony and reconciliation. Such justice focuses on the experience of victims; hence the importance of reparation' (Volume One: 9). The Report identifies one of the most important tasks of restorative justice as being 'to redefine crime: it shifts the primary focus of crime from the breaking of laws or offences against a faceless state to a perception of crime as violations against human beings, as injury or wrong done to another person' (Volume One: 126).

6. 7,128 amnesty applications were received. By October 1998, 4,303 cases had been rejected or denied amnesty because they did not meet the criteria laid down in the Act (Volume One: 276 and Volume Four: 312). The Amnesty Committee's work is not yet complete. Its findings will be added to the Commission's 1998 Report. The Reparation and Rehabilitation Committee devised five measures of reparation, two of which accrued directly to 'victims' identified by the HRVC or the Amnesty Committee. The first, 'Urgent Interim Relief' (UIR) grants of between R 2000 and R4000 (approximately US$ 350–600 at that time), were intended to facilitate access to health care or to meet immediate needs of victims. 'Individual Reparation' grants (IRG) of approximately R20,000 (approximately US$ 3,000 at the time) per year for six years were recommended. The committee also recommended 'Symbolic Reparations', such as monuments and memorials, 'Community Rehabilitation', through 'community-based services and activities', and 'Institutional Reform' (Report, Volume Five: 175–95). Although the Report was submitted to the State President in October 1998, and debated in Parliament on 25 February 1999, at the time of writing, the government has not yet acted to implement the recommendations. To date, some people identified as victims have received UIR payments of between R2000 and R4000. Not all victims qualified. NGOs throughout the country have begun to petition the state on the matter of reparations.

7. The Commission was a costly social intervention: the Commission Report indicates that the budget allocated to the Commission through Parliamentary processes was valued at approximately 156 million Rands for the fiscal years 1995–99 (approximately US$ 26 million). In addition, substantial donations and assistance were received from extra-Parliamentary sources (see Volume One: 300–18).

8. This applies only to 'victims'. Amnesty applicants had to demonstrate a political motive and context for their acts.

9. Figures of 46,696 violations involving 28,750 victims are also given (Volume Three: 4), but no explanation for the discrepancy is offered. The figures I have cited in the text are those usually used.

10. The Commission held different kinds of public hearings including Victim Hearings; Institutional Hearings (into the media, prisons, legal system, health system, business, and faith communities); Special Hearings on Conscription, Children and Youth, and Women; Political Party Hearings, and Event Hearings. 'Special investigations' included secret state funding, chemical and biological warfare, exhumations, the activities of the Mandela United Football Club (of which Nelson Mandela's ex-wife, Winnie Madikizela Mandela was patron and which was accused of numerous acts of gross violations of human rights), the death of Mozambique's President Samora Machel in an aeroplane crash on 19 October 1986 and the crash of the Helderberg aeroplane off the Mauritian coast on 28 October 1987 (commentators had accused the State of causing both crashes). Most special investigations were held *in camera*.

11. The Commission's temporal purview excluded a period of considerable protest by women (Walker 1991; Wells 1991a, 1991b, 1993), culminating in protests against the pass laws in the late 1950s. In 1956, some 20,000 women marched to Parliament to protest against carrying passes. Many were harshly treated. Published materials that focus specifically on women's experiences as political activists in the 1980s are scarce, notwithstanding a fine literature on resistance, 'civil disobedience' and state

violence, especially concerning the violence inflicted on children (see Foster, Davis and Sandler 1987; Chabanyi Mangani and Du Toit 1990; Straker 1992; McKendrick and Hoffman 1990).

12. Twenty-six (7 per cent) of the victims identified in testimonies were not identified by sex. They are not included in the analyses. Note that the data presented in my analysis, like the Commission's Report, do not represent the full extent of gross violations of human rights that occurred in South Africa. The data reflect patterns and trends in testimonies made to the Commission, themselves a product of a self-selecting sample. My data are drawn from the same sample and reflect on it.

13. In order to identify patterns in violations, the Commission drew on the terminology of the infamous Population Registration Act No. 30 of 1950 that required people to be registered as belonging to one of four 'population groups'. My use of the Act's terminology in no way implies acceptance of it.

14. The variation may reflect patterns of regional violence (for example, regional-specific conflicts between the African National Congress (ANC) and Inkatha Freedom Party (IFP) between 1990–94), changes in political cooperation with the Commission (the IFP was initally opposed to the Commission and did not encourage its followers to make statements or to apply for amnesty until late in the process), and/or different patterns of statement collection (the Durban office undertook a more extensive 'statement-taking drive' than did the Cape Town office).

15. 'Acts or omissions that deliberately and directly inflict severe mental or physical suffering on a victim, taking into account the context and nature of the act or omission and the nature of the victim. Whether an act or omission constituted severe ill treatment was thus determined on a case by case basis.' The Commission cites two legal cases 'where it was argued that severe is a relative concept ...' (Volume One: 80, footnote 24).

16. Thirty-four people testified at the East London hearing. They described 32 incidents of violation. Nineteen testifiers (55 per cent of the total) were women and 15 (45 per cent) were men. Eighteen of the women testified about violations inflicted on men.

17. Women constituted less than 1 per cent of amnesty applicants. Nineteen amnesty applications made by women have to date been considered. The acts for which application was made included public violence, unlawful possession of weapons, sabotage, 'terrorism', bombing and murder. Eight, part of a collective application, were rejected on the grounds that they were not individual applications.

18. In general, in most African societies it is considered inappropriate for women to speak publicly or in mixed company about their bodies, bodily functions or violence. In some African societies, talk about past violence is considered suspicious: the pollution caused by violence is considered to have the potential symbolically to attach to the person and may contaminate the community unless purification rites are performed (see Honwana 1999 for a discussion in relation to Angola).

19. A partial record of Thenjiwe Mtintso's life is documented in June Goodwin's *Cry Amandla!: South African women and the question of power* (1984). Mtintso was active in Black Consciousness movements and student politics in the early 1970s. In December 1976, she was issued with a five-year banning order. The Black Consciousness organisations in which she was active were banned in 1977, and Steve Biko, a leading intellectual in the organisations, was killed in police custody in September of that year. Between 1977 and 1978, Mtintso spent ten months in prison for breaking the terms of the banning orders. After having been detained five times, she left the country in 1979, and eventually joined the ANC in exile, where she became a commander in MK. See also Devan Pillay's interview with Mtintso carried in Pillay 1992: 18–19.

20. The Report does not state what proportion of violations were committed by representatives of the state compared with other organisations or institutions.

CHAPTER 2

NB: An earlier version of this chapter has been published in Das et al. 2001. I am grateful to University of California Press for permission to reprint. The chapter on the Women's Hearings in the Commission Report draws on material from the first version of the paper that I presented at the Faultlines Conference in 1996 in Cape Town.

1. Giorgio Agamben eschews the terms 'holocaust' and 'Shoah', arguing that the first erroneously links sacrifice and extermination while the second anticipates divine punishment (1999: 28–31).

2. One of the 'homelands' or 'Bantustans' established by the Apartheid State in terms of the policy of 'Separate Development' that held that cultural differences were irreducible and that different cultures should have their own land and government. Four of the homelands – Transkei, Ciskei, Bophuthatswana and Venda – were declared 'independent'. In fact, the homelands remained heavily reliant on the South African State and were not recognised internationally as independent states.

3. A reference to Sipho Hashe, Champion Galela and Qaqawuli Godolozi, political activists in the Eastern Cape who came to be known as the 'PEBCO Three' after their disappearance in May 1985. Arrested and imprisoned, they were never seen again. In 1994, their deaths were linked to operatives based at the police farm, 'Vlakplaas'. Their widows testified to the Commission at its first hearing in East London on 16 April 1996, the day before Nyameka Goniwe gave her testimony. Applications brought before the Amnesty Committee of the Commission in November 1997 by members of the Security Branch and Vlakplaas operatives revealed that the three men had been tortured and killed in May 1985. Nyameka Goniwe's reference here fits Matthew's disappearance into a local chronology of violence, repression and resistance.

4. Thanks to Jane Taylor for pointing this out – personal communication, 27 August 2000.

5. Organised groups of assassins said to have worked for the state security forces. Many members of the apartheid government continue to deny the existence of such squads (National Party Submission to the Commission, 21 August 1996) although there have been convictions in the criminal courts of two leaders of the police unit C-10 based at Vlakplaas, and testimonies made both in court and before the Commission by witnesses involved in operations at Vlakplaas and in 'covert operations' (see Pauw 1997). The Commission Report found the state responsible for 'the covert training, arming or funding of offensive paramilitary units or hit squads for deployment internally against opponents of the government' (Report, Volume Five: 222).

6. Webster, a social anthropologist, was assassinated in 1989. His companion, Maggie Friedman, testified to the Commission on 3 May 1996 in Johannesburg, accusing the state and legal system of covering up his death. Ferdi Barnard, a member of the Apartheid State's covert organisation, the Civil Co-operation Bureau (CCB), later admitted to a journalist that he had killed Webster (*Mail and Guardian*, 21–27 November 1997: 23–4; Pauw 1997). Barnard was tried and found guilty of Webster's death.

7. Scheub's early work (1975, and Zenani and Scheub 1992) is concerned with *iintsomi*, stories that have mythic or fictional underpinnings. Nevertheless, his analysis is pertinent to my argument regarding oral forms. My Xhosa-speaking informants described testimonies as *ibali* (stories based on fact) or *imbali* (histories). They used the verb *ukungqina* for testify. In Xhosa, the 'Truth and Reconciliation Commission' was translated into '*Ikomishoni yeNyani noXolelwaniso*'. *Xolelwaniso* has implications of forgiveness.

8. This does not apply solely to those that drew from oral literature forms: in both Nyameka Goniwe's and Elizabeth Floyd's testimonies there is little elucidation of the context of repression and resistance in which the deaths that they described occurred.

9. See Hofmeyr (1994), who demonstrates changes in oral historical narratives as a consequence of colonisation and apartheid. Arguing that memory has 'a close mnemonic relationship with place and location', her work examines what happens when 'people lose access to the topography that helps to uphold oral memory' (1994: 160). She shows that oral traditions endure albeit in changed form. The most marked change has been a radical decrease in men's storytelling (usually drawing on historical narratives and told in public spaces) whereas women's storytelling (usually fictional and associated with the residential area of a homestead) continues.

10. The phrase is coined to describe the complex product of speaking and listening to oral performances among Basotho migrant labourers.

11. Idiom was lost in the simultaneous translation of testimonies into English. Nevertheless, the lyric style and repetition characteristic of traditional forms remained in translation.

12. It is not clear from her testimony which organisation he joined: on 8 April 1960, the ANC and PAC were banned. The organisations established bases in neighbouring states and in 1963 the ANC launched its armed wing, Umkhonto We Sizwe (MK – Spear of the Nation). The PAC established APLA (the Azanian People's Liberation Army) in 1967.

13. The time frame in her testimony became condensed at this point and it was not clear how much later she learned of his arrest. In the testimony, it appears that she heard of his arrest shortly after she had left him in the street.

14. Death is considered polluting and after a burial relatives and neighbours wash their hands outside the homestead of the deceased person before entering and sharing food with the family.

15. Members of liberation organisations who had been captured and 'turned' and who served the state.

16. This appears to be a mistranslation. Seven youths were killed by the Security Forces, who described the young men as guerrillas trained in the USSR.

17. My thanks to Linda Waldman for pointing out the absence of representation of men in women's testimonies.

18. I am grateful to Jane Taylor for her suggestions in relation to time – personal communication, 27 August 2000.

19. The mid-1980s were marked by extreme violence throughout the country. In the Cape there were ongoing conflicts between *witdoeke* ('white cloths' – the name given to vigilantes who covered their heads with white fabric) and surrounding squatter camps aligned to progressive political organisations and the UDF. The *witdoeke* were widely believed to be aligned with the police. (See Cole 1987; Report, Volume Two: 306–8, and Volume Three: 463–74.)

20. A rhythmic chanting accompanied by dance performed during diverse forms of protest – marches, rallies, protests, funerals. It was powerful, creating a strong sense of unity and cohesion in a group through physical exertion, an enactment of collective goals and a clear identification of 'the enemy'.

21. People suspected by members of their communities of having been police informers were sometimes set alight and burnt to death. One method, 'necklacing', was to fill a car tyre with paraffin or petrol, put it around the victim's neck, and set it alight.

CHAPTER 3

1. The patterning of testimony bears resemblance to conventions of mourning elsewhere in the world, where it is often women's work to lament the dead. See for example, Nadia Seremetakis (1991), who shows that through rituals performed by women, death is given social meaning.

2. Amnesty applicants, on the other hand, had to demonstrate a political context for their actions.

3. To date some 31,000 people have applied for Special Pensions. Few applications have yet been processed. Administrators are unable to differentiate between male and female applicants (A. van Heever, personal communication, 18 March 1999).

4. The chapter draws on testimonies given at hearings of the HRVC that I attended and on testimonies from Women's Hearings held in Cape Town (7 August 1996), Durban (24 October 1996) and Johannesburg (29 July 1997) that aimed to elicit descriptions of women's experiences of violation, especially rape and sexual violence. Some women, styled as having particular expertise on the basis of their personal experiences and professions, spoke at Institutional Hearings: in this respect, I draw from testimonies given on 21 and 22 July 1997 at a special hearing on prisons in the former prison, The Fort, in Johannesburg.

5. The story of the 'Upington 26' trial, and the campaign to free Mrs de Bruin from Death Row is told by Andrea Durbach (1999) in *Upington*.

6. ARM grew out of the Liberal Party of South Africa. Its formation and activities are described in Hugh Lewin's book, *Bandiet* (1989). Lewin, who had been a member of ARM, was a member of the Commission's HRVC in Johannesburg.

7. Extracts from testimonies by Fatima Meer, Marie Magwaza, Joyce Sikhakhane Ranken and Deborah Matshoba appear in Volume Four of the Report (pp. 282–316), but their names are not included in its victim list (Volume Five: 26–107). In addition, Nontobeko Feni, Nomakula Zweni, Deborah Marakala, Theresa Ramashamola, Jubie Mayet and Thandi Mavuso gave testimonies before the Commission but are not identified in the Report. Theresa Ramashamola and Jubie Mayet may be registered as victims with different names from those they used in testifying: in the Report, Volume Five, on pages 58 and page 93, Zubeida Mayet and Machabane Ramashamola are identified as victims. The absence of the women's names from the list of victims does not indicate that they have not been found to be victims: in some cases, names were not included at victims' behest and in other cases, investigation and corroboration is not yet complete. In other cases, people were invited to testify as expert witnesses and may not have made statements that implicated themselves *as victims* to the Commission.

8. Ms Narkedien was subpoenaed to testify before an *in camera* hearing concerning a bomb-blast on 14 June 1986 at Magoo's bar in Durban, in which three people were killed and 69 injured (Volume Two: 330–1). She had been a member of the cell that planted the bomb. She has been granted amnesty.

9. Bear in mind that until 1996, the post-apartheid government was one of National Unity; distrust of official institutions was, at that time, great. Some testifiers felt that Commission hearings were similar to interrogation. For example, one woman told me that she was afraid of the possible repercussions of witnessing. She had feigned illness in order to leave work and appear before the Commission. Part-way through her testimony she wept and decided not to continue. Later she told me that the earphones of the translation devices reminded her forcibly of the machinery used to shock her during interrogation.

10. According to Commissioner Yasmin Sooka, between 1960 and 1990, 78,000 people were detained under various pieces of legislation (introductory statement prior to testimony by Mrs Salojee, 29 April 1996 in Johannesburg). Many of them were children (Report, Volume Four). See aggregated data presented in Appendix B. For accounts and analysis of torture in detention, see Foster, Davis and Sandler (1987); and contributors to Chabanyi Mangani and du Toit (1990).

11. Together with Sylvia Dlomo-Jele (see Chapter 2), Shezi was instrumental in establishing the support and lobby group, 'Khulumani'. The play, *Now I Am About To Tell My Story*, devised by the group, features Thandi Shezi acting out her experience of appearing before the Commission. She appears in the video made by Khulumani to promote the Commission and the work of the support group.

12. Judith Butler implies that it is not shame but guilt that performs this function (1997a: 25).

13. Alan Feldman (1991) describes similar tactics and consequences for male political prisoners in Northern Ireland.

14. Adrian Vlok, Minister of Law and Order at the time, applied to the Commission for – and received amnesty for – his role in the bombing, Amnesty application number AM4399/96.

15. In a later interview I conducted (15 April 1999), Gunn described the removal of her child as calculated to 'break' her and also to enable the police to 'eliminate' her. She believes that the police, desperate to kill her, had no intention of capturing her alive. She described the vociferous campaign mounted on her behalf by her mother and the ANC Women's League when Haroon was removed. Haroon was returned to her after a judge ruled that if the place in which his mother was incarcerated was unfit for a child, the police were obliged to find a place where the child could be kept with his mother. She was later moved to Caledon Women's Prison where she was held in the hospital so as to be isolated from other prisoners.

16. An anti-apartheid activist who died in police custody in 1979. His family were invited to testify before the Commission but declined.

17. Activists coached one another, describing the torture that they could expect in detention (Donald Skinner, personal communication, October 1995), and devising strategies to resist interrogation or to accommodate themselves to the demands while causing the least possible damage to others. Organisations that were sympathetic to 'the struggle' drew up pamphlets that explained the rights of detainees and described the kinds of treatment detainees could expect (DPSC n.d.; Foster and Skinner 1990).

18. Drawing on Foucault, Butler argues that the body is produced and proliferated 'as an object of regulation' (1997b: 59–60): an understanding that here sheds light on the increasingly wide scope of detention laws and their performative effect, especially in relation to the punishment of children. In their study of the psychological effects of detention in South Africa, Don Foster and Donald Skinner (1990: 228) show that increased repression spurred greater resistance, solidarity and political education among those whom the repressive practices were designed to control. The sense of commitment of some women political detainees and prisoners is portrayed in some of the writings contained in Barbara Schriener's (1992) edited volume, *A Snake with Ice Water*, in which political detainees recorded their determination to continue with the struggle against apartheid.

19. At the time, Sexwale was the Premier of Gauteng Province. One of few political leaders to appear before the human rights violations hearings, he did so in his capacity as leader to introduce the hearings rather than to make a statement about his own experiences of violation.

20. Her comment here indexes the possibility raised by Wittgenstein and explored by Veena Das (see Chapter 2) that one may feel the pain of another in one's body.

21. Notably a comment by political activist Mike Basupo (quoted in Jacklyn Cock's contribution entitled, 'Political Violence' in a volume on violence edited by Brian McKendrick and Wilma Hoffman, *People and Violence in South Africa*, Oxford: Oxford University Press, 1990), and J. Saporta and B. van der Kolk's *Psychobiological Consequences of Severe Trauma: Current approaches*, Cambridge: Cambridge University Press, 1992). See Report, Volume Five: 133.

22. The sense of disorientation and loss that accompany power's shifts is clear in a statement made by Xolile Dyabooi, a young activist from Zwelethemba, to Pamela Reynolds (reported in Grundlingh et al. 2000). Describing the difficulties he encountered after being indemnified and released from prison in 1991, he said, 'And another thing … the transition in South Africa was one of a special kind. It was another kind of transition. So many things just happened. So dramatically. So that resulted in people going without preparations, because most of us were not prepared for such a sudden change. We were thinking we were still fighting. As a result, I feel that we didn't become part, or I didn't become part, of the transition process.'

CHAPTER 4

1. As a means of denunciation and of integration see Fitzpatrick and Gellately (1997); Felman and Laub (1992); Agger (1994); Minow (1998). Coady (1992) argues that testimony's history was not always so positive – his philosophical investigation aims to redeem it. He argues that testimony implicates a trust in the word of others that is fundamental to the cognitive act of communication.

2. Thenjiwe Mtintso's statements about gender discrimination and violation against women are included in five places in the 1998 Report, and extracts from Zubeida Jaffer's testimony at the Woman's Hearing in Cape Town on 8 August 1996 are included in ten places in the Report.

3. I retain 'township' here because residents of Zwelethemba use it, although some use the older term 'location'. As in many of the small towns in the Boland, black residential areas were set at a distance from the main town and consist of little more than houses laid out in grid formation. Some, such as Zwelethemba, have schools, a police station, post office and basic shopping facilities.

4. Some of the former residents have made claims for the return of their property or compensation for its loss to the Land Claims Commission established by the post-Apartheid State.

5. The Commission Report (1998, Volume Three: 447) states that in the 1980s all three men were charged with numerous cases of assault and torture. They denied the charges at the time they were laid and the Attorney General did not prosecute. Van Loggerenberg still resides in Worcester and a number of activists who had brutal encounters with him report seeing him in the town's streets.

6. In the testimonies about Zwelethemba, only Mr Dyasi, whose son, William, had been shot while running from two policemen, did not claim a political identity for his son. When asked about his son's political activism, he replied, 'As far as I know he was a very sweet child. He couldn't [wouldn't] tell where he was going to, he was just going out saying nothing so I had no idea how involved he was or where.' Young political activists in Zwelethemba regard William Dyasi as a martyr in 'the struggle' against apartheid.

7. Extracts quoted here are drawn both from my own notes during the hearing and from the Commission's transcripts of testimonies, which were available only in translation from the Xhosa. My interviews with Yvonne Khutwane were conducted in English and Afrikaans, both of which she, like many others in Zwelethemba, speaks fluently.

8. The state established municipal bars in the townships, the money from which was to be used to augment municipal incomes and so keep rentals on municipal housing low. The institution was widely disliked by progressive youth, and in 1985 there was a wave of arson attacks on municipal bars all over the country.

9. In an interview, she told me that she asked a policeman to drape her coat over her shoulders to spare her mother the sight of her hands cuffed behind her back. Much to her surprise, the policeman obliged.

10. In an e-mail correspondence in response to my questions about the testimonial process, Ms Gobodo-Madikizela said that she identified closely with Mrs Khutwane's experiences, prompting concern for her from some of her colleagues in the mental health field (personal communication by e-mail, 5 April 1999, cited with permission).

11. This appears to be a mistranslation. The house was attacked while she was on trial, having been released from prison on bail.

12. From her Commission testimony, it is not clear whether the child died of an epileptic attack triggered by the arson or in a separate incident. In fact the child's death was not linked to the arson attack.

13. I conducted three formal interviews with Yvonne Khutwane in Zwelethemba and spoke with her informally and telephonically several times between 1997 and 1999.

I discussed her testimony with a number of other people, including youth activists, and, with the exception of one woman, I spoke to the people she named in Zwelethemba. I corroborated material by e-mail with Pumla Gobodo-Madikizela, Wendy Orr, and Martha Minow (see below), discussed the reporting of the case with correspondent Roger Friedman who reports for the *Cape Times*, and spoke with representatives of the Commission regarding her testimony and the debriefing process. I have been unable to gain access to Yvonne Khutwane's file at the Commission as the statements given to the Commission are not yet public documents and are protected.

14. The Cape Town-based Trauma Centre for Victims of Violence had a branch in Ashton at the time of the hearing. A fieldworker offered debriefing to those who testified.

15. Father Michael Lapsley, an Anglican minister and ANC member whose hands were blown off in 1990 when a parcel bomb sent to him in Harare, Zimbabwe, exploded. His life history is recorded in Michael Worsnip's book, *Priest and Partisan*, published in 1996, and he testified before the Commission on 10 June 1996 at a hearing on human rights violations in Kimberley. Lapsley established an initiative called 'Healing of the Memories Workshops' that at that time operated through the auspices of the Trauma Centre. The workshops aimed to effect reconciliation by bringing together people from a wide spectrum of society to discuss and share with one another the personal effects of apartheid. The workshops were modified to provide support for those who had given testimony before the Commission.

16. Findings were made on the basis of statements, corroborating evidence and the balance of probabilities (Volume One: 91, 142). The 1998 Report does not offer summaries of findings.

17. I verified the statement with a Commission employee on 29 March 1999, who confirmed that the deponent included a statement on 'the *threat of rape*' but not about acts of sexual violation.

18. It is not clear whether the men were military police, policemen or soldiers. The English translation offered at the hearing was 'policemen', but Mrs Khutwane recalls that the men wore berets, suggesting that they were military police. The lack of clarity is reflected in the media reports below.

19. Yvonne Khutwane does not recall having been debriefed after testifying, although post-testimony debriefing was a standard feature of the hearings. The files that would indicate the nature of her debriefing are not currently open to public scrutiny and I have been unable to verify that debriefing took place.

20. Minow drew the case from a talk prepared by Dr Wendy Orr, a Commissioner, for the World Peace Foundation South African Truth and Reconciliation Commission Meeting, May 1998 (Minow, 1998: 175, footnote 145, confirmed with Wendy Orr by e-mail correspondence, 13 September 1999).

21. Her reference has dual connotations, alluding both to the extent of Mrs Khutwane's illness – she was too ill to describe her pain – and to traditional healing practices in which the healer divines the source and explanation for illness.

22. The lyric style produced by repetition was characteristic of her telling and has echoes in many of the testimonies offered by women – see Chapter 2.

23. Her child was injured but recovered quickly and wrote the Matriculation examination, passing with a university exemption. The damaged windows were replaced and the sole remaining physical reminder of the petrol bombing is a burn mark on the dressing table.

24. Among exiles, *umgwenya* (singular, pl.: *imigwenya*) was used as a term of respect. In Zwelethemba, it was used as an antonym to describe those who comprised 'the rank and file', or, as one man's phrase, 'the loose molecules'.

CHAPTER 5

1. Throughout the country, deponents implicated an average of 1.4 victims per statement and 1.6 violations per victim (Report, Volume Three: 3).
2. At the time of writing, statements are not public documents and details are not released. On 6 March 2000, I checked a list of names that I had obtained with Mirriam Moleleki, who had taken statements for the Commission in Zwelethemba (see Chapter 6). She was unable to identify five names on the list of 26 women and I have been unable to trace the women. Nine women made statements about their own experiences of gross violations of human rights; eight described violations committed against their sons, three were about husbands, and one about a father.
3. Numbers in brackets refer to statement case numbers.
4. In terms of the Public Safety Act No. 3 of 1953, magistrates had wide-ranging powers to limit the size and scope of funerals. By 1985, the Act had been amended to permit the state to limit the number of mourners, and to specify that there were to be no political speeches or political songs and no flags flown. If a number of people had been killed in the same incident, they could not be buried at the same time. In terms of the 1986 Security Laws Amendment Act No. 13, a person caught and charged with attending a restricted funeral could be imprisoned for up to ten years.
5. Amnesty was refused on the grounds that there was no political motive for Dyasi's killing – decision no. AC/2000/0005, TRC website, accessed 30 January 2002.
6. In a divide-and-rule strategy, policemen were brought from elsewhere in the country.
7. COSAS was banned in August 1985. In terms of the Internal Security Act, anyone found furthering the aims of a banned organisation could be charged with terrorism.
8. To protect people's identities, I have not revealed their names unless they participated in my research or gave testimony to the Commission.
9. Tyawana was invited to testify before the Commission's Special Hearing on Business and Apartheid. He did not make a statement or testify but the story of his arrest is included in the Report. His later attempt to make a statement came too late. His name is not recorded on the Commission's list of victims.
10. Rival taxi associations competed over routes. Different political organisations were embroiled in the war in an attempt to bring it to an end. There is some evidence to suggest that state operatives worked to heighten tensions (see Report, 1998 Volume Three: 495–6) that resulted in considerable violence.
11. On 21 March 1960, in Sharpeville, a peaceful march organised by the PAC in protest against the passes that Africans were forced to carry that circumscribed their residential and occupational rights, became a massacre when police opened fire and killed 69 people. On the same day, two protesters were killed in a similar incident in Langa, Cape Town.
12. Mawethu Mzima's death is not included in the chronology of deaths in Zwelethemba recorded by the Commission. Residents in Zwelethemba say that police killed him after a 'sell-out' mistakenly identified him as youth activist Mbuyiselo Mroxisa. They state that the death led to the series of events that culminated in the death and burning of Mpazamo Mbani.
13. Patricia Henderson, an anthropologist, activist and performer, describes liberation songs as both expressions of loss and as containing peoples' aspirations for the future. She writes, 'In the context of war, fear and death, these songs sung collectively galvanise those immersed in conflict and mobilise them not to lose courage or hope'. She adds that the songs are important in overcoming the social wounds of war, challenging 'hegemonic constructions of peoples' place in political configurations and ... [overturning] people's current objective subjugation' (1992: 1).
14. I know of only three women in Zwelethemba who were members of MK. Only one was recruited while a student and her military training was not completed.

Membership and recruitment was secret and the women were recruited into different cell structures. Cell members still do not know the members of all other cells in Zwelethemba and do not lightly disclose their membership. The weft of secrecy that held cells together is strong. Some members committed actions for which they could still be prosecuted.

15. The relative, Mrs Mfengu, died in 1983. The funeral is frequently cited as a marker of the intensification of local protest and struggle in Zwelethemba.

16. Nowi was 22 at the time. Students who were able to attend schooling regularly and who passed each year could complete the twelve years of schooling until their graduation (matriculation) by the age of 17 or 18 years. Only a minority of black children did so. Nowi missed schooling during school boycotts and protests in 1976, 1980–81 and in 1986–87. During the mid-1980s, schooling was frequently disrupted. The Department of Education and Training (DET) was responsible for the education of those defined as African. In 1982–83, the state spent eight times as much money on educating white students as on Africans (SACHED 1988: 98–101). In 1976, the proportion was substantially higher: for every Rand spent on African children's education, approximately 14 Rand was spent on white children's education (SACHED 1988:100).

17. Maqoma is Xolile Dyabooi's nickname. Dyabooi testified before the Commission on 26 June 1996. He had been detained in 1987 when captured while trying to leave the country to go to exile in Botswana. He was severely tortured, charged and tried for terrorism. He was 21 years old when he began his sentence. He was indemnified and released in 1990.

18. Informal outlets selling liquor illegally.

19. Only two men spoke fluent seSotho. The travel documents each member of the group had been given were stamped with the same date and had been issued in Cape Town. One of the men in the group recalls that he was concerned that the documents might give the group away as they were travelling together. He recommended that they go to Herschel and then Mount Fletcher and cross the border separately so as to avoid suspicion.

20. This was the man who had been unknown to the other members of the group. He was later believed by residents in Zwelethemba to have been involved in the deaths of the seven youths in what has come to be known as the Gugulethu Seven incident (see Mrs Miya's testimony in Chapter 2). Some people believe that he was punished for his alleged activities as an *impimpi* ('sell-out') by being necklaced in Khayelitsha in 1986.

21. This is the only point in all our discussions about her experiences that Nowi admitted emotion. Later she explained her tears as originating not in pain and fear but from her frustration at being helpless.

22. Her suspicions were not ill founded. In 1982, Siphiwo Mthimkhulu, a youth activist, was fed rat poison in detention. His mother, Joyce Mthimkhulu, testified to the Commission on 26 June 1996 in Port Elizabeth. During the Commission's investigations it emerged that the state had sponsored a chemical and biological warfare programme under the project leadership of Dr Wouter Basson, Surgeon General of the Armed Forces (Volume Two: 504–17). Basson applied for, but was not granted, amnesty. A criminal trial that ended in April 2002 found him not guilty on 67 charges ranging from fraud to murder.

23. Local farmers were involved in a volunteer corps in Worcester and activists recall that the corps was particularly brutal in its treatment of young people. The complicity of farmers in violence against activists and the existence of farm prisons have received little attention in the Commission's work.

24. People in Zwelethemba frequently refer to organisations that existed in the 1980s by their counterparts in the 1990s. 'Women's League' here refers to the ANC Women's League, of which Nowi has been a member since it was instituted after the ANC was

unbanned in 1990. In 1988, the Women's League did not exist in South Africa: here, Nowi refers to UWCO.

25. Ntsoake falls into this category: detention without trial was not clearly identified as a gross violation of human rights at the time that statements were being solicited in Worcester and she did not make a statement subsequently.

26. The Promotion of National Unity and Reconciliation Act No. 34 of 1995 stipulated that 'The commissioners shall be fit and proper persons who are impartial and who do not have a high political profile.'

27. I drew on many different research techniques to elicit the data presented here, including interviews with the young women and their kin, informal discussions with the women and with male activists, focus group discussions, and workshops. The women recorded some of their memories in what they called 'Struggle Diaries' and together we made a documentary film in which they recorded past activities and short descriptions of their present lives and hopes for the future. My credibility was consolidated by my relationships with male activists whom the women trusted, by my activities in following up with the Commission on behalf of residents and by the length of time (regular contact between 1996 and 1999 and intermittent visits to 2001) that I worked in Zwelethemba.

28. The study does not question the applicability of its diagnostic criteria to the research population. Idioms of distress may differ across societies and the use of psychology's diagnostic categories may be misleading in cross-cultural applications or in conditions of poverty or in conditions where conflict has not yet ended. (See for example, Bracken, Giller and Summerfield 1995; Young 1995; Honwana and Dawes 1996; Honwana 1999; Sideris 1999.)

29. Traditionally, the family of a man who impregnates a girl before marriage is responsible for the 'damage' and must make compensation.

CHAPTER 6

1. Data presented here is drawn from the autobiographies, all quotations from which are referenced, and from interviews conducted between 1997 and 1999.

2. The Black Sash, an organisation of white women opposed to apartheid that monitored state repression, established and helped fund Advice Offices throughout South Africa. The Worcester Advice Office offered a range of services to residents in the Boland, including basic legal advice. Women working in the Worcester Advice Office also channelled money from the UDF and the Dependents' Conference of the South African Council of Churches to pay the bail of those detained for political activities.

3. The policy declared that in certain areas west of an imaginary line, those classified Coloured had preference in employment. An African could not be appointed to a job if there was a Coloured person to do it.

4. Tumelo's political activities continued. In 1996 he was elected to the Northern Cape Provincial Government. He died in a motor accident on 31 December 1999.

5. In 1975, residents formed the Zwelethemba Residents Association (ZRA) in opposition to the state-appointed councillor system established in terms of the 1971 Black Affairs Administration Act No. 45. By the early 1980s, several members of the ZRA's management committee had become councillors. A new ZRA was established in 1983 and Mirriam served on its executive committee.

6. *Baasskap*, Afrikaans: literally, master condition. Required particular behaviour on the part of those who were, on the basis of their skin colour and racial classification, cast as subservient.

7. According to research notes compiled by the Commission for the media, the incident described here occurred on 27 August 1985.

8. She was notified by the Commission that, as several people had named her in their statements, she might be identified as a victim (personal communication, 6 March 2000).

9. *Boer*, Afrikaans, pl. *Boere*, literally 'farmer'. It is often used as a derogatory term to describe whites, especially Afrikaners and policemen.

10. Sarah Radcliffe and Sally Westwood (1993), Jo Fisher (1989, 1993) and Jennifer Schirmer (1993) describe women's mobilisation against military juntas and dictators in Latin America. Julia Peteet (1997) shows how Palestinian women transformed ideas of motherhood to make demands on the state. Women are frequently depicted as 'mothers' of the post-colonial state in Zimbabwe (see Weiss 1986; Staunton 1990). Nira Yuval-Davis (1989, 1997) provides a stringent critique of nationalism and the representation of women as mothers (see also McClintock 1995). Pnina Werbner (1999) explores the implications of 'political motherhood' for securing new forms of citizenship in the post-colonial state.

11. People who did not have rights to reside in given areas or whose rights had expired could be 'endorsed out': any remaining rights to remain were rescinded and they were sent back to homeland areas (see Platzky and Walker 1987).

12. One was Thandiwe Silere, who became a founder of UWO and the UDF in the Boland (1984), a member of the Executive Committee of the Civic Association (1985), and was employed with Mirriam and Neliswa at the Advice Office in Worcester from 1986.

13. Another story, probably apocryphal, draws on people's attempts to escape from police by hiding in graves. While the story does not fall into the trickster pattern, it elicits hilarity by describing absurdity in the face of adversity. On April Fool's Day, 1997, Mawethu Bikane, a youth activist, told this story:

    When the people protested, the police shot teargas and the people fled. One man ran and hid in an open grave, pretending to be a corpse awaiting burial. Two policemen, chasing people through the graveyard, came upon the open grave with the man lying inside, arms folded across his chest, eyes closed. One policeman said to the other, '*Leef hy?*' [Is he alive?], to which the 'corpse' quickly responded, '*Nee, baas, ek is dood*' [No, boss, I'm dead'].

14. The mode of dressing is part of an intricate code of respect (*-hlonipha*) practised by married women, who cover their heads in public and drape shawls or blankets over their shoulders. Some wear fabric or aprons knotted over their skirts. *Ukuhlonipha* is structured around an elaborate complex of language and spatial avoidance practices. The complex is usually formally taught to young women at marriage. The patterns differ by 'family' [clan affiliation] and with them, the density and intensity of practice.

15. During the ten-week 'hearing cycle' in Worcester, the Commission sought information concerning Worcester and Zwelethemba and surrounding towns (Robertson, Ashton, Rawsonville and Montagu) for the public hearing. The cycle ended shortly after the hearing (24 to 26 July 1996), after which potential testifiers had either to travel to Cape Town or to make their statements through Mirriam Moleleki's offices.

16. In Zwelethemba, kin and the immediate social community are intimately connected. Many residents are linked to one another through ties of kinship, clanship, neighbourhood and place of origin.

17. It is not easy work. For example, after the first democratic elections in April 1994, much of the aid that had been channelled to NGOs and CBOs during the apartheid years was redirected to assist the new government in implementing change. NGOs were severely hampered by funding difficulties and many closed. Some of the bodies that channelled aid money to NGOs and CBOs suffered financial maladministration, as did some of the receiving agencies.

18. The impact of apartheid policies on the domestic sphere, particularly the migrant labour system, homelands creation, forced removals and the pass laws, have been

well documented (see reviews in Wilson and Ramphele 1989, and Platzky and Walker 1987).

EPILOGUE

1. Ian Hacking (1999) has described as 'the looping effect' the process through which people occupy a newly emergent subject position, transforming it through living it. Some of those included in the loop of victim groupings in South Africa are ex-political activists who made statements to the Commission. For example, the Western Cape branch of the survivor support group, Khulumani, is headed by Shirley Gunn (formerly a member of MK, whose testimony is described in Chapter 3). Approximately 5 per cent of the group's membership comprises those who gave statements to the Commission. The group is currently lobbying government to act in relation to reparations.

2. The role of certain male activists – particularly those in the military and in exile – is, on the other hand, lionised, although it should be noted that the political activities of young men who remained in South Africa are seldom properly acknowledged. Museums in particular tend to commemorate the role of men.

APPENDIX B

1. Most questions were put by Helen Suzman, lone Member of Parliament for the Progressive Party from 1961 until she was joined by others in 1974. She retired in 1989.

2. Poqo was a rurally based political organisation that drew its support mainly from Xhosa speakers. In 1963, it initiated a wave of attacks and was banned.

REFERENCES

Abu-Lughod, L. (1990) 'The romance of resistance: tracing transformations of power through Bedouin women', *American Ethnologist*, Vol. 17, No. 1: 41–55.

Agamben, G. (1999) *Remnants of Auschwitz: the witness and the archive*. trans. Daniel Heller-Roazen (New York: Zone Books).

Agger, I. (1994) *The Blue Room: Trauma and testimony among refugee women. A psycho-social exploration*, trans. Mary Bille (London: Zed).

Agger, I. and Soren J. (1990) 'Testimony as ritual and evidence in psychotherapy for political refugees', *Journal of Traumatic Stress*, Vol. 3: 115–30.

Amadiume, I. and Abdullahi An-Na'im (eds) (2000). *The Politics of Memory: truth, healing, and social justice* (London: Zed).

Anderson, M. (1993) 'The sexual abuse of women in South African state custody' (Department of Criminology, University of Cape Town. Unpublished paper).

Antze, P. and Michael Lambek (eds) (1996) *Tense Past: Cultural Essays in Trauma and Memory* (London: Routledge).

Appadurai, A. (1997) 'Fieldwork in the Era of Globalisation', *Anthropology and Humanism*, Vol. 22, No. 1: 115–18.

Arendt, H. (1963) *Eichmann in Jerusalem: A report on the banality of evil* (New York: Viking Press).

Aretxaga, B. (1997) *Shattering Silence: Women, Nationalism and Political Subjectivity in Northern Ireland* (Princeton: Princeton University Press).

Asmal, K., Louise Asmal and Suresh Roberts (1996) *Reconciliation Through Truth: A Reckoning of Apartheid's Criminal Governance* (Cape Town: David Philip).

Augé, M. (1995) *Non-Places: Introduction to an Anthropology of Supermodernity* trans. John Howe (London: Verso).

Balibar, E. (1998) 'Violence, Ideality and Cruelty', *New Formations: The Ethics of Violence*, No. 35: 7–19.

Bar-On, D. (1999) *The indescribable and the undiscussable: reconstructing human discourse after trauma* (Budapest, Hungary: Central European University Press, and Ithaca, NY: Distributed by Cornell University Press).

Battaglia, D. (1999) 'Toward an Ethics of the Open Subject: Writing Culture in Good Conscience', pp. 114–50 in Henrietta Moore (ed.) *Anthropological Theory Today* (Cambridge: Polity Press).

Bell, T. with Dumisa Ntsebeza (2001) *Unfinished Business: South Africa, Apartheid and Truth* (Muizenberg, Cape Town: Understanding our Past).

Benjamin, W. (1992 [1968]) 'The Storyteller', pp. 83–107 in *Illuminations* (London: Fontana).

Bettelheim, B. (1980) *Surviving and Other Essays* (New York: Vintage Books).

Boraine, A. (2000) *A Country Unmasked* (Cape Town: Oxford University Press).

Boraine, A. and Janet Levy (eds) (1995) *The Healing of a Nation?* (Cape Town: Justice in Transition).

Boraine, Alex, Janet Levy and Ronel Scheffer (eds) (1994) *Dealing with the Past: Truth and Reconciliation in South Africa* (Cape Town: IDASA).

Botman, Russell and Robin M. Petersen (eds) (1996) *To Remember and to Heal: Theological and psychological perspectives on truth and reconciliation* (Cape Town: Human and Rousseau).

Bozzoli, B. (1999) 'Public ritual and private transition: The Truth Commission in Alexandra township, South Africa 1996', *African Studies*, Vol. 57, No. 2: 167–98.

Bracken, P, Joan Giller and Derek Summerfield (1995) 'Psychological responses to war and atrocity: the limitations of current concepts', *Social Science and Medicine*, Vol. 40: 1073–82.

Brown, W. (1995) *States of Injury: Power and freedom in late modernity* (Princeton: Princeton University Press).

Burton, M. (2000) 'Making moral judgements', pp. 77–85 in Charles Villavicencio and Wilhelm Verwoerd (eds) *Looking Back, Reaching Forward: Reflections on the Truth and Reconciliation Commission of South Africa* (Cape Town: UCT Press).

Butler, J. (1990) *Gender Trouble: Feminism and the subversion of identity* (London: Routledge).

Butler, J. (1997a) *Excitable Speech: A politics of the performative* (London: Routledge).

Butler, J. (1997b) *The Psychic Life of Power* (Stanford: Stanford University Press).

Buur, L. (1999) 'Monumental History: Visibility and Invisibility in the work of the South African Truth and Reconciliation Commission'. Paper presented at the conference, *The TRC: Commissioning the Past*, University of the Witwatersrand, 11–14 June 1999.

Buur, L. (2000) 'Institutionalising Truth: Victims, perpetrators and professionals in the everyday work of the South African Truth and Reconciliation Commission' (PhD dissertation, Aarhus University, Denmark).

Cavell, S. (1994) *A Pitch of Philosophy: Autobiographical exercises* (Cambridge, MA: Harvard University Press).

Census96, Statistics South Africa: Supercross Version 3.6.

Chabanyi Manganyi, N. and André du Toit (eds) (1990) *Political Violence and the Struggle in South Africa* (Halfway House, South Africa: Southern Book Publishers).

Charman, A., C. de Swardt and M. Simons (1991) 'The Politics of Gender: Negotiating Liberation', *Transformation*, Vol. 15: 40–60.

Clifford, J. (1997) *Routes: Travel and Translation in the Late Twentieth Century* (Cambridge, MA: Harvard University Press).

Coady, C. (1992) *Testimony: A philosophical investigation* (Oxford: Oxford University Press).

Cochrane, J., John de Gruchy and Stephen Martin (1999) *Facing the truth: South African faith communities and the Truth & Reconciliation Commission* (Cape Town: David Philip).

Cock, J. (1990) 'Political violence', pp. 44–72 in Brian McKendrick and Wilma Hoffmann. (eds) *People and Violence in South Africa* (Cape Town: Oxford University Press).

Cock, J. (1991) *Colonels and Cadres: War and Gender in South Africa* (Cape Town: Oxford University Press).

Cock, J. (1992) *Women and War in South Africa* (London: Open Letters).

Cole, J. (1987) *Crossroads: The Politics of Reform and Repression, 1976–1986* (Johannesburg: Ravan Press).

Coleman, M. (ed.) (1998) *A Crime Against Humanity: Analysing the repression of the Apartheid State* (Cape Town: Human Rights Committee, Mayibuye Books and David Philip).

Coplan, D. (1995) *In the Time of Cannibals* (Chicago: University of Chicago Press).

Daniel, E.V. (1996) *Charred Lullabies: An Anthropography of Violence* (Princeton: Princeton University Press).

Das, V. (1987) 'The Anthropology of Violence and the Speech of Victims', *Anthropology Today*, Vol. 3, No. 4: 11–13.

Das, V. (1990) 'Our work to cry, your work to listen', pp. 345–98 in Veena Das (ed.) *Mirrors of Violence: Communities, riots and survivors in South Asia* (Delhi: Oxford University Press).

Das, V. (1995) *Critical Events: An Anthropological perspective on contemporary India* (Delhi: Oxford University Press).

Das, V. (1996) 'Language and body: Transactions in the construction of pain', *Daedalus*, Vol. 125, No. 1: 67–92.

Das, V. (1997) 'Sufferings, theodicies, disciplinary practices, appropriations', *International Social Science Journal*, Vol. 154: 563–72.

Das, V. (2000) 'Violence and the Work of Time', pp. 59–73 in Anthony P. Cohen (ed.) *Signifying Identities* (London: Routledge).

Das, V. and Arthur Kleinman (2000) 'Introduction', pp. 1–18 in Veena Das, Arthur Kleinman, Mamphela Ramphele and Pamela Reynolds (eds) *Violence and Subjectivity* (Berkeley: University of California Press).

Das, V. and Arthur Kleinman (2001) 'Introduction' to Das et al. 2001, pp. 1–30.

Das, Veena, Arthur Kleinman, Margaret Lock, Mamphela Ramphele and Pamela Reynolds (eds) (2001) *Remaking a World: Violence, Social Suffering and Recovery* (Berkeley: University of California Press).

De Kok, I. (1997) *Transfer* (Cape Town: Snail Press).

Desjarlais, R. and Arthur Kleinman (1994) 'Violence and demoralisation in the new world disorder', *Anthropology Today*, Vol. 10, No. 5: 9–12.

DPSC (not dated) *'Unzima Lomthwalo': A handbook on detention* (Johannesburg: DPSC).

'DPSC (1988) *Cries of Freedom: Women in detention in South Africa* (London: Catholic Institute for International Relations), previously published as *A woman's place is in the struggle, not behind bars* (Johannesburg: DPSC/DESCOM).

Durbach, A. (1999) *Upington* (Cape Town: David Philip).

Edelstein, J. (2001) *Truth and Lies: Stories from the South African Truth and Reconciliation Commission* (Milpark, Johannesburg: M&G Books).

El Sa'awadi, N. (1991 [1986]) *Memoirs from the Women's Prison*, trans. Marilyn Booth (London: Zed).

Feldman, A. (1991) *Formations of Violence: The narrative of the body and political terror in Northern Ireland* (Chicago: University of Chicago Press).

Felman, Shoshana and Dori Laub (1992) *Testimony: Crisis of witnessing in literature, psychoanalysis and history* (New York: Routledge).

Fisher, J. (1989) *Mothers of the Disappeared* (Boston: South End Press).

Fisher, J. (1993) *Out of the Shadows: Women, Resistance and Politics in South America* (London: Latin American Bureau).

Fitzpatrick, S. and Robert Gellately (eds) (1997) *Accusatory Practices: denunciation in modern European history, 1789–1989* (Chicago: University of Chicago Press).

Foster, Don and Donald Skinner (1990) 'Detention and Violence: Beyond victimology', pp. 205–33 in N. Chabanyi Manganyi and A. du Toit (eds) *Political Violence and the Struggle in South Africa* (Halfway House, South Africa: Southern Book Publishers).

Foster, D., Dennis Davis and D. Sandler (1987) *Detention and Torture in South Africa* (Cape Town: David Philip).

Gaitskill, D. and Elaine Underhalter (1989) 'Mothers of the Nation: A comparative analysis of nation, race and motherhood in Afrikaner nationalism and the African National Congress', in Nira Yuval Davis and F. Anthias (eds) *Women-Nation-State* (London: Macmillan).

Goldblatt, B. (1997) 'Violence, gender and human rights: An examination of South Africa's Truth and Reconciliation Commission', Paper presented to the annual meeting of the Law and Society Association, St Louis, Missouri.

Goldblatt, B. and Sheila Meintjes (1996) 'Gender and the Truth and Reconciliation Commission: A Submission to the Truth and Reconciliation Commission' (Johannesburg: Centre for Applied Legal Studies, University of the Witwatersrand).

Goodwin, J. (1984) *Cry Amandla!: South African women and the question of power* (New York: Holmes and Meier Publishers).

Griffin, S. (1992) *A Chorus of Stones: The private life of war* (London: The Women's Press).

Grundlingh, Geoffrey, Pamela Reynolds and Fiona Ross (with Amos Khomba, Charity Nana Khohlokoane, Edwin Rasmani, Eric Ndoyisile Tshandu, Mawethu Bikane, Mzikhaya

Mkhabile, Nokwanda Tani, Noluthando Qaba, Nomeite Mfengu, Nowi Khomba, Ntsoaki Phelane, Xolile Dyabooi and Zandesile Ntsomi) (2000) 'Unfinished Business' in W. James and L. van der Vywer (eds) *After the TRC* (Cape Town: David Philip).

Gupta, A. and James Ferguson (eds) (1997) *Anthropological Locations* (Berkeley: University of California Press).

Gurr, R. and Jose Quiroga (2001) 'Approaches to torture rehabilitation', Supplementum No. 1 to *Torture*, Volume 11, No. 1a.

Hacking, I. (1999) *The Social Construction of What?* (Cambridge, MA: Harvard University Press).

Hamber, B. (ed.) (1998) *Past Imperfect: Dealing with the past in Northern Ireland and Societies in Transition* (Derry/Londonderry: INCORE).

Hansard (1960–94) *House of Assembly Questions and Answers* (Cape Town: Government Printers).

Hastrup, K. (1992) 'Out of Anthropology. The Anthropologist as an Object of Dramatic Representation', *Current Anthropology*, Vol. 7: 327–45.

Hastrup, K. (1994) 'Anthropological Knowledge Incorporated', pp. 224–40 in Hastrup, K. and K. Hervik (eds) *Social Experience and Anthropological Knowledge* (London: Routledge).

Hayner, P. (1994) 'Fifteen Truth Commissions – 1974 to 1994: A comparative study', *Human Rights Quarterly*, Vol. 16: 597–655.

Hayner, P. (1996) 'Commissioning the Truth: Further Research Questions', *Third World Quarterly*, Vol. 17, No. 1: 19–29.

Hayner, P. (2001) *Unspeakable Truths: Confronting state terror and atrocity* (New York: Routledge).

Heller, A. (1985) *The Power of Shame* (London: Routledge and Kegan Paul).

Henderson, P. (1999) 'Living with Fragility: Children in New Crossroads' (PhD dissertation, University of Cape Town).

Henderson, P. (1992) 'Songs in civil war: Pietermaritzburg, 1985–1989', Paper presented to the Department of Social Anthropology, University of Cape Town, October 1992.

Henri, Y. (2000) 'Where Healing Begins', in Charles Villa-Vicencio and Wilhelm Verwoerd (eds) *Looking Back, Reaching Forward: Reflections on the Truth and Reconciliation Commission of South Africa* (Cape Town: UCT Press).

Herman, J. (1992) *Trauma and Recovery* (London: Basic).

Hofmeyr, I. (1994) *We Live Our Lives as a Tale that is Told: Oral historical narrative in a South African chiefdom* (London: James Currey).

Honwana, A. (1999) 'Negotiating post-war identities: Child soldiers in Mozambique and Angola'. *CODESRIA Bulletin*, Nos 1, 2: 4–13.

Honwana, Alcinda and Andrew Dawes (1996) 'Children, culture and mental health: interventions in conditions of war' in proceedings of the conference 'Children, War and Prosecution: Rebuilding Hope' (Maputo, December 1996).

House of Assembly (1960–90) *Reports on Parliamentary Questions and Answers* (Cape Town: Government Printers).

Ignatieff, M. (1996) 'Articles of faith', *Index on Censorship*, No. 5: 110–22.

James, Wilmot and Linda van der Vywer (eds) (2000) *After the TRC* (Cape Town: David Philip).

Jeffrey, A. (1999) *The Truth About the Truth Commission* (Spotlight Series, Johannesburg: SAIRR).

Khohlokoane, Charity T.L. (1998) 'Seduction and coercion: the recruitment and involvement of eight Zwelethemba youths in politics in the 1980s' (Unpublished Honours dissertation, Department of Social Anthropology, University of Cape Town).

Kimble, J. and Elaine Unterhalter (1982) 'We opened the road for you, you must go forward: ANC women's struggles, 1912–1982', *Feminist Review*, Vol. 12: 11–35.

Kleinman, Arthur and Joan Kleinman (1994) 'How bodies remember: Social memory and bodily experiences of criticism, resistance and delegitimation in the aftermath of China's Cultural revolution', *New Literary History*, Vol. 25, No. 3: 707–23.

Kleinman, A. and Joan Kleinman (1997) 'The appeal of experience, the dismay of images: Cultural appropiations of suffering in out times' in Arthur Kleinman, Veena Das and Margaret Lock (eds) *Social Suffering* (Berkeley: University of California Press).

Krog, A. (1998) *Country of My Skull* (Johannesburg: Random House).

LaCapra, D. (1999) 'Trauma, Absence, Loss', *Critical Enquiry*, Vol. 25, No. 4: 696–727.

Lambek, Michael and Paul Antze (1996) 'Introduction: Forecasting memory', pp. xi–xxxviii in Paul Antze and Michael Lambek (eds) *Tense Past: Cultural essays in trauma and memory* (London: Routledge).

Langer, L. (1991) *Holocaust Testimonies: The ruins of memory* (New Haven: Yale University Press).

Langer, L. (1995) *Admitting the Holocaust: Collected essays* (Oxford: Oxford University Press).

Langer, L. (1996) 'The alarmed vision: Social suffering and Holocaust atrocity', *Daedalus*, Vol. 125, No. 1: 47–67.

Last, M. (2000) 'Reconciliation and Memory in post-war Nigeria', pp. 315–32 in Veena Das, Arthur Kleinman, Mamphela Ramphele and Pamela Reynolds (eds) *Violence and Subjectivity* (Berkeley: University of California Press.)

LCHR (Lawyers Committee for Human Rights) (1986) *The War Against Children: Apartheid's Youngest Victims* (New York: Lawyer's Committee for Human Rights).

Levi, P. (1989) *The Drowned and the Saved*, trans. Raymond Rosenthal (New York: Random House).

Lewin, H. (1989) *Bandiet: Seven years in a South African prison* (London: Heinneman).

Malkki, L. (1997) 'Speechless emissaries: Refugees, humanitarianism and dehistoricisation', pp. 223–54 in K. Olwig and K. Hastrup (eds) *Siting Culture* (London: Routledge).

Mamdani, M. (1996) 'Reconciliation without justice', *South African Review of Books*, Vol. 46, November–December: 3–5.

Marcus, G. (1995) 'Ethnography in/of the World System: The Emergence of Multi-Sited Ethnography', *Annual Review of Anthropology*, Vol. 24: 95–117.

Masiye, A. (1977) *Singing for Freedom* (Lusaka: Oxford University Press).

Mbembe, A. (2000) 'Memory and African modes of self-writing', paper presented at the International Conference, 'Memory and History: Remembering, Forgetting and Forgiving in the life of the Nation and the Community', University of Cape Town, August 2000. Published online at <www.fl.ulaval.ca/celat/cadre130.htm>

Mbembe, A. and Janet Roitman (1995) 'Figures of the subject in times of crisis', *Public Culture*, Vol. 7: 323–52.

McClintock, A. (1995) *Imperial Leather: Race, gender and sexuality in the colonial conquest* (London: Routledge).

McKendrick, B. and Wilma Hoffmann (eds) (1990) *People and Violence in South Africa* (Cape Town: Oxford University Press).

Meiring, P. (1999) *Chronicle of the Truth Commission* (Vanderbijlpark: Carpe Diem).

Meredith, M. and Tina Rosenberg (2000) *Coming to Terms: South Africa's search for the truth* (New York: Public Affairs).

Mfengu, N. (1997) *My Storie Loop So [My Story Goes Like This]* (Cape Town: Kagiso Publishers).

Millett, K. (1994) *The Politics of Cruelty: An essay on the literature of political imprisonment* (London: Viking).

Minow, M. (1998) *Between Vengeance and Forgiveness: Facing history after genocide and mass violence* (Boston: Beacon Press).

Moleleki, M. (1997) *This Is My Life* (Cape Town: Kagiso Publishers).

Moore, H. (1988) *Feminism and Anthropology* (Cambridge: Polity Press).

Morris, D. (1996) 'About Suffering: Voice, Genre and Moral Community', *Daedalus*, Vol. 125, No. 1: 25–46.

Motsuenyane Commission Report (1993) *Reports of the Commission of Enquiry into Certain Allegations of Cruelty and Human Rights Abuses Against ANC Prisoners and Detainees by ANC Members* (Report made to the African National Congress).

Mroxisa, N. (1997) *Umzabalazo [The Struggle]* (Cape Town: Kagiso Publishers).

National Party (1996) 'Submission to the South African Truth and Reconciliation Commission' presented to the Commission on 21 October 1996.

Ndebele, N. (1994) 'The Rediscovery of the Ordinary: some new writings in South Africa', pp. 41–59 in *South African Literature and Culture: Rediscovery of the ordinary* (Manchester: Manchester University Press).

Ngcwecwe, N. (1997) *Not the End of the World* (Cape Town: Kagiso Publishers).

NGO Coalition (1997) *Submission to the Truth and Reconciliation Commission Concerning the Relevance of Economic, Social and Cultural Rights to the Commission's Mandate*. Submission by NGOS including: Community Law Centre, University of Western Cape; Development Action Group; Legal Resources Centre; Black Sash; Centre for Human Rights (University of Pretoria); NGO National Coalition; National Land Committee; National Literacy Cooperative; Peoples' Dialogue; Urban Sector Network. <http://www.truth.org.za/submit/esc6.htm>

Nicol, M. (1995) *The Waiting Country: A South African Witness* (London: Voctor Gollancz).

Nordstrom, C. (1998) *A Different Kind of War Story* (Philadelphia: University of Pennsylvania Press).

Olkers, I. (1996) 'Gender-neutral truth – A reality shamefully distorted', *Agenda*, Vol. 5: 61–7.

Orr, W. (2000) *From Biko to Basson: Wendy Orr's search for the soul of South Africa as a Commissioner of the TRC* (Saxonwold, South Africa: Contra Press).

Owens, I. (1996) 'Stories of silence: Women, truth and reconciliation', *Agenda*, Vol. 4: 66–72.

Pandolfo, S. (1997) *Impasse of the Angels: Scenes from a Moroccan space of memory* (Chicago: University of Chicago Press).

Pauw, J. (1997) *Into the Heart of Darkness: Interviews with Apartheid's assassins* (Johannesburg: Jonathon Ball Publishers).

Perera, S. (1995) *Living with Torturers, and Other Essays of Intervention: Sri Lankan society, culture and politics in perspective* (Colombo: International Centre for Ethnic Studies).

Peteet, J. (1997) '"Icons and Militants": Mothering in the danger zone', *Signs: Journal of Women in Culture and Society*, Vol. 23, No. 11: 103–29.

Pillay, D. (1992) 'Women in MK', *Work in Progress*, No. 80: 18–19.

Platzky, L. and Cheryl Walker (1987) *The Surplus People: Forced removals in South Africa* (Johannesburg: Ravan Press).

Pongweni, A. (1982) *Songs that Won the Liberation War* (Harare: The College Press).

Radcliffe, S. and Sallie Westwood (eds) (1993) *'Viva': Women and popular protest in Latin America* (London: Routledge).

Rajan, Rajeswari Sunder (1993) *Real and Imagined Women: Gender, culture and postcolonialism* (London: Routledge).

Ramphele, M. (1996) 'Political Widowhood in South Africa: The Embodiment of Ambiguity', *Daedalus*, Vol. 125, No. 1: 99–118.

Rayner, M. (1990) 'From Biko to Wendy Orr: The problem of medical accountability in contexts of political violence and torture', pp. 172–204 in N. Chabanyi Manganyi and A. du Toit (eds) *Political Violence and the Struggle in South Africa* (Halfway House, South Africa: Southern Book Publishers).

Reynolds, P. (1995a) *The Ground of All Making: State violence, the family and political activists* (Pretoria: Human Sciences Research Council).

Reynolds, P. (1995b) '"Not Known Because Not Looked For": Ethnographers Listening to the Young in Southern Africa', *Ethnos*, Vol. 60, Nos 3–4: 193–221.

Rich, A. (1995) *What Is Found There: Notebooks on poetry and politics* (London: Virago Press).

Rosenberg, T. (1992) *Children of Cain: Violence and the violent in Latin America* (Harmondsworth: Penguin).

Ross, F.C. (1996) 'Silence and secrecy: Women's testimonies in the first five weeks of public hearings of the South African Truth and Reconciliation Commission', paper presented to the 'Faultlines Conference', Breakwater Lodge, Cape Town, 4–5 July.

Ross, F.C. (2001a) 'Speech and Silence: Women's testimonies in the first five weeks of public hearings of the South African Truth and Reconciliation Commission', in Arthur Kleinman, Veena Das, Margaret Lock, Mamphela Ramphele and Pamela Reynolds (eds) *Remaking a World: Violence, Social Suffering and Recovery* (Berkeley: University of California Press).

Ross, F.C. (2001b) 'Measuring wrongs with rights: Method and moral in the work of the South African Truth and Reconciliation Commission', paper presented to the ASA conference, 'Rights, Claims and Entitlements', University of Sussex, 30 March–2 April.

Ruddick, S. (1989) *Maternal Thinking: Towards a Politics of Peace* (New York: Ballantine).

Russell, D. (1990) *Lives of Courage: Women for a new South Africa* (New York: Basic Books).

SACHED (1988 [1985]) *The Right To Learn: Struggles for education in South Africa*, prepared by Pam Christie (Johannesburg: SACHED Trust/Ravan Press).

SAIRR (South African Institute for Race Relations) (1960–94) *Race Relations Survey Handbook* (Johannesburg: SAIRR).

Saporta, J. and B. van der Kolk (1992) *Psychobiological Consequences of Severe Trauma: Current Approaches* (Cambridge: Cambridge University Press).

Scarry, E. (1985) *The Body in Pain: The Making and Unmaking of the World* (New York: Oxford University Press).

Scheper-Hughes, N. (1992) *Death Without Weeping: The violence of everyday life in Brazil* (Berkeley: University of California Press).

Scheub, H. (1975) *The Xhosa Intsomi* (Oxford: Clarendon Press).

Scheub, H. (1996) *The Tongue is Fire: South African storytellers and Apartheid* (Madison: University of Wisconsin Press).

Scheub, H. (1998) *Story* (Madison: University of Wisconsin Press).

Schirmer, J. (1993) 'The seeking of truth and the gendering of consciousness: the COMADRES of El Salvadore and the Conavigua widows of Guatemala', in Sarah Radcliffe and Sallie Westwood (eds) *'Viva': Women and popular protest in Latin America* (London: Routledge).

Schreiner, B. (ed.) (1992) *A Snake With Ice Water: Prison writings by South African women* (Johannesburg: COSAW).

Scott, J.C. (1985) *Weapons of the Weak: Everyday forms of peasant resistance* (New Haven: Yale University Press).

Scott, J.C. (1990) 'Voice under domination: The arts of political disguise', pp. 136–82, in *Domination and the Arts of Resistance* (New Haven: Yale University Press).

Scott, J.W. (1991) 'The evidence of experience', *Critical Inquiry*, Vol. 17, Summer: 773–97.

Seremetakis, C.N. (1991) *The Last Word: Women, Death and Divination in Inner Mani* (Chicago: Chicago University Press).

Shifman, P., N. Madlala-Routledge and V. Smith (1997) 'Women in Parliament caucus for action to end violence', *AGENDA*, Vol. 36: 23–6.

Sideris, C. (1999) 'Violation and healing of the spirit: Psycho-social responses to war of Mozambican women refugees', unpublished PhD dissertation, Rand Afrikaans University, South Africa.

Skinner, D. (ed.) (1998) *Apartheid's Violent Legacy: A report on trauma in the Western Cape* (Cape Town: The Trauma Centre for Victims of Violence and Torture).

Skweyiya, T.L. (1992) *Report of the Commission of Enquiry into the Complaints by Former African National Congress Prisoners and Detainees* (Johannesburg: African National Congress).

Smithyman, R. and Glynnis Lawrence (1999) 'Pain and attacks on the five senses', unpublished seminar paper presented to the Department of Social Anthropology, University of Cape Town, September.

Staunton, I (ed.) (1990) *Mothers of the Revolution* (Harare: Baobab).

Straker, G. (1992) *Faces in the Revolution: The psychological effects of violence on township youth in South Africa* (Cape Town: David Philip).

Suarez-Orosco, M. (1987) 'The treatment of children in the "Dirty War": Ideology, state terrorism and the abuse of children in Argentina', pp. 227–46 in Nancy Scheper-Hughes (ed.) *Child Survival* (Dordrecht: D. Reidel Publishing Company).

Suarez-Orozco, M. (1992) 'A Grammar of Terror: Psychocultural responses to State Terrorism in Dirty War and Post-Dirty War Argentina', pp. 219–59 in Carolyn Nordstom and JoAnn Martin (eds) *The Paths to Domination, Resistance and Terror* (Berkeley: University of California Press).

Taussig, M. (1984) 'Culture of terror – Space of death: Roger Casement's Putamayo Report and the explanation of torture', *Comparative Studies of Society and History*, Vol. 26: 467–97.

Taussig, M. (1992) *The Nervous System* (New York: Routledge).

Taylor, D. (1997) *Disappearing Acts: Spectacles of gender and nationalism in Argentina's 'Dirty War'* (Durham, NC: Duke University Press).

Taylor, J. (1994) 'Body Memories: Aide memoires and collective amnesia in the wake of the Argentine terror', pp. 192–203 in Michael Ryan and Avery Gordon (eds) *Body Politics: Disease, desire and the family* (Boulder, CO: Westview Press).

Thomas, B. (1990) 'Violence and Child Detainees', in Brian McKendrick and Wilma Hoffmann (eds) *People and Violence in South Africa* (Cape Town: Oxford University Press) pp. 446–64.

Todorov, T. (1996) *Facing the Extreme: Moral life in the concentration camps* (London: Weidenfeld & Nicholson).

Trouillot, Michel-Rolph (1995) *Silencing the Past* (Boston: Beacon Press).

Truth and Reconciliation Commission (1998) *Truth and Reconciliation Commission of South Africa Report, Volumes One – Five* (Cape Town: Juta).

Truth and Reconciliation Commission (1998) *CD-ROM of the Truth and Reconciliation Commission Website, November 1998* (Pretoria: Truth and Reconciliation Commission).

Turshen, Meredith and Clotilde Twagiramariya (1998) *What Women Do in Wartime: Gender and conflict in Africa* (London: Zed).

Tutu, D. (1996) 'Forward' in H. Russel Botman and Robin M. Petersen (eds) *To Remember and to Heal: Theological and psychological perspectives on truth and reconciliation* (Cape Town: Human and Rousseau).

Tutu, D. (1999) *No Future Without Forgiveness* (London: Rider).

UNICEF (1989) *Children on the Frontline* (New York: UNICEF).

van Heerden, J. (1996) 'The Meaning of the MASA Apology', *South African Medical Journal*, Vol. 86, No. 6: 656–60.

van Heerden, J. (1997) 'Prison health care in South Africa: A study of the prison conditions, health care and medical accountability for the care of prisoners', unpublished M.Phil dissertation (Medicine), University of Cape Town.

Villavicencio, C. and Willem Verwoed (eds) (2000) *Looking Back, Reaching Forward: Reflections on the Truth and Reconciliation Commission of South Africa* (Cape Town: University of Cape Town Press).

Walaza, N. (2000) 'Insufficient healing and reparation', pp. 250–5 in Charles Villavicencio and Wilhelm Verwoerd (eds) *Looking Back, Reaching Forward: Reflections on the Truth and Reconciliation Commission of South Africa* (Cape Town: University of Cape Town Press).

Walker, C. (1991 [1982]) *Women and Resistance in South Africa* (London: Onyx Press).

Walker, C. (1995) 'Conceptualising motherhood in Twentieth Century South Africa', *Journal of Southern African Studies*, Vol. 21, No. 3: 417–37.

Weiss, R. (1986) *The Women of Zimbabwe* (Harare: Nehanda Publishers).

Wells, J. (1991a) 'The rise and fall of motherism as a force in black women's resistance movements', paper presented at the 'Conference on Women and Gender in South Africa', University of Natal, Durban.

Wells, J. (1991b) *We Have Done With Pleading: The Women's 1913 Anti-Pass Campaign* (Johannesburg: Ravan Press).

Wells, J. (1993) *We Now Demand: The history of women's resistance to pass laws in South Africa* (Johannesburg: Wits University Press).

Werbner, P. (1999) 'Political motherhood and the feminisation of citizenship: women's activisms and the transformation of the public sphere', pp. 221–45 in Nira Yuval-Davis and Pnina Werbner (eds) *Women, Citizenship and Difference* (London: Zed Press).

Werbner, R. (1998) 'Smoke from the Barrel of a Gun: Postwars of the dead, memory and reinscription in Zimbabwe', pp. 71–102 in R. Werbner (ed.) *Memory and the Postcolony: African Anthropology and the Critique of Power* (London: Zed).

Weschler, L. (1990) *A Miracle, A Universe: Settling accounts with torturers* (Harmondsworth, Middlesex: Penguin).

White, H. (1994) *In the Shadow of the Island* (Pretoria: Human Sciences Research Council).

Wilson, F. and Mamphela Ramphele (1989) *Uprooting Poverty: The South African challenge* (Cape Town: David Philip).

Wilson, R. (1996) 'The *Sizwe* will not go away: the Truth and Reconciliation Commission, human rights and nation building in South Africa', *African Studies*, Vol. 55, No. 2: 1–20.

Wilson, R. (1997) 'Representing Human Rights Violations: Social contexts and subjectivities', pp. 134–60 in Richard Wilson (ed.) *Human Rights, Culture and Context* (London: Pluto Press).

Wilson, R. (2001) *The Politics of Truth and Reconciliation* (Cambridge: Cambridge University Press).

Winterson, J. (1993) *Written on the Body* (Toronto: Vintage).

Worsnip, M. (1996) *Priest and Partisan* (Melbourne: Ocean Press).

Young, A. (1995) *The Harmony of Illusions. Inventing Post-Traumatic Stress Disorder* (Princeton: Princeton University Press).

Yuval-Davis, N. (ed.) (1989) *Woman-Nation-State* (London: Macmillan).

Yuval-Davis, N. (1997) *Gender and Nation* (London: Sage).

Zalaquette, J. (1994) 'Why deal with the Past?', pp. 8–15 in Alex Boraine, Janet Levy and Ronel Scheffer (eds) (1994) *Dealing with the Past: Truth and Reconciliation in South Africa* (Cape Town: IDASA).

Zenani, Nongenile Masithathu, and Harold Scheub (1992) *The World and the Word: Tales and observations from the Xhosa oral tradition* (Madison: University of Wisconsin Press).

NEWSPAPERS

Cape Times, Monday, 17 June 1996, Barry Streek, 'Spotlight falls on lives of Worcester women activists', p. 2.

Cape Times, Wednesday, 19 June 1996, Roger Friedman, 'Ex-MK man tells of abuse', p. 6.

Cape Times, Tuesday, June 25 1996, Roger Friedman, 'ANC veteran tells of sexual abuse', p. 3.

Mail and Guardian, Friday 21 November 1997, 'More corpses in Winnie's cupboard', p. 2. On-line archive, accessed 2 March 2000 <www.web.sn.apc.org/wmail/issues/971121/NEWS4.html>

Mail and Guardian, Friday 21 November 1997, 'The night Ferdi Barnard told me he killed David Webster', pp. 23–4. On-line archive, accessed 2 March 2000 <www.web.sn.apc.org/wmail/issues/971121NEWS18.html>

South African Press Association (SAPA), Umtata, Tuesday, 18 June 1996, 'MK Commander alleges sexual abuse in ANC exile camps' (Crawford and the Truth and Reconciliation Commission CD-ROM: SAPA/9606/S960618B.htm).

South African Press Association (SAPA), Worcester, Monday, 24 June 1996, 'Woman tells truth body of sexual abuse' (Crawford and the Truth and Reconciliation Commission CD-ROM: SAPA/9606/0960624C.htm).

Sunday Times, Sunday, 31 January 1999, 'Ex-MK men confess to killing student leader', p. 1.

Sunday Weekend Argus, Sunday, 21 April 1996, Christina Stuckey. 'Widow's courage and dignity shines through', p. 6.

The Sunday Independent, Sunday, 21 April 1996, Christina Stuckey, 'Truth Commission hearings reveal the strength of women who overcame barbarism with quiet dignity', p. 4.

The Sunday Independent, Sunday, 5 May 1996, Beth Goldblatt and Sheila Meintjes, 'Journalist did well to recognise that the role of women in the struggle was not just as victims', Letters to the editor.

Worcester Standard, Friday, 28 June 1996, *WVK hoor talle verhale*' ('TRC hears diverse stories').

VIDEO

'We tell our stories the way we like': the wives of the Cradock Four. 1999. Produced, directed and scripted by Taryn da Canha, Gairoonisa Paleker and Lauren van Vuuren. Video. 47 mins. History Department, University of Cape Town.

INDEX

Compiled by Sandie Vahl